Conserving
Natural Value

Perspectives in Biological Diversity
MARY C. PEARL, EDITOR

Perspectives in Biological Diversity Series

also related
METHODS AND CASES IN CONSERVATION SCIENCE SERIES

Thomas Rudel, *Tropical Deforestation: Small Farmers and Forest
Clearing in the Ecuadorian Amazon*
Joel Berger and Carol Cunningham, *Mating in Small Populations:
Insularization and North American Bison*

Series Editor, Mary C. Pearl
Series Advisers, Christine Padoch and Douglas Daly

Conserving
Natural Value

HOLMES ROLSTON, III

COLUMBIA UNIVERSITY PRESS   NEW YORK

Columbia University Press
New York   Chichester, West Sussex
Copyright © 1994 Columbia University Press

Library of Congress Cataloging-in-Publication Data

Rolston, Holmes, 1932–
    Conserving natural value / Holmes Rolston III
        p.   cm. — (Perspectives in biological diversity series)
    Includes bibliographical references (p.   ) and index.
    ISBN 0–231–07900–1
    ISBN 0–231–07901–X   (pbk.)
    1. Nature conservation—Moral and ethical aspects.
    2. Environmental protection—Moral and ethical aspects.   3. Human
    ecology—Philosophy.   I. Title.   II. Series.
    QH75.R65   1994
    333.7'2'01—dc20   94–15628
                                                                  CIP

Casebound editions of Columbia University Press books
are printed on permanent and durable acid-free paper.
Printed in the United States of America

c 10 9 8 7 6 5 4 3 2 1

p 10 9 8 7 6 5 4 3 2 1

Contents

▪▪
▪▪

1. Natural and Cultural Values   1

2. Diversity and Complexity Values   34

3. Ecosystem Integrity and Health Values   68

4. Wildlife Values   101

5. Anthropocentric Values   133

6. Intrinsic Natural Values   167

7. The Home Planet   203

References   *237*
Index   *249*

Conserving
Natural Value

1

Natural and Cultural Values

■■
■■

The Earth is remarkable, and valuable, for both the nature and the culture that occur on it. If visitors from space were to file a report about Earth, volume one might cover the geological and biological phenomena, volume two the anthropological and sociological events. Such a division might seem biased, since evolutionary history has been going on for billions of years, while cultural history is only about a hundred thousand years old. But certainly nature and culture are currently in tandem, with, from here onward, culture increasingly determining what natural history shall continue. Both volumes one and two would be uniquely historical, peculiarly earthbound.

1. NATURE AND CULTURE

There is neither one nature nor one culture. Nature is plural; the ten million species each have their own natures. Each species lives in the world with some degree of uniqueness—whether bats or beetles. There are different levels of naturalness—electronic, ecological, and sexual phenomena. There have been ten thousand different cultures and subcultures, from Druids to yuppies. But within this pluralism, the nature/culture division marks a critical transformation on Earth. We organize our universities this way: the natural sciences, pure and applied, and the humanities, arts, and social sciences.

The physical sciences are true all over the universe; the biological sciences are true all over the Earth. But the distinctly human sciences, such as anthropology, sociology, political science, economics, and (for the most part) psychology, study only one species, *Homo sapiens*. It may seem strange to devote several sciences to just one species. One reason is our special human needs, perhaps another is our arrogance; but this is also evidence of the radical difference being human makes. Unlike coyotes or bats, humans are not just what they are by nature; they come into the world by nature quite unfinished and become what they become by culture. Being human is more than biochemistry, physiology, ecology.

Humans superimpose cultures on the wild nature out of which they once emerged, with radical innovations. Information in wild nature travels intergenerationally on genes; information in culture travels neurally as people are educated into transmissible cultures. Though the higher animals can learn limited behaviors from parents and conspecifics, animals do not form transmissible cultures. In nature, the coping skills are coded on chromosomes. In culture, the skills are coded in people's traditions, in their crafts, religious rituals, or technology manuals. Information acquired during an organism's lifetime is not transmitted genetically; the essence of culture is acquired information transmitted to the next generation.

Information transfer in culture can be several orders of magnitude faster and overleap genetic lines. A typical couple have only two or three children, who inherit their genetic information. But those children are educated by taking classes from dozens of teachers, by reading hundreds of books, using libraries with tens of thousands of books, written by authors to whom they are genetically quite unrelated, who may have been dead for centuries. The children learn from television programs with information coming from all over the world. A human being develops typically in some one of ten thousand cultures, receiving a heritage that is historically conditioned, perpetuated by language, conventionally established, using symbols with locally effective meanings. Cultures may exchange ideas; sometimes people are reared at the crossroads of cultures or well-educated people choose and criticize their cultures.

Animals are what they are genetically, instinctively, environmentally, without any options in what they shall be at all, even if they do make some limited choices. Humans have myriads of lifestyle options, evidenced by their cultures; and each human makes daily decisions that affect his or her character. Natural selection pressures are relaxed in culture; humans help each other out compassionately with charity, affirmative action, or headstart programs. They study medicine to cure their bodily diseases. The determinants of animal and plant behavior, much less the determinants of climate or nutrient recycling, are never anthropological, political, economic, technological, scientific, philosophical, ethical, or religious. Little or nothing in wild nature approaches all this.

Animals do not hold elections and plan their environmental affairs. They do not make bulldozers to cut down tropical rainforests. They do not fund development projects through the World Bank. Or contribute to funds to save the whales. They do not teach their religion to their children. They do not read or write books trying to decide what natural values shall be conserved. They do not try to get clear about the differences between nature and culture, or get confused about whether their actions are natural (a confusion we soon worry about). If we are going to evaluate what natural and cultural values we want to treasure, we must appreciate and criticize human affairs with insight into their radically different character.

We might want, for instance, to insist (as we will in chapter 6) that there are intrinsic wild values. Just because the human presence is so radically different, humans ought sometimes to draw back and let nature be. If so, we will have to debate those who say that all values are anthropocentric (human-centered) or anthropogenic (human-generated) (as we will in chapter 5). All this is quite outside the capacity of plants and animals. Humans can and ought to see outside their own sector, they can relate their species self-interest to other natural values. And only humans have conscience enough to do this; indeed, it seems likely that only humans have conscience at all.

Some will protest that humans too are natural. We have to be careful here, because "nature" and "natural" are slippery words. It is important to identify what the contrast class is.

1. The sense we need when we distinguish between nature and culture is that of spontaneous nature contrasted with deliberated culture. Nature runs by causal law, biological metabolisms, genetic coding, instincts, evolutionary and ecological processes, accidental contingencies. Culture is mind-based in the radically different ways we have been describing. The difference is that between a pair of boots found in the woods, an artifact, which some cobbler thought about and made, and a mushroom, resulting from mere biology, or even a bird's nest, which is made instinctively without deliberation over blueprints or cost. Any human agency, however well intended, is intention nevertheless and interrupts these spontaneous processes and is inevitably artificial, "unnatural." The architectures of nature and of culture are different. In that sense, "man is the animal for whom it is natural to be artificial" (Garvin 1953:378).

2. In a law-of-nature sense, even deliberated human actions break no laws of nature. We cannot break the laws of gravity or electricity. Neither industry nor agriculture break natural laws; they rather employ them in redirected ways. The laws of nature operate willy-nilly no matter what we do. Long ago, at the start of the technological age, the English philosopher Francis Bacon coined the aphorism: "Nature is not to be commanded, except by being obeyed" (1968 [1620]: vol. 1, p. 157, vol. 4, p. 47), and that is going to be true forever, no matter how high-tech our industries become, building rockets and computers. We cannot, for example, break the laws of health in nutrition and medicine, though we can deliberately employ them to redirect our biochemistries and cure diseases, even though, in private life, we often neglect to consider how to employ the laws of health to our welfare. Everything, better or worse, is natural in this sense.

Humans evolved out of nature, and that can confuse people into saying that humans are just natural, since they are products of various natural laws and events operating through evolutionary history, and, since their origins were natural, they continue to be natural. But that is to fall into a "nothing but" fallacy (more accurately the genetic fallacy), which confuses what a thing now essentially is with what its historical origins once were. It cannot take emergence seriously. J. Baird

Callicott makes this mistake: "We are animals ourselves, large omnivorous primates, very precocious to be sure, but just big monkeys, nevertheless. We are therefore a part of nature, not set apart from it. Chicago is no less a phenomenon of nature than is the Great Barrier Reef" (1992:17).

And Lake Michigan, polluted with the effluents of Chicago (by some precocious monkeys), is as natural as the Great Barrier Reef too. Lake Michigan restored (by some conservationist monkeys) is natural too; anything that humans do is natural, no matter whether it is better or worse. There is no contrast class of events, unless perhaps there is the supernatural. So we are not going to get any guidance out of that sense of natural, since any and all cultural values will be natural values as well; any and all cultural disvalues will be natural disvalues too. The products of urban industries, such as disposable diapers and styrofoam cups, are natural values just as much as coral reefs with their polyps and giant clams. Corporate executives deciding to break the standards of the Clean Water Act and pollute Lake Michigan are behaving in accord with nature as much as those deciding to meet or exceed the standards, so as to preserve the integrity of the waters. CEO decisions are as natural as clams feeding underwater off Australia. Whatever pollutants these monkeys discharge into Lake Michigan are as natural as any fishes already there. Pretty obviously, we have just gotten ourselves lost with this sense of natural!

That is because we are not discriminating enough to see that, though they evolve out of nature and its processes, humans significantly evolve *out of* it. "By every conceivable measure, humanity is ecologically abnormal," concludes Edward O. Wilson (1992:272). We need to see the difference in being human, and only after we are clear about that, do we also want to see the senses in which, though evolved out of it, culture has to remain in relative harmony with nature. Then we might want to say that, although all deliberate human behaviors differ from the processes of spontaneous nature, some human behaviors are healthy for humans because they agree with the natural systems with which their cultural decisions interact, and some others not healthy. Or that human-caused extinction of mussels in midwestern rivers, owing to the toxic wastes from Illinois industries, is not natural extinction at all.

3. So we turn next to a relative sense in which what humans do cul-

turally can be natural. We need that sense because we recognize, right at the start, that conservation values are not the only values; there are numerous values autonomous to cultures. We will ask whether and why cultures should preserve any natural values at all, and what kind of balance ought to be reached between natural and cultural values. Using these coordinates of nature and culture, we run a risk of bifurcating values, but the other risk is of being insufficiently discriminating about the two main domains of value that have appeared on our planet.

2. ENTWINED DESTINIES: NATURE SUPPORTING CULTURE

Contrasting nature and culture, we might think that value decisions will therefore involve values in conflict. We often think that within culture. Acting to do A brings less for the developers and more for the environmentalists, or vice versa. Choices are a win-lose game. Economists routinely calculate costs versus benefits. They hope to find ways to use resources so that some consumers are made better off while making none worse off, winners without losers. But they often cannot, and then they ask whether the winners could compensate the losers to see whether there is net gain or loss.

Policymakers, along with economists, ask about opportunity costs. With consumable resources, if you use a resource one way, you cannot use it another way. You cannot eat a piece of pie twice. Either a tract is timbered or made wilderness for recreation, not both. Life is always a balancing of value gain and value loss. If you restore wolves in Wyoming, environmentalists will be pleased; ranchers will lose some sheep. In this view, there must be winners and losers among the humans who are helped or hurt by the condition of their environment.

Further, humans can gain or lose vis-à-vis nature. They cut down a forest to gain timber and make a plowed field; the fauna and flora lose; humans gain. Here we may wonder how much of the time humans ought to win—all or just part of the time. They cannot lose all of the time; but we may also hold that humans ought not invariably be the winners. There must be a net gain for humans if they are to flourish, but that still allows that humans can and ought sometimes to constrain their behavior for the good of plants and animals, or even rivers, canyons, and ecosystems. Indeed, not only in human affairs vis-à-vis nature, but in biological affairs generally, especially in zoology, there must be value capture. When a coyote eats a jackrabbit, the coyote gains, the rabbit loses. At least the individual rabbit loses, though the species may benefit from the pressures of predation.

But sometimes decisions can be win-win. There are nonrival goods. A decision can be good for both management and labor, if it keeps the company as a whole prospering. This is often true with values at stake between nature and culture. In *Caring for the World: A Strategy for Sustainability*, the opening argument laments "People vs. Earth: a No-Win situation," tragically the case today as escalating human growth and resource demands degrade the natural world (World Conservation Union 1990:9). Proper care for the natural world *can* combine with a strategy for sustainability, a win-win solution.

Denis Goulet acknowledges that "nature and human liberty have come to be perceived as opposing poles in a dichotomy" but holds that their seeming opposition "can be subsumed under a larger whole." "The reason is simply that any long-term, sustainable, equity-enhancing combat against poverty requires wisdom in the exploitation of resources." Humans, too, are members of their supporting ecosystems; "those human members cannot become truly 'developed' if their supportive nature is violated" (Goulet 1990:44). This claim is especially frequent among natural scientists. The Science Advisory Board of the Environmental Protection Agency (EPA) concluded: "Although natural ecosystems—and the linkages among them—are not completely understood, there is no doubt that over time the quality of human life declines as the quality of natural ecosystems declines" (Knickerbocker 1991:8). The idea here is that nature provides the life support that is often good for culture. Fauna, flora, and people all need clean air, clean water, good soil. It is hard to have a healthy culture in a sick environment. This is the entwined destinies view where values are often complementary.

Now we can clarify the relative sense in which culture can be natural. Natural and cultural values come in degrees on a spectrum. Although it is true that any deliberated action is unnatural (in sense [1], above), and continuing to set aside the unhelpful truth that all cultural events are natural (in sense [2]), and recognizing that it is human nature to build cultures, about which cultures they have some options, we can notice that some cultures are more, some less in a sustainable relationship with their ecosystems. All cultures modify their landscapes; agricultural and industrial cultures modify landscapes considerably, but they should also acknowledge that no culture can exist without the natural givens—air, water, soil, sunshine and photosynthesis, trophic pyramids, recycling of nutrients, and so on. Such a culture will be relatively natural (in sense [3]).

The goods of culture often require the conservation of natural goods, not only in actual life support, but also in life enrichment. No culture develops independently of the environment on which it is superimposed, no matter how relatively free humans are in their cultural options. In the underlying story of culture there are always distinctive landscape features—for instance, the Shenandoah Valley or the Chesapeake Bay with which the Virginians interact. The Finger Lakes are part of the ethos of central New York state. Shorelines are essential to the quality of life on Prince Edward Island. The British have their moors; the Germans the Black Forest, the Russians the steppes. However much the native wildness is domesticated, humans want some nature preserved, for it comes to express and support the values of the culture superimposed on it. What would Florida be without its flora?

Some deliberated human actions are more in keeping—others less—with how Earth was proceeding prior to human arrival and with how nature yet proceeds spontaneously in independence of humans. Some human actions intelligently fit in with the ecological cycles, while others do not. Humans ought to choose a culture that is sustainable on the land, one congenial to the values achieved over evolutionary natural history and the ecological values that continue still. That is a first principle of intelligent action; no contrast between nature and culture ought to forget such complementarity.

It is true that Earth is now in a post-evolutionary phase. Culture, now more than nature, is the principal determinant of Earth's future; we are passing into a century when this will be increasingly obvious. Indeed, that will be the principal novelty of the new millennium: Earth will be a managed planet (though see chapter 7, sec. 5). But we are not yet in a post-ecological phase; the management of the planet *must* conserve environmental values. Hopefully, such a policy can, in places on

Earth, let nature take its course, let nature evolve. We may have to see to it that the Colorado River continues running through the Grand Canyon by an act of Congress. On those parts of the Earth that we rebuild to our cultural preferences, we will have to conserve the natural values that support such culture. The technosphere still remains a part of the biosphere.

3. RESIDENCE AND RESOURCE:
COMMUNITY AND COMMODITY

Culture may modify nature, but we continue to live on landscapes. All life requires a place; an examined life needs a sense of place. With this sense of place, treating the dirt as a natural resource to be farmed, mined, timbered, or owned is necessary but not sufficient for an understanding of natural value. The question is not that of maximum exploitation of Earth as a big property resource; it is that of valued residence in a community of life. A discriminating account will counter any bifurcation of nature and culture by realizing that humans reside in their cultures within countries, where "country" includes a sense of geographical dwelling place. A person without a country—a landscape as well as a nation-state—is a tragedy. That is the root of the word *nation*, those who are "natives," being born and bred (Greek: *natans*) in a country.

To put this point provocatively, recall how the ancient Hebrews thought of Palestine as a promised land, a land flowing with milk and honey, a land that they were to use justly and charitably, yet still very much a geographical country with which their cultural destiny was entwined. They rejoiced in the natural processes: the sunshine, the clouds and rain, the soil, the seasons, seedtime and harvest, which they marked with festivals. They included the wild beasts in their covenant with God. Subsequently, in the Diaspora, the Jews became a people without a country; and they persistently regarded this as tragic, even though Judaism also became more universalist and less land-based. Alternately, they said that all peoples, everywhere, inhabit lands with promise.

Americans sing "America the Beautiful," glad for purple mountains' majesties and the fruited plains stretching from sea to shining sea. People on the frontier found that they had no sooner conquered a wilderness than they had come to love the land on which they settled. As sung in the musical *Oklahoma*, "We know we belong to the land, and the land we belong to is grand." Of those drawn to the city for livelihood or commodities, many really prefer to live in the "suburbs," so as to remain also near the country, in some place not consummately urban but where there is more green than anything else, where, with the neighbors, there are fencerows and cardinals, dogwoods and rabbits. We cherish our hills of home, our rivers, our bays, our country drives. Real estate agents term these "amenities" with our "commodities," but this is really nature mixed in with our culture. We want greenbelts in cities, mountains on the skyline, parks, seashores and lakeshores, spits, headlands, islands, forests, even wildernesses, including deserts, tundra, and swamps to visit. Most people identify with some countryside; indeed, our affections toward the city are often exceeded by those we have toward the landscapes on which we were reared.

"Resources" contains the idea of taking a natural source and *re*-directing it to our cultural needs. "Resource" is not just a cultural concept, because every living thing must have resources, nutrients that it takes in and sequesters for its own uses. Humans, coyotes, and warblers all require resources, but humans redirect their resources extensively and intentionally to rebuild their environments. They do so with the know-how of transmissible cultures. Within culture we distinguish between what we value as consumers and what we value as citizens. Often we use government to regulate business in order to protect these citizen values that cannot be left to unregulated commerce. The question is not simply one of multiple exploitive uses, but of multiple values to be optimized. We already know this when we think like citizens. Environmentalists add that people need to be "native residents" as well. "*Re*-side" has the root "re" (repeatedly) and "sedere" (to sit); it is where one settles down to live, one's home.

When we begin to think of ourselves primarily as consumers, and secondarily as citizens, and only rarely as residents, we are getting our values topsy turvy. Such insistence on the primacy of residence is sometimes called "bioregionalism," which is well enough as far as it goes, but this sense of geographical place should also involve a *global* sense of residence. Future generations, as we enter the next millenni-

um, must increasingly realize that we are earthlings—of the Earth—
and that this is our home planet, an emphasis with which we will conclude (chapter 7).

Natural selection could certainly select for people who love that
with which they have an entwined destiny; that should convey survival advantage. Formerly, humans hardly knew they inhabited a
planet, but they did know they dwelt on landscapes. They belonged to
"countries," and it seems plausible to think that humans could, over
time, be selected to love their geographical places. Animals feel most
comfortable in their niches. Some observers have noted that people
especially love savanna environments (trees with open spaces, also
springs or streams), because this is the kind of environment in which
humans evolved (Orians 1980). Perhaps, but our capacity to love
places will be flexible, since humans inhabit many different kinds of
landscapes and have the capability to rebuild them to their liking,
often making them savanna-like.

That rebuilding, too, will convey survival advantage. Maybe there
is some selection of those who love culture and conquer nature. Still,
in the end, every culture remains set in an ecosystem. There is no cause
to think that all our emotions are for coping in culture, and none for
loving nature. It must be part of our human nature—the human genetic destiny, if there is such a thing—to make choices that keep the self
happy in its home place.

We are born clean of culture, for any culture can be emplaced in
any newborn. But we are not born free of nature, and in any cultural
education we do ill to neglect those emotions that are native to our
birth. The word *human* is cognate with the word *humus*, because we
are made of dirt and we dwell on earth, on Earth. We need roots as
well as resources. Nature offers resistance to life as well as conductance, and the values that flow on Earth are aroused and energized in
the interplay of both; human values flow in the interplay between natural and cultural values.

The landscape is crucially a "commons," a public good, and that
not just for people but for all the residents of the biotic community,
including nonhumans. Coyotes and warblers cannot be citizens, but
they are residents on the same landscape as ours. They, too, are earthlings. The decisions we make as geographical residents, then, will have
to consider the fauna and flora not simply as resources but as residents

who count for the values they carry. The word *resident* enlarges one's community further than does the word *citizen*. Good citizenship is important. But it is not simply what a society does to its slaves, women, minorities, handicapped, children, or future generations, but what it does to its fauna, flora, species, ecosystems, rivers, beaches, and landscapes that reveals the character of that society.

4. URBAN, RURAL, AND WILD

There are three kinds of environments on Earth: the urban, the rural, and the wild. In urban environments culture has largely replaced nature. In wild environments culture is absent or minimally present. The hybrid zone is rural, where nature and culture blend. "Man is by nature a political animal," said Aristotle (*Politics* I, 2.1253a); the human *genus* may be animal, but the human *differentia* or essence is to build a *polis*, a town. The human habitat is village, town, city, which is another way of saying that human life is political, social, or, more generally, cultural.

The novelty when humans appear is not simply that humans are more versatile in their spontaneous natural environments. Animals take nature ready to hand (so to speak, though few have hands), adapted to it by natural selection, fitted into their niches. Humans rebuild their world through artifact and heritage, agriculture and culture, political and religious decisions. Humans have hands, coupled with their minds; they think about and go to work on their world. *Homo sapiens* is *Homo faber*. Deliberately rebuilt environments replace spontaneous wild ones. This is especially evident in cities. The keyword for this phenomenon, in recent discussions, is *development*.

The values that humans cherish in towns cannot be modeled on values in nature, since there are no templates for towns in wild nature. Nature frees humans to do their own thing. Humans are the creatures that nature did not specialize but rather equipped with marvelous faculties for culture and craft. There must remain a biological understory for our cities, rather like the life of the mind requires ongoing biochemistry; after that, we are on our own. The values of the city are up to us and they ought to be judged by a culturing of those native endowments we call reason and conscience. The city is in some sense our niche; we belong there, and no one can achieve full humanity without it. Cultured human life is not possible in the unaltered wilderness; it is primitive and illiterate if it remains hunter-gatherer or even if it remains at a merely rural level. The city mentality provides us with literacy and advancement, whether through the market with its trade and industry, or through the library and laboratory.

The rural environment is likewise valuable, since no city can be sustained without rural life support. The rural is nature as domesticated, rebuilt for our residence, primarily the cultivated landscape—the agricultural field, the woodlot, the pasture, the orchard, the ranch, the forest watershed, irrigation ditches, the road from place to place, rivers bridged, and nature as generally managed. Forests are cut down or planted, fields plowed, livestock tended, farmhouses and barns built, and so on. The farm feeds the city, and that may be taken as metaphor for the whole support of society in soil, water, air—for the organic circulations of the city in nature. The rural environment is where humans meet nature in a productive encounter, where we command nature by obeying her.

Because of this rebuilding, humans can inhabit environments altogether different from the African savannas in which they once evolved. In the city, and even on the farm, they insulate themselves from environmental extremes by their rebuilt habitations, with central heat from fossil fuel or by importing fresh groceries from a thousand miles away. In that sense, animals have freedom within ecosystems, but humans have freedom from ecosystems. Animals are adapted to their niches; humans adapt their ecosystems to their needs. Humans act using large numbers of tools and things made with tools, extrasomatic artifacts. In all but the most primitive cultures humans teach each other how to make clothes, thresh wheat, make fires, bake bread.

This contribution of labor builds an economy, which is something more than a natural ecology. Humans have hands and build artifacts and cultural value depends on this. This is the "re-" in "re-source," the natural course re-directed by human effort and made into something valuable. That is also why economists often think that markets are the real centerpiece of value. Animals do not labor to make artifacts nor trade their labors and artifacts; but humans do this in markets, and so markets will reveal what work humans have done, what artifacts they value. Value comes with the "development" of the natural givens; that is what happens in rural and urban areas.

Yet this is only half true, since all development depends on the natural givens. Nature is not like an empty glass that only carries the values that human labor puts into it. We value the natural properties on which technology depends; human art has no independent powers of its own. Human craft can never produce any unnatural farms, or towns, or chemicals, or energies. All we can do is shift natural things around, taking their properties as givens. That takes us back to "natural" (in sense [2]), meaning that nothing that humans can do in rural or urban areas breaks natural laws. The rural environment, especially, keeps us aware of how nature serves cultural value, including economic value, because of its rich utilitarian pliability, due both to the plurality of the natural sorts and to their splendid multifaceted powers. Nature is a fertile field for human labor, and that agricultural metaphor (which applies just as well to industry) praises not only laborers but their surrounding environment. Natural properties mix with human ingenuity to assume value.

Though we do not reside in the wild, we wish to conserve the wild, along with the rural and the urban, on our landscapes. Our requirements for wild nature are more difficult to specify than those for tamed nature, but nonetheless real. The scarcest environment we now have is wilderness and, when we are threatened with its possible extinction, we are forced to think through our relationship to it. Do we preserve wild nature only as a potential resource for activity that humans may someday wish to undertake in terms of urban or rural nature? Or are there richer values, both moral and prudential reasons why we ought to maintain some of our environment in a primitive state? A fuller answer must be postponed until chapter 6, but we can lay the groundwork here.

Wild nature is a place of encounter where humans go, not to act on it, not to labor over it, but to contemplate it, drawing ourselves into its order of being, not drawing it into our order of being. This accounts for our tendency to think of our relationship to nature as being recreational, and therefore perhaps idle, since we do not do any work while there. We are at leisure there, often, of course, an active leisure, but one that is not economically productive. We do not convert wilderness to farm or city. Wild nature is not commodity for us, but it does reveal the diversity of the larger Earth community in which we reside, even though we humans cannot reside in wild nature and have resolved not to remake it into *polis* (town). Wilderness brings a moment of truth, when we realize how false it is that the only values, moral or artistic or political, are human values. Wild nature has a kind of integrity; it is creation itself and contact with it is re-creating (a deeper recreational value) because we encounter our sources, beyond our resources.

There nature has intrinsic philosophical and religious value (chapter 5, sec. 1 [14]). Neither religion nor philosophy is present in wild nature, of course, since animals cannot pray or argue. Humans can think about ultimates; they can espouse worldviews; indeed, they are not fully human until they do. No one can form a comprehensive worldview without a concept of nature, and no one can form a view of nature without evaluating it in the wild, deliberating over spontaneous nature and whether and how it can have value. In that sense, one of the highest of cultural values, an examined worldview, is impossible to achieve without wild nature to be evaluated as foil to and indeed source of culture.

Rather interestingly, some analysts, especially economists, speak of the contemporary reevaluation of nature by those who join the Sierra Club, Wilderness Society, or Audubon Society as "urban values." They mean that such evaluation of nature characterizes urbanites more than farmers; they may notice that only after city folk are comfortably fed, clothed, and housed with the produce of rural areas, do they turn to recreate in the wilderness or go birdwatching. But it is revealing too that it is just such urban people, who evidently value the city, are those who also find that they need continuing contact with the wild. In that sense the deprivation of the city awakens a sensitivity to the wild, one that rural people, caught up in laboring over nature, and still having some wild nature in their surroundings, can forget or take for granted. A merely urban person is, we might say, one-dimensional; three-dimensional persons will know how appropriately to respect urban, rural, and wild environments. Many rural people think that such an environment is really the best from which to look in both directions, and they may join environmentalist societies as readily as urban dwellers.

Development seems like a good thing, but we cannot really know what we are doing until we know what we are undoing. What is evident across the American continent, and around the world, is development—condominiums, dams, highways, shopping centers, mushrooming cities, forests cut, lands mined, trash dumps. Less evident is how this cultural development is bringing about a tragedy—the catastrophic collapse of evolutionary developments there since remote geological times. We do value cultural development, and so we want rural and urban areas in which to reside. But irreversible destruction of the generative and regenerative powers on Earth, the loss of the wild, cannot be the positive "development" that humans want.

5. ENVIRONMENTAL VALUES AND HUMAN RIGHTS

Humans have a right to an environment with integrity. Such a right, though novel and loosely specified as yet, includes protection of the air, soils, waters, and essential biological processes, protecting the sustainable productivity of the land, the preservation of biodiversity, protection from toxic substances, access to natural resources essential for life, and perhaps access to public lands and commons. Such a right is emerging now, previously little acknowledged because little threatened (human rights to development are discussed in chapter 6, sec. 4). We discover that there is one more domain of value, always present but only lately consciously appreciated, now so threatened that it must come under political protection.

Perhaps we will need to add an article to the Bill of Rights. The National Wildlife Federation has proposed an "Environmental Quality Amendment" to the United States Constitution. Amending the Constitution is probably politically too difficult, but the idea is logically sound. This right is more likely to be established, within the United States, by other environmental legislation; and, indeed, Congress has passed hundreds of laws to protect environmental integrity on grounds that American citizens have values at stake here that ought to be protected. "The Congress recognizes that each person should enjoy a healthful environment and that each person has a responsibility to contribute to the preservation and enhancement of the environment" (U.S. Congress 1969: sec. 101[c]).

The *Universal Declaration on Human Rights* (UN General Assembly 1948), which contains nothing on the natural environment, could be amended. The UN World Commission on Environment and Development has proposed: "All human beings have the fundamental right to an environment adequate for their health and well-being" (UN World Commission 1987:9).* Pope John Paul II insists, "The right to a safe environment . . . must be included in an updated charter of human rights" (John Paul II 1989:467). In nations revising their constitutions, the right to nature ought to be a constitutional right.

The key words for such a right are still open to discussion. Possibilities include the right to a natural environment with quality, health, and integrity, to a productive environment, to one adequate for well-being, to a sustainable environment without permanent degradation of resources. In addition to a basic right that ought to be transcultural and universal, since everyone needs to breathe air, drink water, have a sustainable food supply, and enjoy a landscape, this right, to some extent, might be time-bound and nation-specific. The detail of application could vary with the degree of environmental alteration that has already taken place historically or with the relative richness of natural resources on differing landscapes.

This new right is important ethically and its need is quite urgent, because if not soon established, many environments with integrity—which presently remain or might be restored—may be irreversibly lost forever. This claim is also philosophically interesting because of the mix of cultural with natural values. "Rights" is a concept that ethicists and politicians have developed over the last four hundred years, as part of the Enlightenment's legacy, with which to protect core human goods. A right is a valid claim that a person can make, or have made on their behalf, to have their interests or welfare taken into account. Rights invoke justice and equality, rather than benevolence or charity. They propose standards below which human life in culture ought not to fall. A typical account of basic rights includes: freedom of physical movement, ownership of property, freedom from torture, a fair trial, nondiscriminatory treatment, physical security, freedom of speech and association, minimal education, political participation, and subsistence. It seems perfectly consistent with such human rights

---

* The United Nations Commission on Human Rights, through its Sub-Commission on Prevention of Discrimination and Protection of Minorities, has underway a study on human rights and environmental problems.

to add that humans have a right not only to the basic life support but also to the quality of their natural environment.

But here we must be careful. Culture, and not nature, is the proper venue for such talk of rights. There are no rights in wild nature. Natural value per se does not include any right to nature. Rather, we value that kind of culture that includes harmony with nature, conserving natural values. To guarantee such a culture, we resolve that humans have a right to a decent natural environment. Claiming such a right will be an assertion *about* nature, not culture, but it will not be an assertion directed *to* nature, the source of these goods; rather, it will be directed to other humans. Rights claims will still operate within the affairs of culture, as these now touch the life-support system. In other words, they will be political claims.

Some sort of inclusive environmental fitness is required of even the most advanced culture. Whatever their options, however their environments are rebuilt, humans remain residents in an ecosystem. But earlier ethics and law never paid much attention to ecosystems because humans had little comprehensive scientific knowledge of ecology, and even less power to affect these processes (although there was environmental degradation in ancient Mesopotamia, and although there is historic natural-resource law).

Lately, owing to human population increases, advancing technology, and escalating desires, we are drastically modifying our life-support system. People's lives may be threatened by these alterations, and this raises ethical questions. Humans now must assert a right to a decent environment. In that sense, if there is any such thing as natural rights, privileges that we possess just by being born on Earth, the right to nature will be foremost among them. Natural right does not refer, as natural rights have typically referred before, to values intrinsic to the nature of personhood, but to instrumental natural givens, intrinsic to human ecology, to which humans have a birthright. Humans have no right to dispossess other people from this natural heritage.[*]

---

[*] Property rights, already on the traditional list, are rights to local sites of occupation and development on parcels of land with surveyed boundaries, on which one has the usufruct, the right to use and enjoy so long as the property is not substantially damaged. But we have not hitherto had to establish rights to the landscape in the ecological sense.

People do not degrade their natural environments except in the course of pursuing cultural values that they desire. No one pollutes a stream just for the fun of it; the pollution is the result of mining, farming, manufacturing, or some other labor that resourcefully uses the natural environment to make it over into some desired artifact. The pollution is an undesired byproduct of the quest for some cultural good. Meanwhile, this byproduct threatens a natural value, the integrity of the ecosystem, which is valuable in the life-support system of that culture. Such disvalue falls involuntarily on many who are not parties to the business transactions of which the pollution is a byproduct. The rights claim here constrains the kinds of labor that are acceptable within culture, by identifying a threshold of environmental quality below which we will not allow cultural development to push us. Artifacts are a good thing, but not if the result is toxic air, soil, or water. Humans may have a right to development, but they do not have the right to development that imperils fundamental natural values. To the contrary, all humans have a right to those values, a right significant enough to constrain development that threatens these values.

6. FUTURE GENERATIONS

Values have to be conserved over time—long periods of time. In the birth-death-birth-death cycle, life goes on by series of replacements, of the deer in the forests, of the people in the towns. The individual, although essential to biology and in ethics, is quite ephemeral on historical scales. Somatic defense and genetic transmission are the only conservation activities possible for most organisms; they are necessary for all. Cultural beings, humans, must also transmit their ideas and ideals, creeds and crafts, skills and sciences to the next generation. In this sense, every species is perpetually an endangered species, humans doubly so because they have to reproduce values at both natural and cultural levels. All of us live one generation short of extinction of self and kind and everything we value, unless we reproduce both our bodies and our thoughts.

Most immediately our personal identity surrounds our body and our own memory traces and aspirations. But we live with our children, remember our grandparents, and see our grandchildren come into the world, who will outlive us. We can dissociate our identity from the immediate level of our own life and reassociate it with our family tradition, even more broadly with our ethnic and national kinds. Still, we may falter thinking of ancestors whose names have been forgotten, or of faceless future nonpersons. Far-off descendants, like distant races, do not have much "biological hold" on us. Across the era of human evolution, little in our behavior affected those remote in time and space, and natural selection, as well as cultural reinforcement, shaped our conduct toward those closer. Making it through the next generation or two was what counted; if we did that, the subsequent generations could take care of themselves.

But when one pauses to consider the life that one "has," only an ignorant person would think of oneself as completely self-sufficient, or that the values one enjoys are purely self-made personal preferences. Or even just those of one's immediate family. We are participants in a shared flow. We inherit values that our forebears conserved for us; we bequeath values to our descendants. Something of Socrates and Jesus, of Newton and Darwin, of parents and grandparents is recomposed when we compose our own personal identity. The main idea in genes is that we inherit so much of what we are from the biological past. The main idea in education is that we inherit so much of what we are from the cultural past. That will be as true tomorrow as it is today. Legacy will become more, not less important, because, increasingly, our actions have lengthened impact. We have to think not just over decades but over centuries, even millennia.

A mature self is able to envision itself in any present moment as enjoying but one slice of a temporally extended life, from birth to death. It is juvenile to value the present so as to devalue the future. A still more mature self realizes that the endpoints of an individual's life are regeneration points in a river of life, which overflows the individual that it flows through. We pass away, but we pass life on. We share a common life with posterity. Though future generations are not available for reciprocal obligations, a common life is transported from here to there.

All the stages are eventually present, and "now" has no favored status in its value significance. The "now" is favored only because we have more responsibility in the present, with consequences for the future. Again, the immature fall into the illusion that the future counts for less, perhaps also misled by what economists call "discounting the future." But this is rather like thinking that the telephone poles get smaller in the distance; the diminishing importance is only an illusion.

We cannot really conserve either natural or cultural values until we break out of that misperception. Farmers who conserve their soil, or teachers who transmit the wisdom of the past to generations to come, statesmen who strive to conserve the democratic way of life, scientists resolutely pursuing the next breakthrough, donors who endow the communities and institutions they have cherished or who give land to the Nature Conservancy, environmentalists who press for wilderness designation all recognize a more enduring community from which the self takes its identity.

To protect our values we must project these values that we enjoy, we must seek to conserve these values for the others with whom we come to have an entwined identity. Love implies a caring about what happens after we are gone. That has natural roots in the urge for parenting; it has cultural roots in the urge to preach one's values to the next generation. Loving is a form of valuing, but love that turns in on itself is unworthy of survival, it will not survive, nor ought it to. Biologically, reproduction always requires some sacrifice—time, energy, risk, and effort spent. Ethically, egoism (that one ought always to do what is in one's enlightened self-interest) is rejected by almost all philosophers. One must, one ought to care for oneself, but in such way that one also cares for others; ethics requires altruism. Only those who care enough to rear and nurture others, children or disciples, will or ought to be represented in generations to come.

The human reproductive urge has been, and remains, a good thing, necessary if there are to be future generations. Yet regeneration can in fact become a bad thing; a paradox of the century in which we are reproducing is that we have reached a point where the conserving of our cultural values requires controlling, possibly even curtailing, our reproduction. The expansion of the cultural realm quantitatively (more and more people) threatens to degrade the realm of the natural (overcut forests, eroded soil, overfished seas) below acceptable levels. Uncontrolled reproduction is cancerous, destructive because it is not sustainable. Conserving cultural values harmoniously with natural values requires that we carry life on only if we limit such generation to the carrying capacity of the natural systems with which we have an interdependent destiny.

We fall into illusion again if we think that we are here somehow being asked to curtail cultural values in favor of protecting natural values; to the contrary, this only extends the entwined destinies view over generations to come. It is no coincidence that environmental ethics and intergenerational ethics are often a single issue, for our survival as races and species and our cultural survival requires a surviving habitat. It is typically, though not invariably, the case that what is good now for the environment is also good for the human future.

Ecology teaches us to expand vastly our notions of connections and cycles, which affect our sense of belongingness and identity. No life form, humans included, can carry itself on through future generations if its environment is not also, at a minimum, sustainable. We can "regenerate" only if our sources are "renewable." We are meeting the prefix "re-" again, now not for the making over of something natural into something human, but, rather, for the making of culture over and over again, this "re-newing" of culture requiring a nature that in turn can be "re-newed." It was a concern for future generations that for many sparked an early involvement with natural conservation. "Development" catches the rebuilding and reproduction of culture, generation after generation, only if we add "sustainable" as a modifier to all acceptable "development" (see chapter 3, sec. 4).

The present is what endures out of the past; the future is what endures out of the present. In an examined life, the deepest levels of meaning are not found merely in the present, but, as in all narrative, when leading features of the past survive, deepen, and cohere to govern across repeated chapters in a whole plot. Or, to move from literary to musical metaphor, life is like the flow of a symphony; the present melody is enjoyed in itself, but it often recapitulates what has gone before and leads on toward movements to come. Life needs the dimensions of retrospect and prospect. We are set in motion with what was delivered to us; we carry it on a bit, but not to its conclusion, we pass from the scene, and our students, disciples, and children carry on. We are trustees of value.

7. ENVIRONMENTAL POLICY

Philosophy and politics, cultural and natural history, mix more than they did before. Thoughts have been increasingly coupled with power. "Philosophy bakes no bread," they used to say. This was never really true, but where power to change the world was limited, people could have what metaphysics they had without much impact on the shape of the world. A people's practice, their technology, was not so close-coupled to their cosmology. The scale of all this has now changed by several orders of magnitude, both the pace and the extent of changes. When our philosophy is "Earth is a big natural resource; exploit it!" we make tractor plows and harvester combines and turn all of the American Midwest into a field for growing wheat to bake bread. We use fertilizers or pesticides that degrade riparian ecosystems. We may ship the wheat to Europe and put rural farmers out of business, affecting for better or worse the rural wildlife half a world away.

A great deal does turn on our state of mind. Our decisions shape our history, the history of others, and even the history of the planet. All this makes an environmental policy more urgent. Such policy is something that humans in their culture can deliberate and set, in contrast to animals who have no environmental policy at all; neither have they any philosophy of conservation. *Policy*, like *ethics*, is a word that belongs in culture, not nature. And the last quarter-century has seen, in the United States and elsewhere, a steady enactment of environmental legislation. There is, of course, a long tradition of natural-resource law, but "ecological values" had little place in it until the second half of this century.

Now the National Environmental Policy Act sets culture in intended harmony with nature in the United States:

> The purposes of this Act are: To declare a national policy which will encourage productive and enjoyable harmony between man and his environment; to promote efforts which will prevent or eliminate damage to the environment and biosphere and stimulate the health and welfare of man; to enrich the understanding of the ecological systems and natural resources important to the Nation. . . . The Congress . . . declares that it is the continuing policy of the Federal

Government . . . to create and maintain conditions under which man and nature can exist in productive harmony. . . .

The Congress authorizes and directs that, to the fullest extent possible: . . . all agencies of the Federal Government shall . . . identify and develop methods and procedures . . . which will insure that presently unquantified amenities and values may be given appropriate consideration in decisionmaking along with economic and technical considerations. [Also they shall] recognize the worldwide and long-range character of environmental problems, and . . . maximize international cooperation in anticipating and preventing a decline in the quality of mankind's world environment. (U.S. Congress 1969, sec. 2, secs. 101–102)

Internationally, the largest summit conference ever held was to set environmental policy, the United Nations Conference on Environment and Development (UNCED), in Rio de Janeiro in June 1992. There were delegations from 178 nations, virtually every nation in the world, 7,000 diplomats and delegates, 30,000 advocates of environmental causes, and 7,000 journalists. More heads of state and government (118) gathered to address environmental policy than had ever gathered in one place before in the history of the Earth. The Convention on Biodiversity was signed as well as the Framework Convention on Climate Change. The conference endorsed *Agenda 21*, over nine hundred pages of environmental and development policy. Cultural diversity prevented as much unanimity as might have been hoped for. Nevertheless, concern about environmental policy ran high.

We can get some insight into the tradeoffs between cultural and natural values by looking at the language of the Rio Declaration, adopted by UNCED. Originally this was to be called the "Earth Charter," but some nations protested that this emphasized Earth too much and people and their development too little—nature more than culture—and hence the name change. The final declaration affirms twenty-seven principles, of which the first is: "Human beings are at the centre of concerns for sustainable development. They are entitled to a healthy and productive life in harmony with nature" (UNCED 1992c). The desired healthy, productive life in harmony with nature echoes U.S. policy. For those concerned with sustainable development, human beings are indeed at the center of such concerns.

But the draft text, eventually rejected, was longer and more explicit. It contained so-called bracketed text, over which there was general agreement but not without some dispute:

[The well-being and dignity of humankind on a healthy planet are at the center of environmental and developmental concerns. Human beings are entitled to live in a sound environment, [in dignity and in harmony with nature for which they bear the responsibility for protection and enhancement] and bear the responsibility to protect, restore and improve it for the benefit of present and future generations]. (UNCED 1992b)

The final, cut version, adopted to achieve a consensus, minimally retains a harmony with nature, but it deemphasizes the human responsibility for the protection, restoration, and enhancement of nature, made clear also by the refusal to call this an "Earth Charter." The final version does also state, in principle 7, "States shall cooperate in a spirit of global partnership to conserve, protect, and restore the health and integrity of the Earth's ecosystem." Otherwise it is largely oriented to the right to sustainable development. Both versions are, we might fear, too anthropocentric, but perhaps political documents always have to err on the side of people values. At stake here is the mix of cultural values (symbolized by the keyword "development") and natural values (symbolized by the keyword "environment") in a struggle that keeps them in subtle balance.

Both the U.S. policy and the UN policy illustrate how environmental policy, philosophically, orients citizens' uses of the commons to make responsible residents. It sets goals for an optimal mix of cultural with natural values. This cannot be left to the good intentions of private individuals, because there are things that individuals can do only if they act in concert. Nor can it be left to individuals in private corporations, such as business, industry, or agriculture. Environmental matters are not private matters; they involve a commons, a common wealth. So they have to be public.

More comprehensively still, environmental matters are more than public, in the usual sense of the word (from the Latin *publicus*, belonging to people). They cannot just be left to other agencies of government, such as the military, or health, education, or welfare agencies, although all agencies of government ought to consider their impacts on environmental quality. The commonwealth is bigger than state or nation, bigger than just people. Environmental policy must be an arm of government, of course, but it is government residing in, superposed on landscape. This is a matter of the whole ecology, the "logic" of the "home," the biotic community entwined with the cultural community. The "commons" (Latin: *communis*) is what is shared by all the community. This commons is bigger than people-public; it is biological-ecological too.

Until now the paradigm for environmental policy in the United States (and elsewhere) has been "multiple uses," and that paradigm may still be lingering in the Rio Declaration. People have a right to use nature for development. But increasingly we are switching to a paradigm of "multiple values" carried by natural systems, to be optimized in their mix with cultural values.

8. BALANCING NATURAL AND CULTURAL VALUES

The world is a complicated and ambiguous place. We are faced with values so diverse in kind and degree, enjoyed or lost by so many people and by animals and plants as well. There is just choice against choice, and who is to say? Are there any rules on which we can approach a consensus? We will not find any calculus here, for mathematical values in equations is too much to expect. But neither is there just confusion. We can make a start. What are some rules of thumb for balancing natural and cultural values? We will start with ten.

1. *Emphasize nonrival cultural and natural values.* This rule does not dodge the issues but tries to get first things first. Culture is a "development" that redoes nature, and it must undo pristine nature, so far as there is intervention and management, but there is still a commons. Where there is a win-win solution, insist on it. If there are win-lose parts to the decision, cultural benefits that require environmental harms, insist on the win-win parts first, cultural goods that coincide with environmental goods. Get those values in place, systemic to the whole; make those nonnegotiable, and then turn to the conflicts. We will return to this principle in closing (chapter 7, sec. 6).

2. *Be careful about compromises.* Nonrival values do not have

to be compromised. But in win-lose parts of the decision, we might think the best rule is compromise. In fact, "compromise" can almost seem a synonym for "balance." But that is not necessarily true, especially where the situation is quite unbalanced already. Compromises often put at risk what they propose to save. The old saying, that "half a loaf is better than none," may be true for those who are arguing over bread. But what if they are arguing over a horse? Some values do not compromise without devaluing them, even destroying them. Consider wilderness designation. About 2 percent of the contiguous United States is wilderness (1.2 percent designated; 1 percent under study). The remaining 98 percent is developed, farmed, grazed, timbered, or designated for multiple use. Another 2 percent might be suitable for wilderness or semi-wild status. So the "balance" is 98–2, or perhaps 96–4. In dispute, we might be tempted to compromise, but then that would make it 99–1, or 97–3. The numbers are only illustrative, indicating that a seeming compromise only further skews the imbalance, at least on this scale. Consider the old-growth forest and spotted owl controversy. Some propose compromise. But how unbalanced is the situation already, due to previous cutting? Half the trees saved would be better than none at all. But the spotted owl might be more like the horse, for if its remaining critical habitat is cut in half, this will not support a viable breeding population; that means no owl at all.

"In politics compromise is the name of the game." Where there is choice against choice, one can expect that positive values will be at stake on both sides; and, in a pluralist democracy, we can often expect that compromise will optimize such values. Compromises can be fair and equitable. We incline to compromise when issues are complex, when there is evidently some value on both sides, when there is a decision required that is impossible to postpone, or where postponing will result in value loss for both sides. Often, too, the facts and projections are uncertain, which makes us less sure of our position. Compromise can win something, while uncompromising "purity" is a sure route to defeat.

But those who are alert to the logic of compromise also know that compromises can mean unbalance and destruction. Compromise is likely to cast the solution in terms of who has interests to adjudicate and is noisy about these. But the better question is: What is of value in the world and how ought we behave so as to optimize those values? Compromise often means that decisions are made in courts (or outside of courts lest courts be invoked), but this means that those who have power to do adversarial work succeed; this may not always be the best way to reach decisions. Adversaries are not always the best optimizers; there is no invisible hand that guides adversarial relations into optimal solutions. There are values here to be discovered, not just interests to be defended.

3. *Protect minority values.* We are wise to guard against some kinds of decisions by simple majority. Just as we do not necessarily split the values half and half, neither do we decide about the split by getting one over half on our side. Democracies have to provide for the protection of minority interests, to protect against hasty and irreversible actions, to insure that there are checks and balances, to protect values that they really do not want to compromise. Democracies may require, for instance, a two-thirds vote before taking particularly important actions, or they may give certain authorities veto power, or they may require different committees or agencies to concur. They may reserve some matters for courts rather than legislators. We might not be wise to declassify a wilderness for logging, given the 98–2 ratio, on a 51-to-49-percent simple plurality, since the change is irreversible and the values at stake among the most rare on the landscape.

4. *Complement economic frameworks with ecological analyses.* The U.S. Congress requires an environmental impact statement to "insure that presently unquantified amenities and values may be given appropriate consideration". Congress also "declares that it is the policy of the United States that" there be "a combination of balanced diverse resource uses . . . without permanent impairment of the productivity of the land and the quality of the environment with consideration being given to the relative values of the resources and not necessarily to the combination of uses that will give the greatest economic return" (U.S. Congress 1976a, secs. 102, 103). One rule for balancing is to get all of the values into the scales, not just the economic ones. This is also likely to make the nonrival values clearer.

5. *Enough is enough!* "Balance" contains the idea of knowing when too much is too much. We want to set that against two other words frequently met in decision making: "maximize" and "opti-

mize." In value theory, especially economic value theory, a rational agent often wants the most—the most profit, the most income, the most for his or her money. But we also reach points of diminishing marginal returns, that is, where more isn't really all that valuable. A major problem in a consumer-oriented society is knowing when to say enough. Growth is a good thing only in regulated contexts; otherwise, growth can be cancerous. "Optimize" is a more sophisticated word than "maximize" because it contains the idea of what is best (optimum), not just what is most (maximum). The best, rather than the most, is often enough.

6. *Identify all affected parties.* When decisions are being made, those who have a lot to gain or lose are likely to be vocal, while those who have a little to gain or lose are likely to be absent. A well-organized minority can outshout, outmaneuver, outlobby a disorganized majority. This may be presented as concentrated benefits or losses versus diffuse benefits or losses, and they will cry that it is unjust to impose concentrated losses on a few in order to gain diffuse benefits for the many. But a careful value analysis can reveal that in aggregate (if we really do wish the greatest good for the greatest number, or the optimal values preserved), the diffused benefits for the many, considered in aggregate and over time, really do outweigh the concentrated benefits for the few. If there are no rights being violated, no injustice being done, the balance requires counting in all the affected parties, not just those present at the hearing.

We do not want to underestimate so-called soft values against so called hard ones, if these really are deep and comprehensive values to be traded against immediate, short-term, special-interest values. One way of putting this in business contexts is that a moral decision maker has to identify not only the stockholders but also the stakeholders, the many who are affected by the decision who are not immediate parties in the business transactions. Another way of putting this is that business has to count the externalities, or the spillover. Where cultural values are at stake, all of the stakeholders are people, but with natural values, most of the stakeholders are not. The animals and plants have no voice in environmental policy. They are not citizens and do not vote. They cannot sue in courts. But they are residents on the landscape, and environmental policy affects them for better or worse. Political decision contexts, in which people are paramount, will have a bias against taking into account the goods of nonpeople. We are not likely to optimize natural values in counterpoint to cultural values while acting on the belief that nature has just whatever value we humans in our particular culture assign to it, no more, no less.

We may need an analog to affirmative action. We say that we ought to weigh more heavily the interests of those at a lower level of well-being (the poor, the uneducated, the disabled), since those at a high level already have enough (the rich, the educated, the healthy). A just society ought to favor the disadvantaged. Why not say, in decision contexts concerning animals and plants, that we ought to favor the interests of those most disadvantaged (the endangered, the powerless, those who have no standing in courts, those who have no rights, those who have no voice), since people are able to look out for themselves and have legislators and judges, family and friends to look out for them?

7. *Insist on sustainability*. With renewable resources, we ought not to have to spend biological capital at all. Soil, air, water, even forests ought to be in as good condition five hundred years from now as they are now, as they were five hundred years ago—or if not, at least in healthy enough condition to sustain both the cultural and natural values that are superimposed on them. Hardly anyone will contest this in principle, yet the principle is routinely undermined in practice.

One reason the practice is difficult to implement is the pressures of business to make a profit in the short term. But even today's business hopes to be in business a decade hence, even half a century hence, and today's businessperson has children and grandchildren that he or she hopes to be in business a century or so hence. Citizens use government to regulate capitalistic business to insure environmental responsibility, to make the playing field level for all. But citizens also have to recognize that democracy can find it a challenge to insist on sustainability, because citizens, no less than consumers, have short-term needs (see chapter 6, sec. 5). Some resources are nonrenewable (coal and oil) and here policymakers must insist on a withdrawal rate that keeps the foreseeable future in mind, and provide a substantial investment for research into substitutes, recycling, or alternative technologies.

8. *Avoid irreversible change*. History is a one-way process in time, so in its strictest sense this rule is impossible. But we can esti-

mate the duration of the impact of policy (a decade for forage, a century for timber regeneration, ten thousand years for soil lost, forever for extinction). The longer the impact, the slower we should proceed. We want all the natural components so that we can put things back as they were, if we have to. There are often unforeseen bad consequences, especially as technology becomes more manipulative, chemicals less biodegradable, and mutagens abound. It is often easier to make changes (flying supersonic transports, burning fossil fuels) than to foresee the results of the changes (climatic changes in the ozone layer or global warming). This is especially true as we approach the carrying capacity of the commons.

A responsibility of those who decide about the commons is to guarantee, so far as possible, that we do not make irreversible mistakes. "To keep every cog and wheel is the first precaution of intelligent tinkering," cautioned Aldo Leopold (1970:190). We should avoid radically closing options. Set that policy which allows us to redeem our mistakes. The chestnut tree and the passenger pigeon are gone forever; the starling and the English sparrow are here to stay. What is next with our acid rain over the Adirondacks, with our CO_2 warming up the climate?

9. *Recognize a shifting burden of proof.* When the first European settlers arrived in New England, their Yankee ingenuity posed little threat to the ozone layer, about which they knew nothing. The twentieth-century manufacturers of aerosol fluorocarbons do endanger that protective layer. Early Virginia farmers hardly knew that the South Pole existed; modern agribusiness in the South can use DDT that makes its way into penguins in Antarctica. The more massive the manipulative power, the nearer industry and agriculture approach the carrying capacity of the commons, the more the unintended, amplifying consequences are likely to be far-reaching. So the burden of proof shifts, and it is now up to those who wish to introduce changes to prove that their changes will optimize the mix of natural and cultural values.

One might have hoped that as our competence increased, risks would diminish. But the depth of upset advances even more, and we remain ignorant of our reach. With ever-higher technology, it seems that our power to produce changes overshoots increasingly our power to foresee all the results. It is easier to make Kepone—a toxic pesticide that Allied Chemical Company discharged into the James

River and Chesapeake Bay and for which in court settlements Allied paid $20 million in fines—than to predict what it will do in the ecology of the James River estuary, easier to mine uranium and make reactors than to predict where the mutagens in the tailings will end up and what damage will result. In a way, our ignorance outpaces our knowledge. So we are asking for trouble unless we slow down the introduction of potentially more potent novel changes without adequate pretesting. The unforeseen consequences outnumber the foreseen consequences, and the bad unforeseen consequences greatly outnumber the good unforeseen consequences, especially as they affect natural values.

We optimize values if we err on the safe side. Those who want to introduce changes have to argue that the risks are minimal, not to presume so, and chance the damage. Sometimes the long-standing patterns of social institutions have to be bent backward to get them straight. It is not enough just to take down the "No discrimination" signs, and otherwise continue business as usual, because the inertia of the past will continue into the future; little will change. One has to examine the prevailing practices and consciously counteract them. This is like throwing an engine into reverse to try to stop it, which one may have to do to stop a juggernaut. In environmental ethics, the human juggernaut has been overriding the welfare of animals, the protection of endangered species, the beauty, integrity, and stability of ecosystems for so many centuries that now we need to reverse ourselves in favor of nature to get it under control. We must shift the burden of proof.

10. *Make latent value judgments explicit.* Environmental values are not new, but they lie on a growing awareness of things before taken for granted, or naively appreciated. We did not realize what the mountain on the skyline meant to us, and in noneconomic terms, until developers threatened to cut it up with roads, take out the timber on the north half, and build a ski resort on the south half. Not until they proposed to drain the marsh could we say that we would rather have it left alone, and even now it is difficult to articulate why. To borrow an old expression, we never miss the water until the well runs dry.

We learn what is at stake only when we learn that it is at stake. We awaken to goods when their opposites threaten, or to inconsistencies in our own value sets when we cannot have our cake and eat it too. Natural values have often long been in place, but not at the forefront of our decision-making process. Now we have to make explicit what was latent. Sometimes making the latent explicit involves defending existing values. Sometimes it requires reversing existing priorities. The multiple-use values that prevail can seem to be the presumed ones, not needing to be argued for, while an increased recognition of natural, but nonuse values can seem to be radical and new, needing argument. But it is not only those who advocate change who advocate values. Those who advocate the status quo do so as well.

And one value can be subtly transformed into another, while the old decision stands and seems to remain unchanged—when new evidence comes in and situations change. A decision seemingly conserved can, in fact and in the light of new evidence, really be a decision remade incrementally by default. Not deciding can be redeciding, and such a latent value judgment needs to be made explicit.

2

Diversity and Complexity Values

■■
■■

Not every natural phenomenon that might be valued lies on Earth. The rings of Saturn are quite a marvel. Io, a moon of Jupiter, is bizarre, perpetually in volcanic convulsions, heated by an eccentric orbit around Jupiter, causing frictional tides. Astronauts, or even tourists, might someday like to visit these places. But Earth's diversity commands our attention. Humans have, increasingly, dramatic powers to affect this diversity for the worse. The diversity and complexity on Earth far and away exceeds any that we yet know elsewhere. We humans, the most complex creature on our planet, live right in the middle of it all, adding a whole new dimension: cultural complexity.

1. DIVERSITY

Earth's diversity includes geological and mineralogical diversity, diverse climates, myriads of different islands, mountains, bays, caves, and on and on. No two landscapes are alike; each canyon or lake has its unique features. And things are constantly changing: the seasons, the rivers, even the mountains. We value this geographical variety. But the biodiversity on Earth is particularly striking—a billion or more species produced over several billion years—and particularly threatened by the adverse effects of cultural diversity. Biodiversity spans levels of organization from genes to biomes. We are concerned with saving species, but also with saving habitats and ecosystems, and germplasm, and with having healthy and robust environments—cumulatively what we will call biological richness. Balancing such a biological commonwealth against cultural richness will prove quite challenging.

The National Forest Management Act requires the United States Forest Service to manage forests so as to "provide for diversity of plant and animal communities" (U.S. Congress 1976b, sec. 6[g][3][B]). The Convention on International Trade in Endangered Species of Wild Fauna and Flora (CITES) protects biodiversity, as does the Endangered Species Act. The Earth Summit in Rio de Janeiro (UNCED) launched the Convention on Biological Diversity, signed by 153 nations, "concerned that biological diversity is being significantly reduced by certain human activities" and "conscious of the intrinsic value of biological diversity and of the ecological, genetic, social, economic, scientific, educational, cultural, recreational and aesthetic values of biological diversity" and "conscious also of the importance of biological diversity for evolution and for maintaining life sustaining systems of the biosphere" (UNCED 1992a: Preamble).

Edward O. Wilson asks, "What event likely to happen during the next few years will our descendants most regret? . . . The one process now going on that will take millions of years to correct is the loss of genetic and species diversity by the destruction of natural habitats. This is the folly our descendants are least likely to forgive us" (1984:121).

How much diversity is there? How much is at stake? We need to measure diversity—existing, threatened, or lost—in order to know what values are at issue. If we cannot measure diversity quantitatively, we can at least narrate diversity descriptively and make some assessment of its quality. The extent of biodiversity is not an easy

question to answer, either in a technical, scientific or in a philosophical, axiological sense. The difficulty rises from its richness, from the
diversity of diversity, if you will.

A first diversity index is the number of species (alpha diversity), or
species richness (something of a misnomer because a simple species
count does not indicate their frequency). The species is thought to be
more real than family, class, or order diversity, because species are the
actual historical lineages through which the natural kinds travel
through time, the breeding populations, as families or classes are not.
There are between 5 and 20 million species now on Earth. Generally,
the number of species increases as one travels from poles to equator,
though Earth is a more diverse planet with species in arctic, boreal,
temperate, and tropical ecosystems, than if it had no climatic diversity. Not long ago it was thought there were only about three million
species on Earth, with approximately half of these identified—4,100
species of mammals, 8,700 birds, 6,300 reptiles, 3,000 amphibians,
23,000 fishes, 800,000 insects, over 300,000 green plants and fungi,
and thousands of microorganisms.

Over recent decades such estimates have been pushed steadily
upward, owing to new discoveries and better taxonomy, mostly in the
invertebrates (Myers 1979; May 1988; Wilson 1992). We may think
that 1,000 new species of beetles represents less diversity than 100
new species of mammals, probably because we judge that mammals
are more complex. Meanwhile, these new species are mostly unde-
scribed, though projections from studied areas indicate that they exist.

Paleontologists estimate that 98 percent of past species are extinct,
so there have been perhaps over a billion species on Earth. One way
to respond to these natural extinctions is to lament that there has been
a large loss of biodiversity; but another way, especially when we
understand how respeciation requires turnover, is to see Earth as an
especially fecund planet. If we add up species historically we have several orders of magnitude more than we have today. We do not discount the past any more than we ought to discount the future. Each
species was, is, will be a good thing in its place and time. Today's
species merely represent a cross-section of the bigger picture.

Tragedy looms; humans threaten to shut down this long-standing
regenerating biodiversity. How many species are at threat? Typical
estimates are that about 20 percent of Earth's species are likely to be

lost over the next century if present growth projections continue, losses about evenly distributed through major groups of plants and animals in the United States and in the world (Council on Environmental Quality 1980, 1:37, 2:327–333). In Hawaii, of the 2,200 native taxa, about 40 percent are in jeopardy. About 56 percent of fish species in the United States and Canada are in need of protection. Threats are especially serious in tropical rainforests.

Another diversity index is the relative abundance of species, often called the "degree of evenness." That is, how frequent a species is in an area. In wild nature, relative abundance is under ecological control; ecosystems are tropic pyramids making it typical that plant species are more numerous than animal species, and some animal species more numerous than others. Ecosystems are so structured that most species are rare. Unfortunately, the infrequent and rare species are more subject to human-introduced stress than are the common or abundant ones. Therefore, the rare tend to be extinction-prone.

Diversity at another level asks how much ecosystems and their species vary within a region (beta diversity). How much community diversity is there? Due to elevation and resulting climatic changes, there may be deserts, grassland plains, montane forests, and arctic tundra all within thirty miles of each other in one region, where elsewhere there may be three hundred miles of nothing but grassland plains. Costa Rica, a small nation no bigger than the state of West Virginia, has more different species than all of the continental United States. This is because of its habitat diversity; there are dramatic elevation changes, the landscape is well watered, and it lies at the crossroads of two continents. Panama has as many plant species as all of Europe.

There are nearly two dozen indices of diversity of various kinds. (Magurran 1988; Pielou 1975). We need some account of whether these species are in diverse genera, families, classes, orders, phyla—in other words, hierarchical diversity. Two species in different phyla (i.e., a beetle and a chimpanzee) offer more diversity than two within the same genus. We will need some regional or global scales. If some species in a system are endemics, that will not affect local diversity indices, but such a local community, with its endemics, adds to the regional diversity, the general idea behind what is sometimes called "gamma diversity." Diversity is low on remote islands, but endemism is high. Isolation allows the few species there to fill new niches under altered patterns of competition. This high endemism, despite the low local diversity, adds to the global diversity. This is particularly true, for instance, in Hawaii (see chapter 4, sec. 4).

How diverse are the interconnections between species? There may be simple or quite complicated food chains, and the latter may give redundance and resiliency, or they may amplify disturbances. If the species are not equally well distributed in location, that will introduce yet another dimension to diversity. Mapping mosaics, or local areas where species occur, works reasonably well for areas covered with plants, but not with animals that move around—unless the animals tend to gather around certain plants. After mapping, we can measure areas and generate some new diversity statistics. Next we will wonder what determines the mosaics, and these factors can be more or less simple or complicated (soil types, rock outcrops, fire history, species competition, competitive exclusion). For predators and prey, the variety of hiding places, nooks, and crannies, is partly a matter of the geomorphology (rock ledges), partly a matter of the vegetation (hollow trees). Is the system climatically diverse (hot summers, cold winters; wet winters, dry summers) or geomorphologically diverse (mountains, plains, lakes, shorelines, desert, tundra), which may or may not be reflected in the diversity of fauna and flora (perhaps affecting the diversity of niches)?

While diversity is largely an objective fact about ecosystems, there will be some subjective decision calls about how many and what different kinds we have. We may run into some disagreements about lumping and splitting. We will have to make some decisions about where to draw the boundary lines, or zones, how long to watch the system. If we observe for ten decades, there can be more diversity coming and going in one of two communities that are equally diverse if we observe for only ten minutes. If the ecosystem is sizable, we cannot make a census of everything in it, and so we will have to have a methodology for sampling populations. If the organisms are arranged in patches (and not randomly), a random sample of space will not give a reliable estimate. So we begin to appreciate both that diversity is complex and that measuring it is no simple thing.

In earlier geological epochs, there were fewer species on Earth than now, but sometimes these were more disparate from each other (a point made forcefully by Stephen Jay Gould [1989]). Nature experiments in some epochs more than others. Diversity is constrained by the requirement that an organism function efficiently. After reaching an operational groundplan, species can be elaborated in kaleidoscopic variations on these basic groundplans.

Diversity is regularly valuable; "variety is the spice of life." Diversity is not, however, ipso facto a value. Were a university to receive an applicant from a foreign country, a young prince who wished to bring along his personal slave, would the university permit this, on grounds that it would add diversity? No, because justice is more important than diversity. Added perversity is not desirable diversity. Diversity is not valuable simply for its own sake. A family does not particularly value having more different kinds of disputes than it did before, if these disintegrate the affections that bind them together.

Some diversity is in fact pointless. If the prince had unusual birthmarks, like no one else on campus, that would not be any reason for admitting him either. Some diversity is superfluous. Discount drug stores already offer so many kinds of shampoo that one more, no better or worse, just different, is hardly a benefit. Nor is another flavor of ice cream in a store than already sells fifty-seven flavors. One might think that nature is even more fecund with beetles than the American industry with shampoos, not knowing when to say enough. But there is a relevant difference; each beetle species is an autonomous biological achievement.

We may not value finding many more parasites or disease organisms than we thought—at least not in terms of human health. We already lament that there are too many strains of flu virus. We may not value two beetle species if the only difference is the location of a few spots and bristles. It is doubtful whether we should value deformed freaks of nature (for example, two-headed calves), even though these are curiosities that people pay to see in sideshows, or that scientists study to understand what went wrong. Introduced exotics add diversity we may not want—dandelions in the wilderness. The primitive character of the wilderness is disrupted by the introduced weed. This subtracts from diversity on national scales, since there are dandelions practically everywhere and few areas pristine and without them. We value diversity that contributes to genuine richness in nature.

Diversity in nature is not simply pluralism. Nature's diversity might just be chaotic. Sometimes nature can seem this way, just a blooming, buzzing confusion. But ecologists know better. Diversity is complemented by integration and unity, and ecosystems are wholes, communities, that incorporate many organisms into networked pyramids. Diversity in ecosystems is not a tight, organismic unity; the integration is more open, within a complementing community. Each species has its own integrity in its niche, and each in turn is webbed into the larger community.

2. COMPLEXITY

The concept of complexity is itself complex, an account of which is even more challenging. We can measure some kinds of complexity (for instance, the number of levels in a tropic pyramid, of gene loci in a genome, of neurons in a brain), but we do not know how to integrate these into an overall measure of complexity. Different kinds of diversity are often graphed for an ecosystem,[*] but we have more trouble producing a graph of ecosystem complexity since overall complexity is not any one thing, or few things, to graph. There is something naive about expecting a simple account of what complexity is, or even some single measure of it. Some measure of the total genetic information (the "bits") present might be a start, but the amount of information does not reveal what the complexities of interactions are.

In fact, a reason often given for the relative immaturity of ecological theory compared with, say, theory in biochemistry is that ecosystems are so vastly complex that they defy anything more than piecemeal analysis. Theories have to simplify and ecosystems are too complex to permit that kind of simplification. Also, the historical nature of ecosystems introduces complex and contingent changes and this makes them impossible to reduce to law-like theory.

We value complexity in organisms, which is likely also to mean complex interrelations in ecosystems. Complex organisms have valuable skills and achievements, such as sentience, learned behavior, and

---

[*] For example, the log-normal curve in a plot of species sequence (species in rank order) against their relative abundance, the shape of the curve giving an estimate of evenness (Magurran 1988:13–15).

cognition, that are not present in less complex organisms. Reptiles can cope in a broader spectrum of humidity conditions than can amphibians. Mammals can cope in a broader spectrum of temperature conditions than can reptiles. Plants have no capacity to make intentional reference, but vervet monkeys learn to give different alarm calls to indicate the approach of different predators: leopards, eagles, snakes. Plants can photosynthesize and monkeys cannot. But learning to give differential alarm calls requires perceptual and neural complexity that photosynthesis does not. Both are valuable, and their difference is not merely that the two processes are diverse; the perceptual/cognitive process cannot be valued appropriately without appreciating its complexity. Nevertheless, the lower organisms fit satisfactorily in their ecosystems; many forms of life are relatively simple.

We Earthlings do not live at the range of the infinitely small (quarks or mu-mesons), nor of the infinitely large (galaxies and supernovae), but we may well live at the range of the infinitely complex. Even microscopic forms of life are quite complex already, to say nothing of the monkeys whose skills we just admired. In a typical handful of humans, which may contain ten billion organisms, there is a richness of structure, a volume of information (trillions of "bits") enormously advanced over anything elsewhere in the solar system, or even, so far as we know, in myriads of galaxies.

In larger animals, complexity increases. The immune system becomes increasingly sophisticated, with acquired in addition to innate immunity. There is increased capacity for centralized control (neural networks with control centers, brains surpassing mere genetic and enzymatic control); increased capacities for sentience using ears, eyes, and noses; increased capacity for locomotion with more complex muscles powering fins, legs, or wings. There is increased capacity for manipulation (arms, hands, opposable thumbs), increased capacity for acquired learning (feedback loops, synapses, memory banks), and increased capacities for communication and language acquisition.

Part of this complexity is the human species—and not only part of it, but in some sense the apex of it. The human being is the most sophisticated of evolutionary and ecological products. In our hundred and fifty pounds of protoplasm, in our three pounds of brain, there may be more operational organization than in the whole of the Andromeda galaxy. The number of possible associations among the ten billion neurons of a human brain, and the number of thoughts that can result from this, may exceed the number of atoms in the universe. This complex brain, and such thoughts, is the basis of all culture, introducing even further complexities that ten thousand cultures in turn bring. The human species is capable of more complexity in its behaviors than any other species. There seems no end to the sorts of scientific and technological discoveries that people can make, novels and poems they can write, adventures and love affairs they can have.

Complexity, like diversity, however, is not always valuable. A watch that is too complex breaks easily and may therefore be less valuable than a simpler one; the fewer moving parts the better. Sometimes with universities, businesses, and governments, the less organization the better. In nature, complexity may be cumbersome. Francis Crick complains that biology, unlike physics, has no "elegance." Organisms evolve happenstance structures and wayward functions that have no more overarching logic than the layout of the Manhattan subway system (Crick 1988:6, 137–142). Stephen Jay Gould insists that the panda's thumb is evolutionary tinkering and that orchids are "jury-rigged" (1980b:20). Evolution works with what is at hand, makes something new out of it, often more complicated in structure than the elegant simplicity of what good engineering would require. Organisms often overspecialize, and this means the loss of flexibility in tracking changing environments. Overspecialists, often too complex to "unevolve" their specialization, are more extinction-prone than generalists.

The composition of ecosystems requires diverse functional roles, for example, autotrophs and heterotrophs, predators and prey. Some parts of the system need to do relatively simple things well, fit into complex systems though they may. Organisms at the bases of trophic pyramids can be of instrumental value just because of their simplicity, like plants that mostly sit around and soak up the sunlight and convert it into biomass with stored energy. There cannot be higher forms all by themselves. They must be superposed on lower forms, embedded in communities. So complexity depends on simplicity.

Still, at the top of the tropic pyramids, evolutionary history has produced animals with skills that are undeniably more complex than those of the lower plants and animals, and these achievements are of higher value. Like diversity, it is important that such complexity fit into a unity, which is typically the case in the integrated organism. The organism moves in a plural, complex world, with degrees of freedom and contingency, but it is just this complex world that calls forth the complex mind and body in which coping is possible, using the cybernetic skills of genes and brains.

In such a world the complexity is narrative, achievements made along particular story lines, which we call species (see chapter 6, sec. 3). Narratives are not statistical affairs; narratives have plots, so to speak, that do not plot well on line graphs. It is going to take a rather more sophisticated logic to appreciate these values. It may be a mistake to look in species histories for the kind of elegance that is displayed in the mathematical equations of physics or in good engineering. If a reason that the skills and achievements of species are not elegant is that they had to be reached historically along story lines, we may judge that it is more valuable to have organismic vitality open and dynamic, proceeding by trial and error, sometimes making mistakes (overspecializing, or jury-rigging a specialized "thumb"), than to have "elegant" optimal solutions without history, autonomy, or adventure. The elegance of the thirty-two crystal classes is one kind of value, not to be confused with the value of life lived in the midst of perpetual perishing—either in nature or in culture.

Ernst Mayr puzzles over the fact that lower forms have the skills needed to survive just as much as higher ones. So, generally speaking, complexity has no survival value per se, because most organisms survive in ways no more complex than before. In that sense "higher," which implies more complex and suggests more value, is a troublesome word in biology:

> And yet, who can deny that overall there is an advance from the procaryotes that dominated the living world more than three billion years ago to the eucaryotes with their well organized nucleus and chromosomes as well as cytoplamsic organelles; from the single-celled eucaryotes to metaphytes and metazoans with a strict division of labor among their highly specialized organ systems; within the metazoans from ectotherms that are at the mercy of climate to the warm-blooded endotherms, and within the endotherms from types with a small brain and low social organization to those with a very large central nervous system, highly developed parental care, and

the capacity to transmit information from generation to generation? (Mayr 1988:151–152)

And who can deny that much of natural value depends on this complexity, integrally related to diversity. In fact, finding both diversity and complexity in natural systems forces us to ask, following Mayr, whether there is some programmatic tendency of nature to produce such value.

3. THE EVOLUTION OF DIVERSITY AND COMPLEXITY

One alleged fallacy, or mistaken way of arguing, is the naturalistic fallacy, so-called, that moves from what *is the case* in natural history to draw conclusions about what *is of value* there. Another alleged fallacy is the genetic fallacy, where one mistakes *present justifications* with *historical origins*. One does not examine an argument by asking a person where he got his opinions. One does not evaluate present worth by probing ancestry. Values are what they are today, regardless of yesterday. Yet dealing with historical systems, process and product do not separate that neatly. The natural values of today may depend significantly on the ecosystemic and evolutionary processes that produced them and in which they remain embedded. We do have to know how we came to have some things if we are to value them appropriately.

Of course, if value is just what we choose to make it, nothing more, nothing less, then origins in the remote past are irrelevant. Value is only in the eye of the beholder. Possibly too, a valueless or even disvaluable process has occasionally produced valuable products, though it would be anomalous if there were a long-standing, high statistical correlation between such a nonvaluable or disvaluable process and its valuable products. We might have some natural values today as a result of accidental natural history in the past.

Possibly nature has some heading toward value. But hard-nosed evolutionary biologists are reluctant to see any such tendency because their theory, as usually interpreted, does not entitle them to see any. Despite the use of "better" with "adaptation," the theory predicts only survivors and leaves entirely open whether the survivors are more diverse or more complex—or have more worth. If the environment is drifting, then species just track drift—buffeted about by aimless geo-morphic processes. If they are diverse, that is because these processes drift about randomly. If they are complex—well, sometimes one can drift into complexity. The only outcome that natural selection can pro-mote is capacity to survive, an independent variable with regard to increasing complexity or diversity. Like a rotating kaleidoscope, there is diversity replacing diversity, but in most species there is just change without any tendency toward either increased diversity or complexity.

We can say that if life starts out simply, there is nowhere to go but up. But life does not steadily have to go up. "Nowhere to go but up" is true at the launching but not thereafter. There is "down," "stable," and "out," and many forms take these routes. The evolutionary process might have achieved a few simple, reliable forms, needing lit-tle modification, and stagnated thereafter, as has sometimes happened in little-changing habitats. Nor is there any account of why the life process, if it happens to ascend, will not happen to descend, earlier more complex, later simpler, devolution after evolution, since up or down is immaterial to survival. Life might have become extinct; many life forms did.

The biological panorama—by this account—has been more or less packed since Cambrian times; it is a scene of steady turnover, but later-coming grasses or crustaceans are not any better than earlier, extinct ones; they are just different. Indeed, in climates growing cold-er or drier fewer species may live there later than did before. There are fewer dinosaurs now than in Cretaceous times, fewer birds than in Pleistocene times. There may result "chance riches," says the paleon-tologist Stephen Jay Gould (1980a), but the system is without value heading. Any values are produced by luck. "Almost every interesting event of life's history falls into the realm of contingency" (Gould 1989:290).

But that hardly seems enough explanation for the observed events of natural history. John Maynard Smith, a theoretical biologist, says, "There is nothing in neo-Darwinism which enables us to predict a long-term increase in complexity." He then goes on to suspect that this is not because there is no such long-term increase, but that Dar-winism is inadequate to explain it. We need "to put an arrow on evo-lutionary time" but get no help from evolutionary theory. "It is in some sense true that evolution has led from the simple to the complex:

procaryotes precede eucaryotes, singled-celled precede many-celled organisms, taxes and kineses precede complex instinctive or learnt acts. I do not think that biology has at present anything very profound to say about this" (1972:89, 98).

Philosophers, meanwhile, must give the best account of this they can. Cold and warm fronts come and go, so do ice ages. There are rock cycles, orogenic uplift, erosion, and uplift again. But there is no natural selection there, nothing is competing, nothing is surviving, nothing has adapted fit, and therefore biology seems different. All those climatological and geomorphological agitations continue in the Pleistocene period more or less like they did in the Precambrian, but the life story is not the same all over again. Where once there were no species, now there are five to ten million. It seems evident that, on average, and environmental conditions permitting, the numbers of life forms start low and end high. That's what evolution does; it tries out mutations, variations, and that means diversity.

E. C. Pielou, a paleobiologist, concludes: "Thus worldwide faunal diversification has increased since life first appeared in a somewhat stepwise fashion, through the development and exploitation of adaptations permitting a succession of new modes of life" (1975:149). Life appears in the seas, then, from the Silurian onward, moves onto the land. Vertebrates took to the air and introduced an entirely new mode of life. In the Tertiary there was a marked increase in diversity due to the rise of warm-blooded vertebrates (mammals and birds), more than making up for the decrease in reptiles and amphibians.

There have been setbacks, followed by recovery. Many factors figure in. Sometimes, the change due to organic evolution is overwhelmed by the change due to climatic cooling or drying. The change due to organic evolution may be accelerated or decelerated by continental drift; continents fused together may provide a bigger area that supports more species, or they may provide more competition that eliminates species that previously evolved on separate land masses. The supercontinent may saturate (some think), and afterward the continents drifting apart may add to the provinciality of the world and facilitate by isolation the evolution of diversity. On the whole, organic evolution has "the result that the present diversity of the world's plants and animals is (or was just before our species appeared) probably greater than it has ever been before" (Pielou 1975:150).

For marine environments, J. W. Valentine, a paleontologist, concludes, "A major Phanerozoic trend among the invertebrate biota of the world's shelf and epicontinental seas has been towards more and more numerous units at all levels of the ecological hierarchy. . . . The biosphere has become a splitter's paradise" (1969:706); there is "a gradually rising average complexity" (1973:471).

According to Francisco J. Ayala, a geneticist, "Progress has occurred in nontrivial senses in the living world because of the creative character of the process of natural selection" (1974:353). Theodosius Dobzhansky, another geneticist, agrees. "Evolution as a whole doubtless had a general direction, from simple to complex, from dependence on to relative independence of the environment, to greater and greater autonomy of individuals, greater and greater development of sense organs and nervous systems conveying and processing information about the state of the organism's surroundings, and finally greater and greater consciousness" (1974:310–311).

The drifting and chance also provides a kind of churning, it agitates and stirs up life; and the nothing-but-chance account omits the cybernetic, hereditary capacity of organisms to acquire, store, and transmit new information. Something is at work in addition to tracking drifting environments. The life process is drifting through an information search; tracking the contingent changes provides an opportunity to make new discoveries. With such a conclusion the value question returns. If the system does produce both diversity and complexity, drifting is not the systemic story, however important it may be in the subplots. Nature is often rather disorderly in its production of order, but it has quite reliably produced order nevertheless.

Contemporary geneticists are insisting that genetic processes are not blind. The evolutionary genetic process is not deliberated in the conscious sense, but it is nevertheless cognitive—somewhat like computers, which, likewise without felt experience, can run problem-solving programs. There is a vast array of sophisticated enzymes to cut, splice, digest, rearrange, mutate, reiterate, edit, correct, translocate, invert, and truncate particular gene sequences. John H. Campbell states, "Cells are richly provided with special enzymes to tamper with DNA structure," enzymes that biologists are extracting for genetic engineering. But this "engineering" is already going on in spontaneous nature. "Gene-processing enzymes also engineer comparable changes in genes in vivo. . . . We have discovered enzymes and enzyme pathways for almost every conceivable change in the structure of genes. The scope for self-engineering of multigene families seems to be limited only by the ingenuity of control systems for regulating these pathways." These pathways may have "governors" that are "extraordinarily sophisticated." "Self-governed genes are 'smart' machines in the current vernacular sense. Smart genes suggests smart cells and smart evolution, . . . the promise of radically new genetic and evolutionary principles" (1983:408–410, 414). All this is evidence of a valuable natural system producing valuable products, both diverse and complex, across evolutionary history—something that humans ought appropriately to respect.

Thinking on these scales, we must observe, however, that there have also been a few (perhaps five) rare but devastating catastrophic extinctions. The diversity of natural history was then decimated. The late Permian and late Cretaceous extinctions are the most startling. Each catastrophic extinction is succeeded by a recovery of previous diversity (Raup and Sepkoski 1982). Although natural events, these extinctions so deviate from the trends that many paleontologists look for causes external to the evolutionary ecosystem. If caused by supernovae, collisions with asteroids, or other extraterrestrial upsets, such events are accidental to the evolutionary ecosystem. If the causes were more terrestrial—cyclic changes in climates or continental drift—the biological processes that characterize Earth are still to be admired for their powers of recovery. Uninterrupted by accident (or even interrupted so), they steadily increase the numbers of species.

What does the setback of diversity do to complexity? David M. Raup, who has best documented these catastrophic extinctions, has also reflected philosophically over them. These periodic cutbacks prepare the way for more complex diversity later on. We first think that the catastrophic extinctions were quite a bad thing, an unlucky disaster. But in fact they were good luck. Indeed, were it not for such extinctions we humans would not be here, nor would any of the mammalian complexity. Life on Earth is so resilient that normal geological processes lack the power to cause widespread extinctions in major groups. But just such a resetting is needed—rarely but periodically (at least on a geologic time scale). We should think twice before judging these catastrophic extinctions to be a bad thing.

Without species extinction, biodiversity would increase until some saturation level was reached, after which speciation would be forced to stop. At saturation, natural selection would continue to operate and improved adaptations would continue to develop. But many of the innovations in evolution, such as new body plans or modes of life, would probably not appear. The result would be a slowing down of evolution and an approach to some sort of steady state condition. According to this view, the principal role of extinction in evolution is to eliminate species and thereby reduce biodiversity so that space—ecological and geographic—is available for innovation. (Raup 1991:187).

There is a big shakeup; this is, if you like, at random; it is, we must say, catastrophic, but the randomness is integrated into the creative system. The loss of diversity results in a gain in complexity. Catastrophic extinction "has been the essential ingredient in the history of life that we see in the fossil record" (Raup 1991:189). The storied character of natural history is increased. Once "we thought that stable planetary environments would be best for evolution of advanced life," but now we think instead that "planets with enough environmental disturbance to cause extinction and thereby promote speciation" are required for such evolution (188).

There is one conclusion we must *not* draw from this. One might say, "Well, if catastrophic extinctions are so innovative, perhaps we need not worry about the anthropogenic ones." Yet that fails to take into account the *radical* differences between natural and anthropogenic extinctions. Anthropogenic extinction has nothing to do with evolutionary speciation. Hundreds of thousands of species will perish because of culturally altered environments that are far different from the spontaneous environments in which such species were naturally selected and in which they sometimes become extinct. In a natural extinction, nature takes away life, when it has become unfit in habitat or when the habitat alters, and supplies other life in its place. Artificial extinction shuts down tomorrow, because it shuts down speciation altogether. Natural extinction typically occurs with transformation, either of the extinct line or related or competing lines. Artificial extinction is without issue. One opens doors; the other closes them. In artificial extinctions, humans generate and regenerate nothing; they only dead-end these lines. There can be little respeciation on toxic soils and none at all on asphalt.

4. RARITY

Does something being rare increase its value? If so, we might make a species more rare to enhance its value. Certain butterflies occur only in isolated hummocks in the African grasslands. Formerly, unscrupulous collectors would collect a few hundred, then burn out the hummock to destroy the species, thereby driving up the price of their collections. We might make things less valuable if we made them more common. If bald eagles were as common as starlings, seeing one would not be so exciting. Both these things are true: rare things can have their value escalated; common things can have their value decrease. But we do not want to make rare species rarer still; to the contrary, we are glad to have eagles, once rare, now more common. Rather obviously, we need a philosophical analysis of rarity. Like diversity and complexity, rarity cannot ipso facto be a value indicator. Rarity piques curiosity, but rarity does not assure value. Children seem to think that green M&Ms, which are few in the candy packages sold, are more valuable than the other colors, especially the ordinary brown ones. But this is childish; the perceived value is an illusion. Similarly, postage stamps have no value increase by their rarity alone; the fact that there are few of them cannot make them really more valuable. Yet it is not childish to value glimpsing a wolverine, nor to contribute money toward saving that rare species.

The HIV virus was once rare; we are alarmed that it is becoming more common. Forest fires, relatively rare, would not be more valuable if more common. It is bad for some good things to be rare; it is good for some bad things to be rare (even if they add diversity when they occur). Some good things are good so long as they *are* rare. Some bad things are not so bad so long as they are rare (like the catastrophic extinctions). If forced to choose between saving a turkey and a whooping crane, we will save the whooping crane. Why? "Because the crane is rare." That is a good answer, but it is not enough.

Let us begin with a descriptive account of rarity (Cain 1971; Colinvaux 1978; Stebbins 1980; Krukeberg and Rabinowitz 1985). If rarity has a variety of causes, we might value different rare species or events differently. In ecosystems, normally a majority of species are infrequent; some will be moderately common, and a few will be abundant. A few will be quite rare. One species might just be getting started; another, once more common when climates or ecology were different, might be almost naturally extinct (relict species). Bristlecone pine (*Pinus longaeva*) was widespread during the late Wisconsin glaciation. Most species are relatively rare throughout their timespan on Earth. This may be because the species is specialized for a narrow niche. Unusual species grow on selenium soil, where other plants find it difficult to compete. A number of species (endemics) occur only in limited geographical areas.* Presumably some species are not all that well adapted; they survive briefly and go extinct.

Some rarity seems to be the result of sheer accident—as when a vagrant Laysan albatross showed up in San Francisco, 5,000 miles from its home in the Midway Islands. This may be true even of entire populations. The Iowa Pleistocene snail, *Discus macclintocki*, relict from preglacial times, survives in a population of a few thousand in northeastern Iowa's nonglaciated driftless area, notably in a cave in Bixby State Park. The species was first described as a fossil and later found to have survived the Ice Age. The species survives by double good luck; some snails chanced to live in a (relatively) small, nonglaciated area and, later, during subsequent warming, some chanced to live in cool environments, like cave openings.

A rare species may just be hanging on; perhaps it never really flourished. If a species is naturally rare, that initially suggests the possibility of its insignificance in an ecosystem. The Devil's Hole pupfish, *Cyprinodon diabolis*, is known only from a single location, an unusual desert spring, about the size of a swimming pool, in western Nevada. Nearby Ash Meadows, a seepy oasis in the desert, supports twenty-six endemic plants and animals. These are odd places, springs in the desert, or caves in driftless areas, and the fish and snails are barely there.

After learning such facts about rarity, we might even come to an indifferent conclusion. Desert fishes and Iowa snails are a fluke, there by luck already—living fossils. What survives or perishes does so by chance, which therefore has nothing to do with what is valuable. Nature has no standards of "value," and there is no reason to think that she has been protecting treasures in the desert or in Iowa caves,

---

* A species may be endemic to a continent and common–like Douglas fir (*Pseudotsuga menziesii*). Nevertheless "endemic" typically refers to a small area; a narrow endemic sometimes locally common, yet often infrequent or rare where found.

conserving them either because they had value in themselves or because humans were coming. So there is no cause for humans particularly to care about this scanty, chance selection of desert fishes and cave snails. If these species come to an end, they have already gone on long enough, and they are all accidental in the first place. Rare they no doubt are, but is that any reason why we should care?

Rarity, as such, is not a valuable property in plants, fish, snails, or in human experience. Some rarity is by genetic deformity, such as albinos. Hunters sometimes refuse to shoot albino deer, thinking they ought to save such rare animals; but there seems no particular value in saving genetically defective deer. Maybe these species, though not exactly defective, are not all that effective either. They could be genetically depauperate.

Yet perhaps we are on the wrong track. Reflecting more deeply, naturally rare species, as much as common species, signify exuberance in nature. The rare species need not be defective or ineffective at all. It can be a biological achievement, a bit of brilliance, a problem resolved, a threshold crossed. The endemic species, perhaps one specialized for an unusual habitat, represents a rare discovery in nature, before it provides a rare human adventure in finding it. If everything were common, there could not be as much diversity as there is; ecosystems, with their limited carrying capacity partitioned among a few species, all common, would be simpler, less rich, less interesting. In fact, rarity makes diversity possible. The fact that many species are rare means that there can be more species.

And most of them can be quite competent. A rare species does not have once to have been common, nor to have the possibility of someday becoming common, to be a good thing where and as it is in its microclimate or specialized niche. It does not have to be important functionally in an ecosystem to be valuable in its own right. What it does need is competence in its niche, whether small or large. Though sometimes species are relatively depauperate, it does not follow that most of them have less biological integrity than common species; they may simply but competently occupy smaller niches.

The rare species of fishes, snails, or flowers—if one insists on a restricted evolutionary theory—are random accidents (as also are common ones), resulting from a cumulation of mutations. But this mutational fertility generates creativity and, equally by the theory, surviving species must be satisfactory fits in their environments. A broader theory also predicts that niches will multiply over time, and that the occupants of these niches will be fewer and at the same time more diverse. We probably go astray to emphasize luck as the only reason the anomalous desert fish or cave snails are still there. The argument begins to move toward another conclusion if we look for a remarkable biological competence instead.

In the case of the desert pupfish, speciation is still going on. We initially suppose that desert fish are dead ends in the evolutionary process; the few remaining fishes are anomalous relics. But that is to misjudge the story. Fishes speciate extensively and explosively; there are more species of fishes in the world than of all other vertebrates (mammals, birds, reptiles, and amphibians) combined. In less than 5,000 years, since ancestral Lake Manly in Death Valley dried up with the retreat of the glaciers, different *Cyprinodon* species learned to survive in quite different environments—in shallow streams and marshes, in groundwater springs, in water as salty as the sea, in thermal springs, in springs where water levels fluctuate widely, in hot artesian wells dug by humans. Some survive in environments that fluctuate widely from cold winter rains to summer heat. About all *Cyprinodon* seems to need is water—any kind, place, amount—and time to adapt to different circumstances.

Though a place like Ash Meadows is a freakish anomaly, the life that prospers there has extraordinary vigor, forced to ingenious modes of adaptation. Accidental life is matched with tenacity of life. The hardy, sprightly *Cyprinodon diabolis* has been clinging to life on a small shelf of rock for 10,000 years or more. No other vertebrate species is known to exist in so small a habitat. This species has evolved in probably the most restricted and isolated habitat of any fish in the world. We begin to wonder if there is not something admirable taking place as well as something accidental, something excellent because it is extreme—and rare because it is excellent.

The rare species offer promise and memory of an inventive natural history. They do pique our curiosity; they are exotic and entertaining because they are rare. But that does not yet get at their real worth, which is that they are extraordinary manifestations of survival. That is why glimpsing a wolverine in the woods is exciting in a way that seeing a rare postage stamp in a collection is not. The postage stamp is no achievement. The surviving snails and pupfish are remarkable success stories. Even more poignantly than the common species, rare fauna and flora provide evidence of life persisting in struggling beauty, flourishing, pushing on at the edge of perishing. The rare creatures—if one opens to a wider, philosophical perspective—offer a moment of perennial truth. Life is a many-splendored thing, and extinction of the rare dims this luster.

5. BIODIVERSITY AND THE COMMONS

While biodiversity can be appreciated philosophically, humans must face the economic facts of life, which are that people are needy, especially in underdeveloped tropical nations, where much of the biodiversity happens to occur. Perhaps Nevadans and Iowans are wealthy enough to save their "useless" pupfish and snails, but most of the world has to make resources out of their biodiversity. If we are going to conserve intrinsic natural value, we are also going to have to balance in the industrial, agricultural, medical, and other uses to which these species can be put.

Consider the case of the developed versus the developing nations (the so-called North-South split). The developing nations, poor financially, have much biological wealth. That can become financial wealth, but the trouble is that it is often exploited by the First World. For instance, horticulturists in 1962 took a wild tomato (*Lycopersicon chmielewskii*) and bred it into and enhanced the commercial tomato for American agroindustry, resulting in $8 million a year in profits, for which Peru, the "owner" nation, was paid nothing.

This situation can be corrected—some now propose—if we attach economic value to this biodiversity. For, after all, these natural resources are national resources, are they not? They belong to the peoples in whose territories they are found. Users ought to pay what they are worth. That will transfer money from the First to the Third World and help correct the economic injustice, and it will make these plants and animals important to these peoples, thereby assuring conservation.

But we need to be careful. When biological values (plants in the Amazon), found in nature, start to mix with commercial values (biotechnology in industries), arising from culture, this raises two different questions about ownership, one of Earth's biodiversity, another of technology. These were principal issues in the Convention on Biological Diversity. The Convention insists that "states have sovereign rights over their own biological resources" and that "the authority to determine access to genetic resources rests with the national governments and is subject to national legislation" (UNCED 1992a, Preamble, Article 15).

The Convention recognizes "patents and other intellectual property rights," but also insists that "access to and transfer of technology . . . to developing countries shall be provided for and/or facilitated under fair and most favorable terms" (Article 16). Signatory parties bind themselves to "sharing in a fair and equitable way the results of research and development and the benefits arising from the commercial and other utilization of genetic resources" (Article 15). Developing nations felt that they had, in the past, been deprived of benefits that flowed from genetic resources that were really theirs in the first place. A total of 153 developing nations, as well as the industrial nations, agreed—except for the United States. (The United States did, at a later time, sign the Convention.)

While fair use of Earth's genetic resources seems equitable, and the United States was much lambasted for being the sole holdout, there is also an important principle involved. Historically, wild plant species, seeds, and germplasm have been considered in the public domain, whereas developing nations are now claiming ownership by the country of origin. Vandana Shiva, the director of the Research Foundation for Science, Technology, and Natural Resource Policy, in Dehradun, India, complains, "The US . . . has freely taken the biological diversity of the Third World to spin millions of dollars of profits, none of which have been shared with Third World Countries, the original owners of the germplasm." "The total contribution of wild germplasm to the American economy has been US $66 billion," despite the fact that "this wild material is 'owned' by sovereign states and by local people" (Shiva 1991:260–261).

Can *natural* resources be *national* resources? Certainly, they often can. Nonrenewable resources (ores, minerals, petroleum) are owned by the nation-state in which they happen to be found, indeed by private individuals and corporations within such states. Likewise with biotic resources. Nations and individuals own the forests on their land; farmers own the crops in their fields. If we follow this logic, we can understand the complaint.

> Thus, the North has always used Third World germplasm as a freely available resource and treated it as valueless. The advanced capitalist nations wish to retain free access to the developing world's storehouse of genetic diversity, while the South would like to have the proprietary values of the North's industry declared a similarly 'public' good. The North, however, resists this democracy based on the logic of the market. . . . There is no epistemological justification for treating some germplasm as valueless and common and other germplasm as a valuable commodity and private property. (Shiva 1991:257–260)

But biotic resources are less evidently subject to ownership than patents, if one refers to the species, to the natural kinds. Shiva is right in that there is no justification for treating some germplasm as valueless, but there is a justification for treating wild germplasm as commons and manipulated germplasm as private property. There are several important epistemological differences. One is between what we have on Earth by gift of wild nature and what we have as a result of human labor; another is between renewable and nonrenewable such gifts, still another is between a token of a natural kind and the type itself.

One may own gold on one's land, token samples of a type, but no one owns gold as a natural kind; no one owns the structure of the atom. One may own land with wild tomato plants on it, and thus the particular plants, but does anyone own the DNA coding within *Lycopersicon chmielewskii* or the species as a historical line? The value of wild germplasm is not owned by the peasant farmer any more than by the modern agriculturalist, nor by a Third World nation any more than by an industrial nation. The democracy Shiva calls for equates alleged ownership of wild species, and freely sharing them, with alleged ownership of agricultural and industrial patents, and freely sharing them.

That misunderstands as equivalent what are not, wild species on the one hand and the products of human labor on the other; the one is a commons and the other is property. This is not, contrary to her allegations, "double standards" and "double-speak" (p. 261); it discriminates an important difference between what we inherit on the planet by natural history and what we achieve by our cultural labors.

We pay Saudi Arabia for oil found there, a nonrenewable resource, though we do not pay for the use of any hydrocarbon organic petroleum structures. We do not pay Afghanistan for the use of the bread wheat species (*Triticum aestivum*) that historically originated there, nor do we pay Mexico for the use of corn (maize, *Zea mays*), nor have we paid Ecuador and Peru for tomatoes (*Lycopersicon esculentum*) and potatoes (*Solanum tuberosum*). Two of the most widely grown crops in South and Central America are bananas (*Musa paradisiaca* var. *sapientum*) and coffee (*Coffea arabica*). Bananas originated in Malaysia, coffee in Ethiopia. New World and Old World peoples do not pay for these exchanges, they are the common heritage of humankind.

The original wild species merely happen to be first found inside national boundaries, boundaries drawn incidentally to the location of such species, sometimes drawn after such species were first identified and utilized. Taken from such initial locations, such species are subsequently grown elsewhere. We do thereafter pay for those productive labors. Where labor has been deliberately expended to alter a native wild type, as is done by plant breeders, the issue is conceptually different; the laborer is worthy of his or her work.

Many will worry that the logic of this argument comes out the wrong way for Third World peoples. We do lament the inequitable distribution of wealth in the world, and Third World voices may be right that there is something unfair about it. No one wants uncritically to defend profiteering industrialists. But philosophers have to follow their logic where it leads them whether they want to go there or not. Conservation based on unsound logic will come undone sooner or later. Surely there is a sounder logic by which equitable conservation can be achieved.

Careful readers will have noticed that the UNCED's Biodiversity Convention, though it insists on "sovereign rights to exploit natural resources," avoids the explicit language of ownership. It speaks instead of "access to genetic resources," ambiguous enough that it can be interpreted as ownership, but not necessarily. Patent holders control access to what they own. By parity, it can be argued that nation-states own the species to which they give access. But consider another case, a contrasting one. Landowners may control access to their property, even though they do not own the wildlife on it. From this perspective, sovereign nations may control access to their territories, even though they do not own the wild species on their landscapes. So we have wild species owned by no one, valuable to all, but located on landscapes within particular countries, who control access.

In 1991 Merck Pharmaceuticals signed an agreement with the National Biodiversity Institute of Costa Rica, a national agency. The institute is attempting to identify all wild plant species in the country, do a preliminary screening, and make agreements with pharmaceutical companies for further use of promising plants. Merck provided $1 million over the years 1991–1992 and will get, in return, the exclusive right to screen the collection. The principle here is not that the Costa Ricans own the plants, but that they have the right to give or withhold "permission to collect" on their soil, for which they can be paid. In the Merck case, this money will go to fund the collection. In other cases, it could go to fund on-the-ground conservation.

An agreement whereby profits of the industry using wild biodiversity resources go to assure conservation of what remains makes perfectly good sense, oblivious to national boundaries, because these are global commons conservation problems and opportunities. Ownership issues and rights to exploit ought to be reconceived as a commons that we are all obligated to protect. Developed and developing country alike, as well as industry, have obligations to save the commons if they are to share it. These species belong to us all.

6. RICHNESS

The value issues turn finally on what we can comprehensively call "richness." Value issues run all the way from the pragmatic to the spiritual—all the way from, "It's my resource, and I want to sell it," to "Praise God for a sublime creation!" The values are diverse and complex, and differently owned by both the wild fauna and flora in themselves and by humans who encounter them. Richness is a pluralism of values, but one is even more rich if these values are integrated, not just aggregated, or, at least, if one has some overview of just where the riches lie.

That richness is valuable is almost tautological; it is foolish to ask, "Well I am rich, but do I have anything of value?"—unless one is stipulating some special meanings for value and richness. Still, the category of richness helps us integrate this diversity and complexity. These riches are instrumental, psychological, organismic, ecological, geological. They are individual, communitarian, systemic, holistic. Utility is part of the picture, but there are dimensions of value richness at multiple levels. Four are paramount.*

1. The complexity and diversity, the rarities in nature, as well as the commons enrich human lives in myriads of ways. Their mix supports the natural life-support system on which humans depend. Nature has economic value, recreational value, scientific value, aesthetic value, genetic diversity value, historical value. Encounters with nature can be restorative, therapeutic; they can build character. We enjoy learning of nature's diversity and of the unity in that diversity; we appreciate both the stability in natural systems and also their spontaneity and contingency. Nature is a foil for culture, which is built in dependence on and exodus from nature. Nature has philosophical and religious value (Rolston 1988:1–27). We will enlarge these themes in chapter 5.

2. There is richness in animal life. Most theories of value have been human-centered. If something doesn't help or hurt humans, it doesn't count. But this is too narrow a perspective. Animals evidently defend their own lives. They have a good of their own, suffer pains and pleasures like ourselves. They, too, have psychological experiences, that is, felt experiences, interests, and preferences that can be satisfied. Although the biological sciences have sometimes treated animals as if they were nothing but machines for human use and consumption, the progress of science has smeared the human-nonhuman boundary line. Animal anatomy, biochemistry, cognition, perception, experience, and behavior, and evolutionary history are kin to our own.

Animals, at least the higher ones, have conscious experiences, though they are not self-conscious in the way we humans are. It is

---

* For another study on richness, see Miller 1982.

arbitrary not to count this part of the richness of life on Earth. Animals have many skills. Fish-eating bats can catch fish by sonar at night, homing in on the noise of a ripple in the water. Coyotes can sniff scent posts and know what other coyotes have passed that way. All these are animal riches. We will return to this in chapter 4.

3. There is richness in organismic life. Plants too can be better or worse off, as can all the lower animals, regardless of whether they feel anything at all. In fact, most of the richness on Earth is of this kind; the plants, insects, crustaceans, and nematodes form far more of the biomass than do the vertebrate animals. An organism is doing well when there is a proper functioning of the organism as a whole, its parts interrelated, with an adequate supply of nutrients, needed shelter, and so on. We need language here that is not exclusively oriented to psychological states, much less human experiences. "Healthy" is an example, since trees can be healthy or diseased. "Flourishing" is a word first applied to flowers, and, by extrapolation, to animals and humans. "Well-being" serves also as a general category of prosperity for plants and animals alike.

One might think that plants cannot be rich, certainly not like humans can be rich. Plants cannot own anything; they do not consider themselves wealthy or poor. True, but the point here is to break out of the psychological restrictions on felt experience and to see that a forest full of plants, shrubs, herbs, that are flourishing does constitute a richness. Botanists regularly use the expression "a rich woods," meaning just this sort of place, where the soil is fertile, the rains favorable, the climate moderate, and the flora grow in profusion. The soil of Iowa, for instance, was called "black gold" by early settlers; it grew grass luxuriously and in fact there was really more wealth there than in the more barren, though sometimes gold-laden, badlands further west.

A rich woods does not become so when humans walk through it, though a human who owned such a woods could count that among his riches. Many orders and families are represented, with varied metabolisms, making all sorts of fruits and seeds, making all those interesting chemicals that Merck Pharmaceuticals is screening in Costa Rica—of use to the plants whether to Merck or not. Plants grow rapidly; the vegetation is lush. Again we see why richness in nature is not like having a collection of stamps, or choices of shampoos, since in the latter two there is no flourishing.

4. There is richness in natural systems. Ecosystems are the fountain of all this creativity. Diverse members are included in community relations, there is conflict, resolution, harmony, integrity. There are resources useful to members of the system (not just for humans). The system is sustainable, there is recycling of nutrients, resources, energy; there is resilience and generativity. An ecosystem is a productive system. Individual plants and animals defend their continuing survival; species increase their numbers. But the evolutionary ecosystem spins a bigger story, limiting each kind, locking it into the welfare of others, promoting new arrivals, increasing kinds and the integration of kinds. Plants and animals increase their kind but ecosystems increase kinds, superposing the latter increase onto the former.

Communal processes—the competition between organisms, more or less probable events, plant and animal successions, speciation over historical time—generate an ever-richer community. Hence the evolutionary toil, elaborating and diversifying the biota, that once began with no species and results today in five million species, increasing over time the quality of lives in the upper rungs of the tropic pyramids. All this is systemic richness; the system has potential that is unfolding from the actual. One really has riches when one has not simply products but the processes that produce products. That is like having the goose that lays the golden eggs, and the goose is more valuable than the eggs.

Once more, we see why richness in nature is not like having a large collection of stamps, or lots of shampoos, since the latter are just merely sets, aggregations, groups with no real integration between the members. By contrast, the big collection of fauna and flora in the Amazon basin is an ecosystem. This is why you cannot have this richness in a zoo or a botanical garden. There is no richness in the interconnections, no creativity in the relationships, no autonomy defended, no storied history in a stamp album lying on the coffee table, or on the shelves of shampoos, or in zoo and botanical garden. There is no system that produces the gold, no prolific system. But that is the principal natural value, the principle of natural value.

7. BALANCING BIODIVERSITY VALUES AND
CULTURAL VALUES

People seldom destroy species just for the hell of it. They want to use the land for agriculture or grazing, to cut down the trees to build houses and furniture, or trap the tigers and sell their hides. So there is an often opportunity cost of preserving the biodiversity. Perhaps some richness in cultural values may be desirable at a sacrifice of natural values. Gaining goods for people is very important, not the only thing, but perhaps the main thing in any value decision. Are there guidelines for balancing value judgments here—continuing those in chapter 1?

1. *Protect biodiversity ecosystemically*. Since the diverse species are not simply aggregated collections, a piecemeal approach is not likely to work well. It might work where there is an endemic plant in a small area around which we can build a fence, and a ten-acre conservancy with just that plant in mind will suffice. Most species are what they are where they are; they depend on the integrity of their larger ecosystems. If the ecosystem is flourishing, the member species will look out after themselves. What one needs for grizzly bears, or bald eagles, or whooping cranes is habitat on regional scales.

The federal Endangered Species Act is the most celebrated piece of biodiversity legislation, but perhaps what we really need is an Endangered Ecosystems Act. Admittedly, it might be difficult to enact, owing to the complexity of values at stake when Congress considers legislation that affects whole regions. But Congress has mandated that the national forests be managed with biodiversity a consideration. Similarly, we need to make clear that regional biodiversity is at stake, not just an isolated species (that is, all the richness of old-growth forests, not just the spotted owl). The welfare of some one species is only an indicator of much more biodiversity. We are not just trading one cultural value against one natural value (owls against jobs), but some limited cultural value (this part of the timber industry) against a regional ecosystem of old-growth forests.

2. *Protect keystone species*. Species that play vital roles in the ecosystem ought to receive greater protection. Ecologists often identify so-called keystone species. These can be big animals, such as predators, that exert a profound structuring influence on the ecosys-

tem—like pumas and jaguars in Central and South America (Terborgh 1988). Or they can be invertebrates that are at the base of the food chain pyramids, like the plankton in the sea, often quite sensitive to toxic substances. The beaver is a mid-sized keystone species.

3. *Protect speciating in process.* Protect biological hot spots, places where speciation is still going on, or groups that are still speciating actively. The changes that humans have introduced into the North American landscape probably mean, alas, that vertebrate speciation under natural selection has been essentially stopped for the larger terrestrial mammals. But this might not be true among the fishes. The desert pupfishes considered earlier provide evidence of this. Often where speciation is under way, differences between species will be marginal and we will be inclined to think these are just populations or varieties and that saving them does not matter. But just the reverse could be true. Nature is quite creatively at work in such locations, and it is more, not less, important to save such places than other areas where speciation may have come to a standstill.

4. *Protect charismatic species.* Enlightened conservationists will, at first, probably demur. There is no particular reason to favor the cute and cuddly species, or the big, fierce ones, over the ugly or inconspicuous and unassuming ones. The U.S. Fish and Wildlife Service, in earlier years, was directed to focus its attention on saving the species to which Americans were attracted; the directive received much criticism. But we need to understand what the word "charismatic" means. The root in the Greek language is *charis*, grace, which conveys the idea of being fortunately, even providentially gifted. Every species in nature has its skills and accomplishments; we admired the tenacity with which the Iowa snails and the Devil's Hole pupfish cling to life. But we also have to recognize that some species do represent more evolutionary achievement than others, often those on the top trophic rungs. They may or may not be important for the roles they play in ecosystems as keystone species. They are, however, especially gifted—the whales and dolphins, or the big cats, or the primates. If we have to choose between saving a gorilla species and saving a beetle species, we save the gorilla species.

Careful readers will notice that this principle is likely to be in tension with the preceding one. The charismatic species are not likely to be undergoing active speciation, while species actively undergoing speciation are not likely to be charismatic.

5. *Protect naturally rare species.* The naturally rare species are likely to be extinction-prone. These may be quite stable in their limited populations; apart from human interventions, they might be around for a hundred thousand years. But they do not absorb human-introduced stresses well. That is why rare species are often indicators; they are the first to pick up stresses in the system. Such species, being naturally rare, are not likely to be keystone species. Perhaps they do not have clearly identifiable functional roles in ecosystems at all.

The small whorled pogonia, *Isotria medeoloides*, is known to occur at only seventeen sites in eastern U.S. forests, and three account for half the population. Since its discovery in 1814, it has been found at only forty-five sites, where it is mostly now extinct. It is difficult to think that the Appalachian woods miss it. But we do respect the rare, not for the rarity as such, but the particular bit of botanical brilliance that this flower does uniquely represent, and which is now only rarely present on Earth. We would not allow, therefore, a common cultural value (another shopping mall) to override this natural rarity, even though we may think that the needs of people are more important than odd wildflowers.

6. *Protect species over individuals.* Individuals can be replaced, but species cannot; extinction is forever. The well-being of a species, even though it is a so-called insignificant one, can be more important than the well-being of animals that we think are significant, even charismatic, if only individuals are at stake. Off the coast of California and isolated from the mainland, San Clemente Island has a number of endemic plant species. The U.S. Fish and Wildlife Service and the U.S. Navy, which controls the island, planned to shoot thousands of feral goats to save three endangered plant species: *Malacothamnus clementinus*, *Castilleja grisea*, and *Delphinium kinkiense* (as well as to protect ecosystem integrity). That would kill several goats for each known surviving plant. By herding and trapping, 14,000 were removed, and about a further 15,000 were shot. Many were in inaccessible canyons, which required their being hunted by helicopter.

The Fund for Animals filed suit to prevent this. But the court judged, rightly, that protecting endangered species justifies the killing of the goats, which are not endangered and which are replaceable, as well as exotic to the island. If the tradeoff were merely one on one, a goat versus a plant, the charismatic goats would override the plants. Goats are among the most nimble and sure-footed creatures on Earth, which is why they were so hard to eradicate. But the picture is more complex. The well-being of plants at the species level outweighs the welfare of the goats at the individual level.

7. *Keep biodiversity in the commons.* Biotic national resources are also the common heritage of humankind. It is a mistake to try to privatize or nationalize biodiversity. Biodiversity belongs to us all, and it is the obligation of all who use it to protect it. Of course society has to work out property rights of various kinds: real estate, mineral rights, water rights, access rights for screening potentially useful wild plants, patent rights for protecting biotechnology, and on and on. But such rights are superposed on a commonwealth, a commons that nobody owns, or, better, that we all own, or, better still, such rights are subsidiary to the community of life in which humans are residents. Another way of putting this is that any human possession of biodiversity is in imperfect ownership. We have what lawyers call the usufruct of the landscape, but our ownership is limited by the common goods also at stake there. Even if a community of people supposed that they have, as a public, the right to destroy "their" biodiversity, this needs to be argued before a still more public court of opinion than just the citizens of the political territory where the biodiversity happens to be located.

8. *Do not jeopardize biodiversity to postpone solutions to social injustice.* The UN Conference on Environment and Development made it clear in the language of Agenda 21 and the Biodiversity Convention that the biodiversity problem is also one of social justice. Biodiversity cannot be saved with half the world starving. But the Convention ignored how unjust social structures within nations, and also internationally, will often prevent goods obtained by sacrificing biodiversity from benefiting the poor in any long-term way. It is futile to sacrifice biodiversity to benefit the disadvantaged unless the social structures and the prevailing economy are just enough to make it probable that this transfer will reliably take place.

Failing that, the issue is a smoke screen that merely protects vested interests; it sacrifices needed social reforms, keeping in place a social disvalue, and sacrifices natural values to do so. The basic needs of nearly all can be met if the system were more equitable and just. Social injustice condoned does not justify destroying natural values, as yet little appreciated and in the commons. Rather than address the real problem, unjust distribution of what is already being produced in the society, we turn instead to developing, and destroying, marginal wild areas to feed the poor. We lose species, but their loss is part of no stable, long-term strategy for the solution of human problems here; to the contrary, these values are lost because humans do not have any viable strategy for solving their own problems. They have only an illusion of solution. Nine times out of ten, the way to feed the hungry is by a redistribution of produce from lands already developed, not by exploitation that degrades the lands on which the biodiversity remains (see chapter 5, sec. 3).

9. *Protect the most fundamental values, whether natural or cultural.* We ought to consider whether the goods purchased by sacrifice of biodiversity are basic to human needs, rather than novel, peripheral, or even just desirable. We might jeopardize biodiversity where humans are malnourished (and there is no other social solution); we ought not to jeopardize a species to produce a new brand of shampoo or new flavor of ice cream. We ought to consider the extent and duration of the human goods achieved (is the malnourishment problem fixed for the indefinite future, or just postponed a decade?), how equitably the goods are distributed (the malnourished are fed, but are the rich still getting richer?). We can ensure that the decision is carefully made by placing it where there are many checks and balances, where there is public participation in the decision by all parties affected, by making sure that the witness of competent experts is heard, by not acting precipitously, nor leaving earlier decisions in place after new information arises. Perhaps we will require a larger majority for irreversible decisions that jeopardize biodiversity. We will do all we can to ensure that the fundamentals at stake get weighed for what they are really worth.

10. *Protect biodiversity with triage.* We will only be able to do so much and therefore we can optimize values by making our efforts maximally efficient. One way to do this is to sort the species into three groups: a first group that, unfortunately, are probably going

to go extinct even if we try hard to save them. A second group is jeopardized but will probably make it through even without our help, at least in some locations. A third group will probably go extinct unless we intervene. This strategy is called triage; a version of it has been used in war, where medical resources are in short supply. One abandons the most desperately injured, cruel though this may seem, because they will probably not survive in any event. One abandons the least injured, as they will probably make it. One concentrates resources where medical help will most probably make the difference between life and death.

This maxim comes last, not because it is most important, but because it is appropriate when the other considerations have also been weighed. It ought not, for instance, override an ecosystem-oriented strategy. Or an effort to find solutions to injustices in society that imperil biodiversity. Or attention to keystone or charismatic species, or to speciation under way. But one ought to be as effective as one can be, other considerations being equal. If one is up against the limits of conservation resources that a society is willing to provide, then triage is both prudent and moral.

In humans, the richness on Earth has become conscious of itself. Humans can appreciate this richness, as no other species can. That enriches, so to speak, the richness even more. Humans can also creatively produce their own novel diverse and complex cultures, eminently a rich thing. But would it not be indeed a tragic failure of human culture, especially of our modern technologically advanced human culture, if it were further to degrade the biodiversity achieved over the millennia, leaving a depauperate Earth. We would not only be impoverishing ourselves; we would be impoverishing the planet. We would not be *Homo sapiens*, the "wise" species at all.

3

Ecosystem Integrity and Health Values

▪▪
▪▪

More than 130 nations have established 6,500 major protected areas, covering nearly five percent of Earth's land surface (United Nations 1990). Such areas, designated for protection of their native biological integrity, will perhaps never exceed ten percent of the Earth's surface (there are also marine areas). There is as much concern, or more, for the regional landscapes—the ninety-five percent rebuilt for culture or put to multiple uses. The nations collectively—178 of them—have tens of thousands of laws and regulations that concern the health of their landscapes. It is hard to have a healthy nation or economy, or even to be a healthy person, in a sick environment. Because culture revises natural systems we need laws to regulate people and protect nature.

Hardly a day goes by without a newspaper report of some environmental threat. The United Nations Conference on Environment and Development brought every nation on Earth together because we need action urgently and analysis to guide action. If we act now and think later, we may be misguided. To be healthy and wealthy, we need to be wise, environmentally.

1. INTEGRITY AND HEALTH

Aldo Leopold enjoined, "A thing is right when it tends to preserve the integrity, stability, and beauty of the biotic community. It is wrong when it tends otherwise" (1968 [1949]:224–225). We are legally obligated as well. The U.S. Congress ordered the restoration and maintenance of "the chemical, physical, and biological integrity of the nation's waters" (U.S. Congress 1972a: sec. 101). Congress singled out the waters, especially threatened, but Congress wants integrity on the landscape as a whole, which it often calls "environmental quality." Congress has also set as national policy "the health of the oceans" (U.S. Congress 1972b: sec. 202).

Leopold also speaks of our "responsibility for the health of the land" (1968 [1949]:221). That, too, has been enacted into legislation. The National Forest Management Act, the Wilderness Acts, national parks legislation, legislation about old-growth forests, acid rain, pesticide and herbicide pollution, overuse of fertilizers, loss of wetlands, fire policy—all these are about the health of the environment.

Let us look more closely at ecological integrity and land health (Karr and Dudley 1981; Ballentine and Guarraia 1977; Costanza, Norton, and Haskell 1992; Westra 1994). Both integrity and health are combined fact-value words. Both convey the idea of wholeness and of unbroken functioning. Both combine the general and the specific. A person may be generally healthy, but there are specific tests about this or that disease. Both terms are a little strange applied to ecosystems. "Integrity" usually refers to a person's character; seldom do we use it of rivers. "Health" usually belongs in medical environments. Possibly "health" is too organismic a term to extrapolate to communities, either social or biotic. Still, we do speak of a healthy nation—at least metaphorically. What does health mean when translated to ecosystems, which do not have organismic identity, but are more loosely organized?

Are integrity and health in ecosystems synonymous? A person with an artificial arm is healthy, though their bodily integrity has been marred. Can ecosystems, after substitutions of artifacts, still be healthy? There is an immediate disanalogy. A person prefers bodily natural health. We repair breakdowns, but we do not rebuild the healthy body. We refuse to design bionic or genetically reengineered people. We only go to doctors when we are sick, or for checkups. By contrast, we do not want entirely natural ecosystems. If there is to be any culture at all, especially a modern culture, we want to transform wild nature into rebuilt environments. We labor every day to make something better out of wild nature, not just fixing something sick. We do not revise our bodies like we revise wild nature.

A flourishing culture requires much revamping of wild nature. However, if this goes too far, then the natural system can collapse. We have to identify a pristine biological integrity, present ideally in wilderness areas, hopefully in protected areas, and contrast that with a culturally modified biological integrity, which we will try to maintain all over the landscape. This is land health, even when pristine integrity has been compromised in order to support various forms of cultural integrity.

Perhaps we cannot be rigorous about integrity; the idea is soft, visionary, suspect because it cannot be made operational. Although integrity can mean a number of different things, yet we use many such paradigmatic concepts to conserve values: justice, freedom, love, democracy, rights, or privacy. *Diversity* and *complexity*, even *nature* and *culture*, are slippery words. All these are system-wide words, symbols that orient us—open concepts, not subject to calculus, but that does not mean they are sloppy and under no logical control. They give general directions.

Biological *integrity* is an ecosystem's ability to maintain "a balanced, integrated, adaptive community of organisms having a species composition, diversity, and functional organization comparable to that of the natural habitat of the region" (Karr and Dudley 1981). Biological *health* is the state in which the genetic potentials of an ecosystem's member species are realized as organisms flourish in their niches, with the integrated systemic condition dynamic and stable. The systemic capacity for self-repair when perturbed is present. "An ecological system is healthy and free from 'distress syndrome' if it is stable and sustainable—that is, if it is active and maintains its organization and autonomy over time and is resilient to stress" (Costanza, Norton, and Haskell 1992:9). Biological *integrity* has as a baseline index the ecosystem originally there, while biological *health* may, but need not. There may be culturally introduced replacements, if these thereafter function with minimal management intervention.

Ecosystemic integrity is historical but not a once-upon-a-time, long-ago matter; it is always dynamic and ongoing. From time to time, even natural systems have had their integrities upset (when volcanoes exploded, or tsunamis destroyed them), and integrity then had to re-evolve. We do have faith that natural systems are, on the whole, as evolutionary and ecology theory both teach, places of adapted fit. We presume that the pristine system had its integrity, and that such integrity, in place or restored, will continue dynamically into the future.

Descriptively, the ecosystem is functioning well; there is cycling and recycling of energy and materials. The member organisms are flourishing as interrelated fits in their niches. The system is spontaneously self-organizing in the fundamental processes of climate, hydrology, photosynthesis. There is resistance to, and resilience after, perturbation. The system does not have to be constantly doctored. "Health is the capacity of the land for self-renewal. Conservation is our effort to understand and preserve this capacity" (Leopold 1968 [1949]:221).

Such a system will produce natural values, as well as support cultural values, and such productivity and support is the bottom line. Neither recycling, nor resilience, nor even self-organization are of value in themselves merely, but only as they systemically make productivity possible. These features are valuable, value-able, because they have the ability to *produce* value. There is systemic value, something in addition to intrinsic or instrumental value, a creative potential that steadily becomes actual. Integrity and health maintain this creativity. Biological integrity differs from health in its emphasis on an original or native complement of species and ecosystem processes.

Integrity and health, though symbolic ideas, can guide specific research and policy strategies. We set pollution standards, for instance, above which threshold there is evident deterioration of fish and waterfowl reproduction. Dissolved oxygen may not fall below 5 milligrams per liter in coldwater fisheries. We can study the food

chains, measure energy cycling and materials recycling, measure population rises and falls, recovery rates, and so forth, to find out, scientifically, what interconnections constitute and preserve biological
integrity.

Highly modified once-natural systems, now requiring steady management, such as farmlands, which must be plowed, seeded, weeded,
fertilized, harvested each year, cannot be said to have native biological integrity. They can perhaps have some kind of agricultural
integrity, if they can be managed sustainably, and if their operation
does not disrupt the surrounding natural systems (rivers, forests,
native fauna and flora in the fencerows, edges, fallow fields, pastures,
rangelands). Areas put into agriculture or industry or to urban uses
will always have to enveloped by natural systems, or else the system
will crash.

An unhealthy system will have "reduced primary productivity, loss
of nutrients, loss of sensitive species, increased instability in component populations, increased disease prevalence, changes in the biotic
size spectrum to favor smaller life-forms, and increased circulation of
contaminants" (Rapport 1989:122). Monocultures have little health.
Pushed more and more into artificiality, there isn't any ecosystem left
at all. A cornfield two miles square is almost like a twenty-acre park-
ing lot full of cars. The individual corn plants might be healthy enough
but they are just parked there by humans, like potted plants on the
porch. There are hardly any ecosystemic connections at all, past the
sunshine. Even the fossil water is pumped from a half-mile below.

The purely natural system no longer exists anywhere on Earth;
there is even some DDT present in penguins at the South Pole. But
only about 25 percent of the landscape, in most nations, is under permanent agriculture; a large percentage is more or less rural. There are
wild plants, escaped introductions; there is photosynthesis; the insects
and birds go their way. Complete unnaturalness, the totally artificial
environment does not yet exist either. How much naturalness is present on a landscape? Consider the following criteria:

1. What is the historical genesis of processes now operating on the
   landscape? Were they introduced by humans, or do they continue from the evolutionary and ecological past? The more doc-
   toring, the less likely there is health.

2. What is the species constitution compared with the original makeup? The more the fauna and flora is depauperate, the less integrity and health.

3. How much cultural energy is required for the upkeep of the modified system? The more such management requires large amounts of labor, petroleum, electricity, fertilizer, pesticides, the further we are from a system that has integrity or health.

4. How much self-organizing nature remains? What would happen without humans? Would the system reorganize itself, if not to its pristine integrity, then at least to a healthy system?

5. How much restoration has taken place? How much time has passed since the historical genesis was interrupted? Naturalness recoups, as we will recognize in the discussion of restoration.

How much naturalness do we value? Natural value is what is most at threat; cultural value is in plentiful supply (though unfortunately often maldistributed and wasted). The trend at the end of the twentieth century, headed into the twenty-first, is an escalation of development that threatens the integrity and the health of ecosystems worldwide. Such developments in culture are likely to have less integrity just because they are misfitted to their supporting biological integrity. We might find ourselves healthy but not rich environmentally.

Hands-on planetary managers will argue that it is futile to try to maintain pristine natural areas. In the future, we will increasingly have managed nature, or have no nature at all (see chapter 7, sec. 5). Global warming proves that. "Used" ecosystems are the only kind there are; there are no unspoiled ones available. All we can do is to see to it that used ecosystems are not abused. There are no unmanaged systems, just varieties and degrees of management, so why care? But this is a counsel of despair, based on a half-truth. Humans rebuild and manage the natural environments they overtake in culture across a spectrum, but this does not mean that there cannot remain ample wildness with its all but pristine integrity, nor that there cannot be both biotic integrity and health on the landscapes we inhabit, a health had by simply conserving natural value rather than by hands-on high-tech management. We have not yet been reduced to nothing but environments that have to be constantly doctored and engineered.

2. STABILITY AND HISTORICAL CHANGE

Stability, too, requires analysis, both as to matter of fact and value. In fact, it may be objected, ecosystems are not stable; they are subject to seasonal perturbations, episodic upsets, and they evolve historically over time (Botkin 1990). Nor, even if they were stable, would this ipso facto be of value. Stability is sometimes a value; one values a stable society. Stability is also sometimes a disvalue; a society without novelty cannot develop. Sameness can be boring. Neither is change, however, ipso facto valuable. Would it not have been better if Leopold had recommended the dynamism of the community? How do we get stability and historicity into valuable balance?

In earlier days, ecologists believed that diversity and complexity were systematically coupled to stability. This seemed plausible. There will be redundant pathways, checks and balances, statistical averaging of behaviors and responses over many species. Predators can switch prey, herbivores can migrate from one food source to another, and so forth. There is much reason to believe that ecosystems are often like this; but they are not always so (MacArthur 1955; May 1973; Goodman 1975; Van Voris et al. 1980). As a law of nature, or even a generalization, the stability-diversity theory has exceptions; it may not even be the case usually. Simple systems can also be stable; increased complexity can sometimes reduce stability. A complicated machine is more likely to fail than a simple one (if that is a fair analogy). If we value diversity because it is coupled with stability, we will have to do this on a case-specific basis. Sometimes, we must value stability independently of diversity.

Ecosystemic stability (like complexity, diversity, integrity, health) is both a general paradigm and a measurable characteristic at particular levels. Ecosystems may be *constant*, that is, little-changing in some dimensions. Temperatures change rather little in some tropical forests; species richness or evenness may remain about the same. One ecosystem might be steady because the climate is constant, another despite a changing environment because feedback loops adjust the system to the changes. Ecosystems may be *persistent*, that is, last long periods of time with little changes in species and their interrelationships. Ecosystems may have *inertia*, that is, resist external perturbations; this will probably be because of negative feedback loops that dampen changes.

Ecosystems may be *elastic*; if so, they return rapidly to their former state after perturbation. This may depend on the *amplitude* of the perturbation, both the area disturbed and the degree of displacement. Ecosystems sometimes have *cyclic stability*, that is, they oscillate periodically about some central mean, or they may have *trajectory stability*, that is, they may move steadily along routes of succession or, more vector-like, have historical tendencies (Orians 1975). Ecosystems may be cycles on cycles at close hand but really, over longer times, spirals that stretch out directionally (somewhat like a stretched-out spring). We can get numbers for some of these dimension of stability.

The stability of ecosystems is not a frozen sameness.* A trajectory stability recognizes that some ecosystems may be steadily changing over time. Ecosystems undergo successions, periodically rejuvenated—disturbance, early, middle, and late succession, climax. But, depending on how frequent and extensive these interruptions are, succession can be more ideal than real. If interrupted often enough, ecosystems wander through contingencies as much as they steadily develop. Ecosystems may be stable within bounds, within which they wander; but, when unusual disturbances come, with enough amplitude to knock them out of bounds, they are displaced beyond recovery of their former patterns. Then they wander until they settle into some new equilibrium.

Lately, with the popularity of chaos theory, some ecologists insist that ecosystem histories are more random walk than they are stable dynamism. Against the sheer random walk hypothesis, there is no doubt that ecosystems are full of cybernetic subsystems, species lineages that transmit information over time, generation after generation. Coded in the genetics and expressed in the coping behaviors of its member species, ecosystems will have the capacity to adjust to interruptions that come often enough to be remembered in the genet-

---

* On a few occasions, the national parks have thought of creating "a reasonable illusion of primitive America" (A. S. Leopold et al. 1963:4). This may be appropriate in certain places (such as the pioneer homesteads in Cades Cove in Great Smoky Mountains National Park), but it is ill-conceived as a general conservation policy. According to the Florida Department of Natural Resources (on brochures distributed at these parks), "Florida state parks are managed to appear (as closely as possible) as they did when the first Europeans arrived." But we do not want to conserve only illusions of eighteenth-century, or even pre-Columbian, America. Conservation, as we say later, is not going back to something.

ic memory. If climatic changes or novel species invasions are not too overwhelming, we expect that ecosystems that have long persisted will persist longer. Nothing succeeds like success.

To understand stability and historical change, we must place them on a scale. The time frames of some ecological changes are the familiar ones of spring, summer, winter, fall, or rainy and dry season. But there are sometimes longer cycles; in Africa, tourists and ungulates both prefer *Acacia* woodlands and gallery forests, but such woodlands are destroyed by aging and by elephant damage. Then wildlife populations diminish, and the reduced grazing pressures allow new *Acacia* seedlings to sprout, which can only get established over a decade or two, during which there may be no animals to see (Walker 1989). The forests of Yellowstone National Park that were burned in 1988 are regenerating, but only our great-grandchildren will see them restored as they were a decade ago.

Integrity is process as much as it is product. Integrity in ecosystems includes the capacity to evolve. Stability, and nothing more, would squelch this creativity. On a big enough scale, ecology meets evolution. Or, perhaps we should say, the evolution going on all the time becomes evident. The cycles of ecology become the spirals of evolutionary history; there are trends that unfold diversity and development, as we have recognized, so historical change is made possible by the stability that also permits and supports variation. The idea of an ecosystem being temporarily displaced from its equilibrium by some upset (a hurricane, a fire), to which equilibrium it soon returns, is only a half-truth. There are other possible responses: the ecosystem may restructure after the upset; the upset may hasten historical trends that were already at work more slowly; or it may introduce new historical directions, if it permits some species to get established that would not otherwise have done so. There is not simply one stable state that an ecosystem should always have; ecosystems are always on historical trajectory.

Meanwhile, on the scale of deep time, some processes continue on and on, so that the perennial givens—wind and rain, soil and photosynthesis, life and death and life renewed—can seem almost forever. Species survive for millions of years. Mountains are reliably there generation after generation. The water cycles back, century after century. Leopold knew well enough that, in an evolutionary time frame, relative stability mixes with change. "Paleontology offers abundant evidence that wilderness maintained itself for immensely long periods; that its component species were rarely lost, neither did they get out of hand; that weather and water built soil as fast or faster than it was carried away." That is why "wilderness . . . assumes unexpected importance as a laboratory for the study of land health" (1968 [1949]:196).

Human life is lived on the scale of ecology, long though these scales sometimes are. A human life is eight decades, more or less; those of our immediate experience include our grandparents, parents, children, grandchildren, covering perhaps a century and a half. On these scales there is stability in nature, and we do not want cultural changes that the natural dynamism of ecosystems cannot absorb. Leopold uses the word "stability" in the time frame of land-use planning. On that scale, nature typically does have a reliable stability, and farmers do well to figure in these perennial givens.

Our national histories cover many centuries, during which we must be prepared for natural systems to change. Even national histories hardly reach the scale of major evolutionary changes (several thousand years); evolution is nevertheless part of what we value in nature, though it differs by several orders of magnitude in pace of change from what we value in culture. Human time fades into deep time, time mixes with near-eternity; that is one reason we value pristine nature so highly.

It may also be true that Earth, from here onward, is entering a post-evolutionary epoch; Earth will become increasingly a "managed" planet. If humans wish a society with integrity, such management, for the foreseeable future, continues to require integrity and health in ecosystems, keeping them stable in the midst of historical change. Further, if humans wish optimal values conserved on Earth, such management ought to conserve appropriate biological integrity forever.

3. COMMUNITY

These ideas—integrity, health, stability, historical development—are valuable because they feed into the concept of the "biotic community." "All ethics so far evolved rests upon a single premise: that the individual is a member of a community of interdependent parts." But ethics has previously focused only on human society; we need now to learn community in environmental ethics. "When we see land as a community to which we belong, we may begin to use it with love and respect. . . . That land is a community is the basis concept of ecology, but that land is to be respected is an extension of ethics" (Leopold 1968 [1949]:203, viii–ix). We must bring nature and culture together in sustainable relationship.

We first need an account of what communities are in nature. Then we have to mix science and conscience, both ecology and social science with values that we want to, and ought to, conserve. A biotic community is a dynamic web of interacting parts in which lives are supported and defended, where there is integrity (integration of the members) and health (niches and resources for the flourishing of species), stability and historical development (dependable regeneration, resilience, and evolution), where the achievements of the past are carried forward and enjoyed in the present, with variations leading to creativity in the future (a cybernetic, transmissible heritage). Communities are plural; there must be many members. But communities are not sheer pluralisms. All community members have relationships; but some may be little related to some others. If there is excessive pluralism, however, there will be diminished integration in the community. A community is not possible without individuals, but a community puts individuals in vital relationships with others. Individuals are not possible without communities.

None of us has any doubt that there are cultural communities, and that they are highly valued because they nurture our human values (mixed, no doubt, with many disvalues). But neither should there be any doubt that there are biotic communities, and that these, too, are of high value (possibly also with mixed disvalues). These systems are the fountain of life. There is no community on the moon. But community is the miracle of Earth—as it has been for almost forever.

Some will protest that the idea of biological community is problematic. Ecosystems can seem to be little more than stochastic processes, hardly communities in a scientific sense, much less communities that count morally. A seashore, a tundra is a loose collection of externally related parts. Much of the environment is not organic at all (rain, groundwater, rocks, nonbiotic soil particles, air). Some is dead and decaying debris (fallen trees, scat, humus). These things have no organized needs; the collection of them is a jumble, hardly a community. There are organisms in relationships, but each defends its own life and there is only fortuitous interplay between organisms. An ecosystem is a matter of the distribution and abundance of organisms, how they get dispersed here and not there, birth rates and death rates, population densities, moisture regimes, parasitism and predation, checks and balances. But there is really not enough centered process to call community. There is only catch-as-catch-can scrimmage for nutrients and energy.

Following this line of thought, an ecosystem is the necessary habitat for all the diverse species and organisms that we value, and we may value it as context that we resourcefully use to make values. But this is to value it only instrumentally to the flourishing of plants and animals. And this flourishing, in turn, we may value really only as a resource for the human community. The integrity really is not in the ecosystem; it is in the individuals that reside in it, to which the systemic processes are tributary. The integrity, therefore, really is not all that much in nature; it ultimately resides in culture. In nature, the systemic processes are pushing and hauling between rivals, opportunists moving through their environments, or there is just indifference and haphazard juxtaposition, something we cannot escape but nothing we should particularly admire. Ecosystems do not have enough integrity to be called communities. They are just jumbles.

So it may seem as if concern for ecosystems is secondary, instrumental to a respect for human and nonhuman life. An ecosystem is too low a level of organization to be the direct focus of concern. To make an analogy with culture, however much society supplies a context of support and identity, the focal point for value is the high point of individuality: the person. By parity of reasoning, though there are no persons in nonhuman nature, we should count the nearest thing. The moral focus in ecosystems (assuming that at least some nonhumans count morally) should be the high point of integrated complexity: the organism. So we will value higher animal lives, and their environments, only because these environments support these valued animals. And what really has integrated complexity is humans in their cultures.

But to say that and nothing more is to misunderstand ecosystems.

An organism has a kind of integrity that ecosystems do not have. Ecosystems have another kind of integrity that organisms do not possess. Organisms are tightly integrated; the heart is closely connected to the liver, and the genome and the brain are unified control centers. Communities are neither organisms nor superorganisms; they are communities, common unities. The community connections, though requiring an adaptive fit of organisms in their niches, are more loose than the organismic coactions. But that does not mean they are less significant. Internal complexity, an organismic self, arises to deal with a complex, tricky environment, the world as foil of self. The skin-out processes are not just the support, they are the subtle source of the skin-in processes.

Everything will be connected to many other things, sometimes by obligate associations, more often by partial and pliable dependencies; among some components, there may be no significant interactions. There will be shunts and criss-crossing pathways, cybernetic subsystems, feedback and feedforward loops, functions in a communal sense. The system is a kind of field with characteristics as vital for life as any property contained inside organisms. The individual, the species, and its environment are not in accidental aggregation; the ecosystem is the depth source of individual and species alike. Although conflict is part of the picture, the organism is selected for a situated environmental fitness. A bear fits a forest just as much as its heart fits its lungs. There are differences; the heart and lungs are closely coupled in a way that bear and forest are not. Still, the bear requires its forest community; the bear-organism fits there, as surely as its organs fit together to compose a bear.

Some suggest that organisms, or their biochemical molecules—proteins and genes—are "real," while ecosystems are merely collections of interacting individuals, epiphenomenal aggregations. This is a confusion. Any level is real if there is significant downward causation. Thus, the atom is real because that pattern shapes the behavior of electrons; the cell because that pattern shapes the behavior of amino acids; the organism because that pattern coordinates the behavior of hearts and lungs; the community because the niche shapes the morphology and behavior of the foxes within it. Genes are the coding for coping in ecosystems; that makes them what they are where they are, and it makes ecosystems as real, as ultimate, as any genetic self. Far from being unreal, ecosystems are the fundamental unit of development and survival.

An ecosystem systematically generates a spontaneous order that exceeds in richness, beauty, integrity, and dynamic stability the order of any of its component parts, an order that in turn feeds (and is fed by) the richness, beauty, and integrity of these component parts. Though these organized interdependencies are "loose" in comparison with the "tight" connections within an organism, the equilibrating ecosystem is not merely push-pull causal forces. It is an equilibrating of values.

There are cultural communities, too, with many relevant differences from natural communities. Natural communities proceed by genetic transmission and natural selection; social communities proceed by neural transmission and social (rational, moral, economic, political) selection. Natural communities are held together by causal relations; human societies are held together also by meaning relations. The relationship between individual and community within culture differs from that within nature. Individuality in persons is more highly developed than individuality within aspen trees or squirrels. New patterns of community relationships emerge in culture. Wild animals do not grant and claim rights, for instance. Nor do they ask about forgiveness when they sin and break community norms. Wild animals do not discuss environmental philosophy, organize classes and read books on conserving natural value, or call Earth Summit meetings alarmed over the fate of the planet. So we do not want to be indiscriminating about the differences between these communities.

These differences are so dramatic that some say that, although ecosystems are biotic communities, they are not moral communities, and therefore, their values can be only instrumental to the communities that really count, that is, human communities. John Passmore claims that only human communities generate obligations:

> Ecologically, no doubt, men do form a community with plants, animals, soil, in the sense that a particular life-cycle will involve all four of them. But if it is essential to a community that the members of it have common interests and recognize mutual obligations, then men, plants, animals, and soil do *not* form a community. Bacteria and

men do not recognize mutual obligations, nor do they have common interests. In the only sense in which belonging to a community generates ethical obligations, they do not belong to the same community. (1974:116)

Passmore is assuming that the members of a morally bound community must recognize reciprocal obligations. If the only communal
belonging that generates obligations is this social sense, involving
mutual recognition of interests, then the human community is the sole
matrix of morality, and the case is closed. But we are asking a value
question. We are basing our ethics on values we want to optimize, not
just on mutual recognitions of interests. So we have opened the question Passmore thinks closed. We have steadily been finding natural
values present in biotic communities. We do not want to extrapolate
criteria from cultural to biotic communities, any more than we extrapolate criteria from biotic to cultural communities. We do not decide
morality for humans by watching the beasts or the birds. Nor do we
decide whether monkeys and parrots are valuable by seeing whether
they enter into moral relationships. Rather, we seek criteria appropriate to each kind of community.

How to trade gains in culture against losses in ecosystemic communities is often puzzling. As a general rule, humans count enough
to have the right to flourish within ecosystems, but they do not
count so much that they can degrade or shut down ecosystems—not
at least without a considerable burden of proof that they are obtain-
ing greater value in culture in exchange. All human culture will modify ecosystems: an agricultural ecosystem will at times have to compromise the native integrity of ecosystems; an urban-industrial community will have to be built on lands once wild but where the
wildness has been displaced. Nevertheless, our human communities
are, and ought to be, sufficiently contained within these satisfactory
ecosystems that embrace society. If this cannot be a rule with which
to judge the past in our now greatly modified, rebuilt environments,
at least it can help envision the future (see chapter 5, sec. 2). From
here on, an important ethical constraint in environmental decisions
is concern for the integrity, stability, and beauty of biotic communities.

4. SUSTAINABILITY

Sustainability has become a keyword in analyses of ecosystem integrity and health, as well as of cultural communities. The UN World Commission on Environment and Development declared, "Sustainable development is development that meets the needs of the present without compromising the ability of future generations to meet their own needs" (1987b:43). The idea was first applied to agriculture and forestry, but later to water use, allowable pollution levels, to industry, urbanization, and national policies and strategies. "Sustainable" is regularly coupled with "development," and this suggests that, as a conservation philosophy, it is a code word for continued growth.

We may worry about sustained growth but then be reassured that growth (a quite biological word) is a good thing. Healthy organisms must grow, flourish; and growth is not problematic if sustainable. After all, we were just insisting that ecosystems develop historically; and ought we not to say something similar about culture? We value cultural systems too that are stable in their historically developing growth (Douglas and Schirmer 1987; Redclift 1987; Reganold, Papendick, and Parr 1990).

On the other hand, growth for most animals is a juvenile phase. Populations in ecosystems usually do not grow; in a healthy population, the death rate about equals the birth rate. In fact, nongrowth can sometimes be the healthy state. We wish to sustain some kinds of development throughout life (growth in knowledge, character, interpersonal relations); we seek some kinds of social development (more justice, better education, better science). But there are some kinds of development that we want to stop. Adult humans cease to grow taller (and they ought not get any fatter). Maybe there ought not always to be a Greater Los Angeles. There is not going to be any Greater California or United States. Neither sustainability nor growth nor development are ipso facto value words (no more than complexity, diversity, rarity, and the others). We are glad to have library holdings growing; we are sad to find a cancer growing. And should we be glad or sad to find our income always growing? Our business making more profit? Our consumption growing? Is there an "enough" some-where?

The UN World Commission on Environment and Development pleads that we must have development because most people do not have anywhere near enough. Such development, fulfilling needs, will carry on in generations to come:

> Humanity has the ability to make development sustainable. . . . The concept of sustainable development does imply limits—not absolute limits but limitations imposed by the present state of technology and social organization on environmental resources and by the abil-ity of the biosphere to absorb the effects of human activities. But technology and social organization can be both managed and improved to make way for a new era of economic growth. . . . Meet-ing essential needs requires not only a new era of economic growth for nations in which the majority are poor, but an assurance that those poor get their fair share of the resources required to sustain that growth. (1987:8)

That is humane enough, but there is here no concern for the integri-ty of ecosystems, nor for biodiversity. The concern is for justice in sharing the produce of the Earth now and in future generations. Nor is there concern about escalating human populations; the only goal is meeting essential human needs by sustainable growth. The Earth is regarded as a natural resource and a sink for wastes; what really counts is meeting people's needs. Most people do not have enough yet for two reasons: not enough is produced; and what is produced is not equitably shared. It is clear here that sustainable development is for people; the commission anticipates much more growth, people increasingly making a resourceful use of the Earth, as fast as technol-ogy can arrange it. Nature, while not ultimately important, is (in the literal sense) provisionally important. People are definitive, thereby discounting natural values. *

Perhaps there is a better way of defining sustainable development. According to the UN commission's definition, sustainability is a rela-tionship within culture that is satisfied if future persons have ongoing equitable development opportunities. What we wish to sustain might

---

* The report does elsewhere say, "Utility aside, there are also moral, ethical, cultural, aesthetic, and purely scientific reasons for conserving wild beings" (13).

be gross national product, or population growth commensurate with crop increases, or per capita income. Any condition of nature that supplies such opportunities will be acceptable, though this will, for the foreseeable future, require some natural conservation. A better definition would envision a relation between culture and nature whereby only that cultural development is acceptable that continues to sustain ecosystemic integrity, or, perhaps, more minimally, health. Natural values would be constraints on social values, not just contributory to them. We should be as interested in sustaining ecological balance as in sustaining increased agricultural or industrial development.

"Sustainable development," J. Ronald Engel tells us, "may be defined as *the kind of human activity that nourishes and perpetuates the historical fulfilment of the whole community of life on Earth*" (1990:10–11). That puts human and biotic communities together comprehensively. If we wish to optimize values overall, this outlook is more promising. Everybody counts—plants, animals, and people. There is no mention of growth at all in this account; within the human community we are not so much concerned with industrial or agricultural growth as with sustaining communities in which people are "fulfilled." Beyond that, what is sustained is the entire community of life. These communities need not grow, though they will *flourish* and perpetuate.

Sustainable development differs from the spontaneous self-organizing of wild ecosystems, or even self-healing rural systems. Natural systems flourish all by themselves, without any human input. Sustainable development is a "human activity," Engel tells us. There will be continued human input external to the much-modified natural system. There will be careful management, and the managerial activity will see to it that everybody is fulfilled. On the ninety-five percent of the landscape that humans rebuild with their agriculture and culture, humans will be energetically active; the only criterion is that what they actively do results in prosperity for all—fauna and flora, nations and people.

Engel's hope sounds vaguely reasonable so long as it is kept reasonably vague, but on closer analysis one wonders whether the fulfillment of the human community is historically possible with the simultaneous fulfillment of the whole biotic community. When Iowa is plowed to plant corn, it can hardly be said that the grasslands of Iowa reach their historical fulfillment. The bison must scatter, and there will be fewer bobolinks—sacrificed that Europeans may build their culture on the American continent. The most we can say is that Iowans can and ought to sustain their agriculture within the hydrology, soil chemistries, nutrient recycling processes, and so on, that operate on the Iowa landscape. But there is no sustainable development of Iowa agriculture that leaves the natural history unblemished. Legitimate human demands for culture cannot be satisfied without the sacrifice of nature. That is a sad truth. Maybe the UN commission had already figured that out.

But the UN commission has played down respect for the integrity of natural systems, and that leaves us wondering if even the health of natural systems is likely to be good, so long as humans are bent on meeting escalating human needs above all else. There is reason to think that agriculture in Iowa has gone too far: there is no national park, no national grassland, no national forest, no wilderness in the state; soil (the "black gold") is being lost at a rapid rate; wetlands are being destroyed; free-ranging bison are extinct in the state. State parks and other conservation areas contain fragments of prairie, but statewide there is less than 0.1 percent of the native prairie left, only one acre in a thousand. There is hardly any mesic prairie at all, once the natural glory of the state. All this development is a good thing, by the UN criteria, if it meets people's essential needs (growing corn and wheat), provided only that future generations can grow crops there, too. Now we do begin to wonder if the sustainable development approach can appreciate natural values, and if, given its fixation on growth, development really is going to be sustainable. Sustainability can sometimes be a green cloak thrown over business as usual, warned that it needs better long-range planning.

Sustainability ought, in fact, to be a warning flag that helps us consider how much is enough. The great new norm for the next millennium is sustainability, and human society is, at present in most of both the developed and the developing countries, nowhere close. When Columbus arrived in the Americas in 1492, there was a vast amount of wilderness, as well as indigenous peoples who had been sustained by the landscape for ten or twenty thousand years. In the five hundred years since, there has been an explosion of European culture rebuilding the landscape, and that rebuilding has now reached a point where further expansion of culture at the price of nature will be counterproductive, even for culture. The next five hundred years simply cannot be like the past five hundred years, without a tragic loss of natural values that will harm humans as well as the nature that today remains on the landscape.

Remembering the root of "satisfactory," we are far past the point where enough is enough, and the mix of cultural and natural values ought not to be further skewed. It is already so disproportionate that in most areas the natural values are the ones in short supply. These natural values ought to be preserved for their own sake, but when they are preserved for their own sake they simultaneously enrich the culture that is otherwise impoverished of natural values. What we really value is a satisfactory community, with a balance of natural and cultural values, and to take sustainable development as a paradigm, though it seems humane, is unlikely to give us a satisfactory community, either biotic or cultural.

The cultural phase of human history not only must be superposed on natural history, it must also adapt and rebuild that natural history to its own benefit. From here onward, any society that we can envision must be scientifically sophisticated, technologically advanced, globally oriented, as well as (we hope) just and charitable, caring for universal human rights and for biospheric values. This society will try to fit itself in intelligently with the ecosystemic processes on which it is superposed. It will also have to redirect those processes to its benefit. In that sense, nature must be harmed if culture is to continue. Culture is a post-evolutionary phase of our planetary history; it must be superposed on the nature it presupposes.

At the same time, humans should build sustainable cultures that fit in with the continuing ecological processes. So the first principle of culture is that it rebuild wild nature; the second is that culture ought to be sustainable on the ecological processes that support it. The third principle of culture is that it ought appropriately to respect the nature that is the original source of our being, a "Mother Nature" that has generated myriads of diverse and complex life forms that are also members of the community of life on Earth.

Having worried about Iowa, we can close on an optimistic note. It is possible to have nature, modified by culture, still flourishing on prairie landscapes. The South Platte River had few cottonwoods before the Europeans arrived. The spring floods washed them out. But now the waters are regulated, owing to upstream dams, and cotton-woods abound. Birds and wildlife have moved in—whitetail deer, blue jays, mockingbirds, wild turkeys, cardinals. Bald eagles overwinter and eat fish from the reservoirs. Waterfowl feed on irrigation ponds, migrating through spring and fall, sometimes nesting there. This seems a sustainable situation.* The riparian ecosystem is not what it was in presettlement days, it has been altered to another dynamic equilibrium. Nevertheless, many regard the change as an improve-ment. The system has health, though it does not have (pre-European) integrity. There is a required human input, regulation of the flow waters, but this will continue for the foreseeable future. Here too, however, there is threat of going too far. Further drying up the Platte would send the whole riparian system into a degenerating spiral.

5. RESTORATION

Where human interference has degraded ecosystems, what about restoring them? In legislation such as the Water Quality Act of 1965 and the Clean Water Act of 1987, we intend that once-polluted sys-tems, when the toxics are removed, will be rejuvenated and return to health. Often, if we cease the interruption, natural systems will be self-healing; but, especially if systems have been pushed far from their equilibriums, or if species have been exterminated, or soils lost, the damage may require managed repair. We may need clean up and fix up. One goal of the Endangered Species Act is recovery of the endan-gered populations; U.S. Fish and Wildlife officials are instructed to form a recovery plan. As just noted, there are only scraps of native prairie remaining in the U.S. Midwest and people have become con-cerned to restore prairie (Jordan 1991; Jordan, Gilpin, and Aber 1987).

All this commendable activity poses some philosophical puzzles (Cowell 1993). These arise from the various senses of what is natural, examined in chapter 1, as they affect natural value. In the first sense,

---

* One unfortunate side effect is that sandhill cranes, which prefer to roost standing in shallow river waters, are discouraged by vegetation nearby in which predators may lurk.

everything that humans do deliberately, being a cultural activity, interrupts spontaneous nature and is in that sense therefore unnatural. But what if humans come in and deliberately repair a degraded prairie? That is a cultural activity; there are work crews organized by the Society for Ecological Restoration. They sketch groundplans for what they will put where; they work at it, often long and hard. Then there it is: behold, a prairie! As good as new. Or is it? A prairie is a phenomenon of spontaneous nature, but this restored prairie? *People* built it. Perhaps it is an artifact, in which case it cannot be wild nature. Hence, a rebuilt prairie is a contradiction in terms. There it is: A faked prairie!

Lest you shake your head at how philosophers, arguing about words, can produce a puzzle anywhere they please, and are only causing trouble, casting doubt on a perfectly commendable activity, we hasten to point out that this matter has considerable relevance. As soon as you accept, uncritically, this rebuilt prairie as the real thing, having all the values of the original, there will arrive a delegation from the mining company, who want to mine the coal under the last remnant of real prairie that *does* exist. If you object that there is little prairie left, and refuse to license the mine, they will reply that they will, after mining, put the prairie back like it was. Almost every development project that disrupts natural systems, in order to get a permit, has to meet certain legal restoration criteria. Often, if one area is destroyed, such as a fishing stream or a wetland, there will be a requirement for mitigation, met when they create another fishing stream or wetland somewhere else. Or to put nature back when they finish.

Unfortunately, restorations are seldom as good as the original. The diversity of species may not be there, nor the complexity of ecosystemic interrelations. So the restored ecosystem will lack integrity. Once, I was deciding where to hike, looking at trails on either side of the road below Independence Pass near Aspen, Colorado. Reading the trail signs, I found that one trail headed into an old-growth forest; the other headed into a forest that had been replanted about a half a century before, after logging. Instantly, I knew which trail I wanted to take. Recent studies in Appalachian forests have found that, though the dominant trees may come back, the forest undercover is only about one-third as rich as it was before, even where there are some efforts at restoration (Duffy and Meier 1992). I look for rare mosses, and I had considerable doubt that the Forest Service restoration team had replanted any undiscovered species of rare mosses! Still, I was glad that the forest had been replanted, even though I chose to hike in the pristine one. So the first point to make is that restorations, although valuable, are not as valuable as pristine nature, because they are simply not as rich (Westman 1991; Roberts 1993).

But more value is at stake, and this turns on a philosophical rather than a technical point. Even if the restoration were one hundred percent, what then? Eric Katz calls restorations "the Big Lie!" (1992). Robert Elliot complains, "Faked nature!" (1982). This is because the historical genesis of the system has been interrupted, and, even though both Katz and Elliot approve of restorations, they insist that the value of even a perfect restoration is always in principle something less than the value of pristine nature, since it is not the handiwork of nature but of humans, who have cleverly restored it. The proper response to make in a restored forest is not, "How marvelous a work of nature! Nature is superb! Just look at those mosses festooning the trees." Rather, we exclaim, "What clever landscape architects. Superb job of restoration! Why, I would never have known. Just look at the moss festooning those trees; it looks like its been there for centuries. They really fooled me!" Even a perfectly restored nature isn't the genuine article it can only be an artifact. The imitation, however accurate, is not authentic nature.

To work our way out of these troubles, notice that there are all kinds and degrees of restoration. At the one extreme, if a forest has been clearcut, or stripmined, there is nothing there; the landscape is blitzed, so any new forest is a complete replacement, a replica. This would be like replicating the Niña, one of Christopher Columbus's ships. The replica is made from scratch and has no historical continuity at all with the original. This is not really restoration at all, but replication. On the other end of the spectrum, if the forest has been cut by selection of a few trees here and there, and new trees replanted to substitute for these, there is restoration.

A restoration is the original, once damaged and now restored. A replica is a new creation, without causal continuity to the old one. While replicas can exist simultaneously with originals, restorations obviously cannot. We do speak—loosely—of the new forest being a restoration, whether it was rebuilt from scratch, or simply facilitated by replanting removed trees, with much of the forest continuing uninterrupted. But, speaking more carefully, replicas are replacements, while restorations continue much of the historical continuity. Restoration of a famous painting, such as da Vinci's *The Last Supper*, is not making a replica and passing it off as the original. By the same token, restoration of a famous natural area, such as Thoreau's Walden Pond, ought to be a careful and respectful rehabilitation. The result is nature *restored*, not nature *faked*.

The comparison with an artwork is somewhat misleading, however, because in nature we restore by rehabilitating. The painting, which is an artifact, does not heal itself when restored; it is a passive object. Strictly speaking, one does not rehabilitate paintings. But nature, as a community of living beings and processes, may, once we put the parts back in place, heal itself. Revegetating after strip mining cannot properly be called rehabilitation either, because there is in fact nothing left to rehabilitate. But one can rehabilitate a prairie that has been not too badly overgrazed. Overgrazing allows many introduced weeds to outcompete the natives; perhaps all one has to do is pull the weeds and let nature do the rest; that is undoing as much as doing. Overgrazing allows some native plants to outcompete other natives, those that once reproduced in the shade of the taller grasses. So perhaps, after the taller grasses return, one will have to dig some holes, put in some seeds that have been gathered from elsewhere, cover them up, go home, and let nature do the rest. Maybe all that is needed is to just put the seeds in the weed holes to aid in rehabilitation. In the restoration of art, there can be no analog to this self-healing (Gunn 1991; Sylvan, 1994).

The naturalness returns. The restoration ceases to be an artifact. In the days before high-tech medicine, many physicians who were congratulated on their cures used to say, modestly, "Really, I just treated you, and nature healed you." When a doctor sets a broken arm, he just holds the pieces in place with a splint and nature does the rest. He is not really to be congratulated for his skills at creating arms. He arranges for the cure to happen naturally. One does not complain, thereafter, that he has an artificial limb. Likewise with restoration. It is more like being a midwife than being an artist or engineer. You arrange the raw materials back on site, and place them where they can do their thing.

The point is that restorations do not fake so much as facilitate nature, help it along, mostly by undoing the damage that humans have introduced, and then letting nature do for itself. As the restoration is completed, the wild processes take over. The sun shines, the rains fall, the forest grows. Birds arrive on their own and build their nests. Hawks and owls catch rodents. Perhaps you return some otters, locally extinct, and put them back in the rivers. But, after a few generations, the otters do not know they were once reintroduced, they behave instinctively as they are genetically programmed to do. They catch muskrats as they can; population dynamics is restored and natural selection takes over. The adapted fits survive in their niches.

Succession resumes. In due course, lightning will strike and wildfire burn the forest again, after which it will regenerate itself. Even a new species could evolve. If such things happened decades, centuries, millennia after some thoughtful humans had once facilitated a restoration, it would seem odd to label all these events as artifacts, lies, fakes. Perhaps the best way to think of it is that the naturalness of a restored area is time-bound. Any restoration is an artifact at the moment that it is deliberately arranged, but it gradually ceases to be so as spontaneous nature returns—but if, and only if, humans back off and let nature take its course.

Nevertheless, the unbroken historical continuity in natural systems is important to humans. That, after restoration, we back off to let nature take its course proves that we wish that the course of nature had never been broken on the landscape we now conserve. We are glad to have broken arms healed; we would just as soon never have broken arms. Though the spontaneity of natural systems might all return, the historical discontinuity can never be repaired. In that respect, the restored area does suffer permanent loss of natural value. Natural systems, like human beings, are not replaceable in their historical identity and particularity. They are characteristically idiographic and deliver their values in historical process, diminished in value if interrupted. Restoring does not restore this interruption. If one is appreciating the present spontaneity of wild nature—the plant or animal in its *ecology*—that can be returned, and will, after complete restoration, be present undiminished. But if one is appreciating the *evolutionary history*—the plant or animal in its historical lineage—even though the genetics may be back in place, there still interrupted wildness. The forest is no longer virgin, no longer pristine, and, in a sense, it is less "real."

"Restore" connotes the idea of putting something back as it was earlier. However, we need to be clear what this something is and what it is not. We are not resetting the forest to what it was a century ago. That suggests going backward in time, and is simply impossible. We can not replace the past. We are only capable today of putting back in place products of nature (i.e., seeds, seedlings, nutrients, species, soils, clean waters), and, with this, encourage the reappearance of what we are really putting back: natural processes. Restoration cannot be a backward-looking activity, though, to be sure, one does have to look to uninterrupted systems to discover what was once there.In fact, restoration must be a forward-looking event to rehabilitate for the future.

We cannot go back in history and undo the undoing we humans once did. We cannot go back to yesterday as though we could restore pre-Columbian America. We ought not do so even if we could, because culture is a good thing on the American landscape and that would diminish value. But we have erred in our excess, in our ignorance, in our insensitivity, in our haste, in our greed; we have lost natural value. Facing up to that loss, often we do want to restore ecosystemic integrity and health. The sin, however, once committed, is done forever. The only recourse is restitution, and such restitution is both possible and desirable.

Sometimes we will restore for pragmatic reasons, since we have often found that the degradation of ecosystems harms us people as well. Sometimes this will be an altruistic restoration, putting it back for the sake of the wild others who may re-reside there. Such restoration is restitution, a moral word. We make restitution where we ought not to have destroyed values. This includes natural values as surely as cultural ones. Restoration as restitution, moreover, is going to increase our human sense of identity with nature; we are going to appreciate the biotic community we have studied and helped to restore. We will be more careful elsewhere about our harmony with the natural systems that we will continue to disturb. That sense of identity and harmony is not inauthentic at all. It is the fundamental imperative of conserving natural value.

6. BALANCING INTEGRITY AND HEALTH VALUES

Continuing the rules of previous chapters, can we say more toward making this land ethic operational?

1. *Land health and human health are nonrival values.* Although settled lands cannot retain their original pristine integrity, all lands can and ought to be healthy. Fortunately, in conserving the basic givens, what is good for the biotic community is good for the human community, and vice versa. We all need clean water, clean air, soil fertility, nutrients recycled, stability in landscape processes, and so forth—birds and wildflowers, as well as city and rural people. If one seems to be facing a tradeoff between health for humans and land health, one is probably mistaken about what is healthy for humans. It might seem, for instance, that human health can be favored by putting more pesticides on the fields, even if this is killing nontarget species. But we may find that the toxics are building up adversely for people, too, or that the nontarget species were contributors to land health in ways of which we were unaware.

This is not mere coincidence; humans are, after all, biological beings; they evolved on landscapes and reside in an ecology. Our biological metabolisms, like breathing oxygen and drinking water, were going on in our ancestors, human and nonhuman, for many millions of years. The cytochrome c molecules, which we use in respiration, are found in organisms ranging from yeasts to people. Humans and nonhumans alike use adenosine triphosphate (ATP), biotin, riboflavin, hematin, thiamine, pyridoxine, and on and on. So we can expect that what makes an environment unhealthy for animals will be unhealthy for people. People do not differ much from animals in the kinds of molecules they need reliably flowing through their bodies. There will be differences of threshold and nutritional needs, of course, but the fundamental processes of biological and ecological health are no respecters of persons.

2. *Human integrity is enriched by environmental integrity.* While the previous maxim has been true since humans evolved, several million years ago. The present one is time-bound; it has become more true than before in the past century, and it becomes more true every decade. This one has for millennia been only partly true in the sense that, as we have lamented, cultural integrity has historically

also required the sacrifice of environmental integrity. There is no sustainable development of Iowa agriculture that leaves the natural history of Iowa unblemished. Human integrity was then enriched by environmental sacrifice.

Now, however, the former half-truth is becoming more and more the full truth. There are fewer and fewer cases where human integrity can really be enriched by the sacrifice of environmental integrity. We need to shift the burden of proof to any who believe so. There may be such occasions yet—if, say, permanent solutions to human needs could be found by converting a tract of forested land to agriculture, with continued environmental health, even though some values in the pristine forest were lost. But this has to be argued, and it is unlikely. It is unlikely because nations have been settled for centuries, if not for millennia; the prime lands for residence and agriculture have long since been claimed, and the remaining lands are probably marginal. We turn next to the better solution.

3. *Do not jeopardize land integrity and health to postpone solutions to social problems.* The no-jeopardy maxim remains an imperative with land integrity and health. The world is full enough of societies that have squandered their resources, inequitably distributed wealth, degraded their landscapes, and who will be tempted to jeopardize land integrity and health as an alternative to solving hard social problems (see chapter 5, sec. 3). Such a solution really fails to face up to where the ill health is: in the social system, which is forcing an unhealthy relation to the landscape. Too often, marginalized peoples will be forced onto marginal lands, lands that are easily stressed, both because by nature they are marginal for agriculture, range, and life support, and also because by human nature marginalized peoples find it difficult to plan in the longer term. They are caught up in meeting their immediate needs; their stress forces them to stress a fragile landscape.

Prime agricultural or residential lands can also be stressed by being forced to produce more and more, because there is a growing population to feed, or to grow an export crop, because there is an international debt to pay. Prime agricultural lands in southern Brazil, formerly used for growing food and worked by tenants who lived on these lands and ate their produce, have been converted to growing coffee as an export crop, using mechanized farming, to help pay Brazil's massive debt, contracted by a military government, since overthrown. Peoples forced off these lands were resettled, aided by development schemes fostered by the military government, in the Amazon basin, on lands really not suitable for agriculture at all. The integrity of the Amazon, to say nothing of the integrity of these peoples, is being sacrificed to cover for misguided borrowing and spending. Meanwhile, the wealthy in Brazil pay little or no income tax, which might be used for such loan repayment.

4. *A toxic threat is trumps.* The volume of pollution dumped into ecosystems has escalated markedly and the kinds have changed dramatically. From 1941 through 1977 the volume of manufactured synthetic chemicals increased 350 times in the United States, with many of these quite toxic. Even the most resilient local ecosystems cannot absorb our exhausts, pesticides, and herbicides. Even global currents cannot flush out aerosol fluorocarbons or the waste that falls as acid rain. Nor can the rivers absorb the pollutants. The more such pollutants are hazardous the more they need to be regulated, and the more they are poisonous the more they are absolutely to be forbidden. If one values health and integrity, poison really is a red flag.

There is room to discuss what counts as acceptable risk, especially since minute pollutants are the most expensive to remove, but surely our policy ought to bias in favor of health—human health coupled with land health. Given the pressures of market competition, industry will be pushed to dump wastes cheaply. Policy needs to counteract this, else poisons will be foisted unwillingly upon millions of persons not party to the benefits of particular business transactions. Especially in view of time lags here, involving the build-up across decades of small amounts of poisons, or delayed effects, the margin of error ought to favor human and land health by a wide margin.

The more permanent the poison's effects, the more it counters large amounts of immediate goods. Plutonium remains lethal for fifty times longer than any civilization has yet survived, five times longer than even *Homo sapiens* as a species has yet survived. Poisons in the groundwater are almost impossible to remove. Since a poison erodes life and health, a little toxic threat overrides a lot of the pursuit of happiness. We live with the moral imperative "Thou shalt not kill," and life shortened or impaired is life taken.

5. *Community overrides consumption.* We are all willy-nilly consumers. But it is just as true that we have to have a safe place to be, a place healthy enough to support consumption. We are all residents of places. We can move around, but not if we run out of safe places to run to. We cannot all always be running from places we have fouled and made unsafe. Every stable, safe, sustainable residing place has to be a community, not just some location at which we consume. There is no reason to prefer consuming over residing as the first fact of life. It is just as important for the bottom line to be green as it is for it to black. Indeed, it is more important, because people can live without money but not without air. They cannot live without food, but food is produced by natural processes, which require biotic community, before it is marketed in supermarkets and bought with money.

In the same way that personal health is essential for our survival, environmental health is not something optional, a luxury. Environmental health is health for all life, supporting organismic health. The only context in which human health is possible is ecosystemic, taking place in a healthy community. That does not mean that we must not consume; it means that consumption cannot be the overriding value of our existence. Consumption must be constrained by the larger sense of community. Everyone has the right to live; no one has the right to jeopardize the community of life. No one can claim a right to increased consumption if this jeopardizes the health of us all.

6. *Preserve processes more than products.* Critics charge that environmentalism is too preservationist. Environmentalists are backward-looking. They want to hang on to a romantic ideal of nature, rather than boldly face a new future that humans now have the opportunity to create. They suffer from failure of nerve. They want natural history museums, and this, while providing an amenity value, does not face the living present, where the work of the world has to go on. People have to be fed, clothed, housed; development is urgent, conservation an elitist luxury.

But this misunderstands what natural value involves. We value ongoing natural processes, kept in place on the landscape, as real today as they ever were, and no less important. The only means to this preservation is to keep products of evolutionary history there, such as trees, fungi, insects, earthworms, but we value these products because, continuing from the past, they make the future possible. They continue the natural processes on which everything of value depends. Conserving health in living systems is never a matter of safeguarding products, things, species, so much as it is of safeguarding the larger historical processes. Such processes take the past, produce the present, and project us into the future. What we are preserving in the present is our future as much as our past.

7. *Restore in order to conserve.* There will be much temptation to say that, alas, things have gone too far; it would have been better once upon a time do otherwise. But now we must let bygones be bygones, and accept what has unfortunately been done. Nicholas Rescher holds that "the environment has had it and that we simply cannot 'go home again' to 'the good old days' of environmental purity." He deplores "an unwillingness to face the prospect of environmental degradation as a permanent reality, an ongoing 'fact of life' " (1974:91). An abused ecosystem is the only kind of ecosystem there is.

While we perhaps cannot return to pristine purity, we can certainly return to vigorous environmental health. Permanent environmental degradation need not be accepted as a fact of life. That is a self-fulfilling prophecy. In fact, restoration biology is a more courageous approach for the future. It does not seek to go back to the "good old days" but to make restitution because it now and henceforth values environmental integrity and health, and because it values cultural integrity as well. We can change these facts of life.

8. *Respect systemic historical change, more than episodic, contingent change.* Not everything that happens in nature is natural in the same way; not every event is essential to ecosystem health and integrity. Keystone species are more important in the roles they play. Likewise, some events in nature are more important for maintaining the ecosystemic processes. We value keeping the food chains in place, the nutrients recycling, the water pure, the air clean, keeping natural selection in place, populations in equilibrium. But there can come episodic interruptions in nature that are not particularly part of the systemic processes. We may still want to let nature take its course, especially if humans are not put in jeopardy by these events, but we should not try to argue that everything that happens naturally is vital to ecosystemic health.

We must exercise caution here, however, because we can be mistaken either way. Formerly, we put forest fires out; they seemed bad, destroying ecosystems, when lightning by chance happened to strike. We have learned that lightning and fire are vital parts of ecosystemic health. Forests, if ready to burn, are in fact rejuvenated by fire. But it does not necessarily follow that there should be no fire management at all, because, while we have reason to think that on statistical average lightning fires will benefit the forests, there is no particular reason to think that every such ignition is the most healthy event possible at that particular time and place.

So a fire management plan for national forests (as distinguished from wilderness areas) can be quite consistent with respecting the health and integrity of ecosystems, especially those that are entwined with human cultures. That was at issue, for instance, in the Yellowstone fires of 1988. In some respects they were natural, in some respects they were catastrophic, aggravated by a century of fire suppression and fuel buildup. The Park Service policy, which was generally, and wisely, to let the fires burn, came into conflict with those who argued that fires of this scale, intensified by the misguided suppression policy, were anomalous fires and ought to be put out.

On July 21, 1987, 175-mile-an-hour tornado winds destroyed 15,000 acres in the Teton Wilderness of Wyoming. There is no particular reason to think that the forest was adapted to endure storms of such freakish wind velocity, nor that such a storm contributed to its health and integrity. The lodgepole pines there are adapted to fire, with their serotinous cones. The pines are also adapted to windstorms, which come every winter. But they are unlikely to be adapted to storms that come only once every five hundred years. Since this is a wilderness, we will leave it as a natural laboratory. But in a national forest, restoration could be in order.* We want wilderness areas pristine, but we can facilitate land health in the natural forests.

9. *The more fragile a landscape, the lighter it ought to be treated.* Natural ecosystems have considerable stamina, but not equally so. Some are less stable by nature. Some, stable enough by nature, are especially vulnerable to human interruption. An example of the latter is the tundra. Industrial society developed in Europe and the

---

* We humans hardly have to form an ethic for David Raup's scale of natural catastrophe, every 26 million years or so.

eastern United States where (and in part because) the soils were fertile, the climate temperate, the waters abundant. This sort of ecosystem is especially self-healing and those environments took a lot of punishment and offal. Society moved into the arid West, took its agriculture with it, and the result was a dustbowl. We have discovered, often sadly, one environment can absorb kinds of exploitation that another cannot. When farmers moved into the Amazon and tried methods of farming that had worked in more temperate and fertile southern Brazil, or that were recommended by North American development officials, the land quickly failed.

Fragility alone, like rarity, is hardly a value word. But it has a way of figuring in a constellation of natural qualities that we need to consider to preserve the health and integrity of ecosystems. We may resolve to place our civilizations on fragile landscapes with less insult. The fact that they are fragile, as we earlier warned about species that are rare, does not mean there is any lessened integrity. Quite to the contrary, especially where these environments are harsh or highly competitive, this can mean that there is more, not less biological achievement in the life that does manage to survive there.

A discovery in the twentieth century is that Earth is a fragile planet—not in and of itself, because life has persisted several billion years, hanging tough in the midst of its trials. But, when confronting the fearful powers of the human mind and hand, Earth is more fragile than we thought. The German astronaut Sigmund Jähn exclaimed, "Before I flew I was already aware of how small and vulnerable our planet is; but only when I saw it from space, in all its ineffable beauty and fragility, did I realize that humankind's most urgent task is to cherish and preserve it for future generations" (in Kelley 1988:141). Health and integrity are always fragile things—too soon destroyed by those who are careless about what they value. That is true of human beings and it is equally true of our planet.

4

Wildlife Values

■■
■■

We have direct encounters with life that has eyes; our gaze is returned by another concerned outlook. The relation is I-thou, subject to subject, more lively than experiencing a flower, I-it, subject to object. There is somebody there behind the fur or feathers. Values, elusive in the preceding chapters, are here right before our eyes, right *behind* those eyes. Animals hunt and howl, find shelter, seek habitats and mates, care for their young, flee from threats, grow hungry, thirsty, hot, tired, excited, sleepy. They lick their wounds. "Man is the measure of things," said Protagoras long ago (Plato, *Theatetus*, 152), and humans have often believed him. But these animals do not make man the measure of things at all.

Here we are quite convinced that there are natural values, independently of cultural values. Still, humans are the only moral measurers of things, and how should we count these wild, nonmoral beings? Perhaps such a conscience ought not to be used simply to defend the interests of *Homo sapiens*, any more than simply to defend one's individual self-interest. Whatever matters to animals, matters morally. We ought to try to measure the values out there.

One opposite of "wild" is "controlled," a positive value in our society. We control ourselves and our children; we police the streets and guard property boundaries. Life gone wild is life gone amok. In that context, wild can mean "not civil," and we, who are civilized, do not want to be uncivil, uncontrolled. But another opposite of "wild" is "tame," and that certainly sounds drab. Wild affairs, not under our control, bring the adventure of excitement and the unexpected. The essential idea is a process "outside the control of humans," and that may be a bad thing in culture, usually, but a good thing in nature, usually.

1. LOWER AND HIGHER ANIMALS

Darwin once penned himself a note, "Never use the words higher and lower" (Darwin 1903 [1858]). Certainly, they are difficult words, not only descriptive but value-laden (recall Ernst Mayr's puzzlement, described in chapter 2, sec. 2). While bald eagles are an endangered species, so are 129 species of American freshwater mussels (or 43 percent of the approximately 300 total species). Is it more important to save the eagle than ten dozen species of mussels? But the mussels are adapted fits in the Clinch and Tennessee Rivers, as well developed in the central United States as anywhere on Earth. Perhaps eagles and mussels are just both there, and neither is higher or lower. Of the animal biomass on our planet, 90 percent is invertebrates, who account for 95 percent of all animal species.

Nevertheless, Darwin could not avoid the use of the terms. "Man may be excused some pride at having risen, though not through his own exertion, to the very summit of the organic scale" (1895 [1871]:619). In *On the Origin of Species*, he concludes, "Organisation on the whole has progressed" (1964 [1859]:345). Yet Darwin does make a reservation: "I do not think that any one has a definite idea of what is meant by higher, except in classes which can loosely be compared to man" (1903 [1858]).

That is not as arbitrary as it might at first seem, if we list the characteristic features that the nonhuman vertebrates, especially mammals, share with humans: learned behavior, advanced cognition, adaptability in diverse habitats, acquired as well as innate immunity, powers of sentience, felt experience, numbers of neurons, language acquisition. These are advances that do enrich the world (Griffin 1981, 1984). We inescapably conclude that eagles are more conscious than mussels. They see us and can be frightened; mussels have no eyes and cannot run, though, if irritated, they use their "foot" to dig themselves into the mud. There is something higher here at work, not just because consciousness is nearer to humans, though it is that. Eagles may have no psychological ego, no self-image, but they are *subjects*, the core category here.

Intelligent space visitors, had they visited Earth before humans evolved, would even then have maintained that eagles are more conscious than mussels. Though both eagles and mussels survive in their niches, there is a level of natural value expressed in eagles that has not been achieved in mussels. The evolution of psychological subjects (eagles, chimpanzees) is as much an objective fact about evolutionary history as is objective lives without subjectivity (mussels, plants). Objective lives have some skills (mussels filtering water; plants photosynthesizing) that subjective lives lack. But that does not diminish the complexity of subjective life as a higher value.

Such animals are called "charismatic megafauna," literally, big animals with much grace (chapter 2, sec. 7). This idea goes back to religious concepts of creation, that such animals have been especially gifted with talents. Members of the Xerces Society will insist that butterflies have their own grace. Instrumentally, grass and mussels are more important in ecosystems than eagles or panthers. Without invertebrate activity the ecosystem would stop in a few months. Nevertheless, the charismatic species, often at the top trophic rungs of ecosystems, have high intrinsic value, animal excellences that embody superb evolutionary achievements. Just their relative rarity indicates how far up the rungs of the pyramid they are.

It is a mistake to value such charismatic animals only as our cousins, who partially approximate humans. We and they do share many of the higher evolutionary achievements. But they are not subhumans, to be respected only if we find something humanlike in them—nonhumans about like imbecile humans, monkeys about like morons. It would be as bad to judge morons as though they were about like monkeys. The animal excellences are not valuable as poor imitations of what is later achieved in humans. It is not a matter of appreciating them by reduction from our own experience to something simpler, but of comprehending competence and virtuosity not our own.

A mother free-tail bat, a mammal like ourselves, can, using sonar, wend her way out of Bracken Cave, in Texas, in total darkness, catch 500–1,000 insects each hour on the wing all night, and return to find and nurse her own young, one pup amidst millions of others, densely packed (500 pups to a square foot) along walls and ceilings deep in the recesses of the cave. That skill expresses, in bat ways, an advanced, alien form of perceptual skill that humans express perceptively in other ways, such as our eyesight, rich in color vision, which we use for location, or our linguistic powers, which we use for communication, both substituting for the bat's sonar.

We do not want to measure nonhumans by human standards, though we sometimes want to measure nonhumans and humans by comparable standards. We also frequently run past our capacity to argue by analogy from the value of our experience. There are quite alien forms of life, with whom we can hardly identify experientially.

> *Octopus* is a mollusc that a primate can recognize as a fellow creature. It is very easy to identify with *Octopus vulgaris*, even with individuals, because they respond in a very "human" way. They watch you. They come to be fed and they will run away with every appearance of fear if you are beastly to them. Individuals develop individual and sometimes irritating traits . . . and it is all too easy to come to treat the animal as a sort of aquatic dog or cat.
>
> Therein lies the danger. It is always dangerous to interpret an animal's reactions in human terms, but with dogs or cats there is a certain reasonableness in doing so. We are mammals too. . . . The octopus is an alien. It is a poikilotherm, never had a dependent childhood, has little or no social life. It may never know what it is to be hungry. . . . The animal, it is true, learns under conditions that would lead to learning in a mammal but the facts that it learns about its visual and tactile environment are sometimes very different from those that a mammal would learn in similar circumstances. Simply because it is evidently intelligent and possessed of eyes that

look back at us, we should not fall into the trap of supposing that we can interpret its behavior in terms of concepts derived from birds or mammals. This animal lives in a very different world from our own. (Wells 1978:8–9)

Those who take one evolutionary route in sentient experience are precluded from the direct experience of alien routes, which also have their integrity. Humans can recognize that integrity, even though participation in it remains foreign to us. We can grant that the octopus is a center of experience, a subject (while we doubt that a mussel is), and respect a wild life with which we cannot empathize. Each particular organism-subject itself has its own integrity, its integrated experiences and achievements.

We can even wonder if there are sometimes animal virtues. These charismatic megafauna have open instincts. They are agents whose behavior is, to some extent, up to them. They move through a world with surprises; they are flexible and change their plans. This requires animal decisions, in contrast with stereotyped behavior in the lower animals. Perhaps this can involve resolution, endurance, courage, cleverness, even wisdom. These are animal excellences, though not moral virtues, and we may be reluctant to fault those who fail to be so excellent. But we may cheer for those who succeed, and think that their successful coping involves something further than the mere deterministic outplay of genetic coding. Perhaps the dominant wolf does express some virtues that are to be admired, and perhaps the females that mate with him sense this. Such flexibility can convey survival advantage, even though the lower animals mostly survive without it. Animal virtues, achievements that an animal makes during its lifetime, something more than mere genetic unfolding, are not implausible; those who are familiar with animals suspect that they are there.

We do not want to be discriminatory, unfair, in our ethics, to treat living beings unequally because we may misperceive what values are there. But neither do we want to be undiscriminating, blind to the advanced achievements, to the excellences, even the virtues that are so superbly expressed in the lofty animal world. Those alert eyes indicate all this. Young and full of trigger-itch, Leopold once shot a wolf, mortally wounding her. "We reached the old wolf in time to watch a fierce green fire dying in her eyes. I realized then, and have known ever since, that there was something new to me in those eyes—something known only to her and to the mountain" (1968 [1949]:130).

2. ANIMAL RIGHTS?

Is it possible that these wild lives have rights? John Muir lamented, "How narrow we selfish, conceited creatures are in our sympathies! how blind to the rights of all the rest of the creation!" (1916:98). We can appreciate his rhetoric, but can we take seriously the rights of the alligators in the swamps in the midst of which Muir was then reveling? Leopold said, more soberly, "A land ethic . . . does affirm their right to continued existence." They "should continue as a matter of biotic right" (1968 [1949]:204, 211). But Leopold's proposal is even more difficult; he proposes rights for plants, soil, rivers.

Charles S. Elton, an ecologist, believes "that animals have a right to exist and be left alone" (1958:143). The philosopher Arne Naess says of animals that "in principle each of them have the same right to live and blossom as we and our children have" (1984:266). A sign in Rocky Mountain National Park urges visitors not to harass the bighorn sheep, "Respect their right to life."

All these people are groping to claim that biological existence confronts humans with a value that it is *not right* for humans always to destroy. We want to claim that too, but, frankly, we have to face the fact that there are no *rights* in nature. A right is a person's entitlement to have other persons treat that person in certain ways, such as the right to vote, or own property, or to a fair trial. A right is a valid claim that a person can make to have his or her interests and welfare taken into account in the society in which he or she lives. Legal rights are enforced in courts, or they ought to be. *Rights* is a political word. But the concept of rights, which has worked so well to protect human dignity proves troublesome when we turn to the biological world. Nature knows no rights. Nature is not civil. There were no rights over the millennia of evolutionary time—nor are there today, outside the human sector. Trees, grasses, wildflowers do not have rights, nor can they recognize the rights of others. They do not assert argued claims and entitlements against each other. Nor do rivers or canyons, clouds or mountains.

The mountain lion is not violating the rights of the deer he slays. Even the lion who eats a human is not violating that human's rights; *he*, the lion is not guilty of reprehensible behavior for which he can be shamed or brought into court. The mountain lion can establish no relationships outside wild nature. Meanwhile, if national park service officials made no effort to rescue the victim, they would be morally as well as legally reprehensible. The victim has a right to be rescued. But it would be the humans that were faulted, not the lion. Rights go with legitimate claims and entitlements, whereas there are no titles or laws that can be transgressed in the wilderness. Rights go with appeals to moral agents. Nature is amoral, though valuable.

Perhaps rights, though absent in wild nature, are generated when humans arrive and encounter the higher subject-animals, where there is somebody there (Regan 1983). Still, animal rights are not natural in the sense that they exist in spontaneous nature. They cannot be an independent natural value out there in the wild. Meanwhile, by constructing the concept of rights, ethicists discover a way to protect values present in persons. Extending this to animals, if there are animal rights, they seem to be there only when persons come on the scene— generated by the encounter of moral agents with sentient life. If so, rights, which are clearly present in (or assigned to) persons, should also be found (or assigned) when persons encounter higher sentient animals. Rights would then not be objective in the animals, but only relational, constituted by the human-animal encounter.

Such rights would be cultural products, brought by persons who extend rights from culture to nature. Such an intervention-generated right would be stronger than a legal right, binding independently of law, but not natural. Humans must sometimes affect sentient life adversely or beneficially, and when we do either, we might say that some animals gain a right, otherwise unknown in nature, to flourish in their own way. Such rights would require felt interests, rotating around a pleasure-pain axis. Such rights would go with a sense of intrusion on experience, present in the higher forms and vanishing lower down. Is this way of conserving natural value going to be plausible and effective?

As much as we wish positively to defend animal lives, we must answer negatively. Rights transfer uncertainly to wild animals. A cultural discovery is being deployed in the attempt to make this fit wild animals. But since the proposed objects of moral concern have non-personal values, much of what we wish to protect in humans is not there in animal nature. To say that x has rights seems like a statement of fact. But it is really a valuation, embedding a prescription, claiming to have located something of value in the alleged possessor of rights. If there are no rights there, what values are there? We do not want to transfer a value from culture to nature; we want to discover what is there to value.

We need to accentuate a different positive. Animals do have interests, desires, needs, and health at stake; there are things that are vital to them, whether we have intruded or not. Some things have, as biologists phrase it, survival value. Those animal lives defended are not only important to them; we humans ought to consider such values in deciding how to behave when we intrude. If we reconsider the sign not to harass bighorn sheep, "Respect their (right to) life," we can give this account: What an ethical visitor directly respects is their life, an objective fact in the wild, discovered there, valuable to the animal and positively evaluated by the human who encounters such life. The words in parentheses can be subtracted without loss of logic or fact. They are not theoretically important.

It is really more "natural" to say that animals have goods. Goods exist in wild nature, while rights do not. The goods of sentient animals are better examined with a concept of health or interests satisfied (or, more technically, utilities, or, more philosophically, integrities). Briefly, their welfare is what counts. But if that is so, what we really want is a vocabulary of value. Animals enjoy values intrinsic to themselves, and when humans arrive, appropriate respect for those values generates an ethics. "Rights" is a noun and can look like the name for something that an animal or a human has, additionally to hair, teeth, skills. But there is no reference to anything biologically present; a right is more like a person's having "money" or "status," that is, these things are intersubjectively, sociologically real, used to protect values that are inseparably entwined with personality. We might try to stretch such rights and project them out of culture onto wild nature. But this does not work convincingly if we move far from analogical contexts. The concept breaks down because nature is not culture.

Furthermore, "right" is also an adjective, used to name forms of behavior engaged in by moral agents. All that "rights" (the noun) really does is state some of the claims about "right" behavior. When we are making moral judgments, we want to focus on the behavior of the human agent, and not on something moral ("a moral right") that the wild animal possesses, although we do need to discover an intrinsic value—its life—that we moral agents ought to protect. Environmental ethics uses "rights" more as a term of convenience; the real convictions here are about what is "right." The issues soon revert to evaluations of right behavior, and we are better advised to dispense with the noun *rights*. We should use only the adjective, *right*, arising when moral agents encounter nature and find something valuable there. It is sometimes convenient rhetorically but in principle unnecessary to use the concept of rights at all.

Rights is a political concept, right for the human that lives in a *polis*, a rebuilt, cultured environment, but not right for the nonpolitical animals who remain wild. Rights protect life in culture where persons desire liberty for the pursuit of happiness in their nation-states. Persons have life choices to make, opportunities to develop, careers to choose. These are the options of culture, which rights need to protect. But wild animals, if they also have their freedoms and excellences, are what they are genetically, without cultural options. Rights have proved among the most powerful of the political and ethical concepts of recent centuries, as a way of protecting personal dignity. So it may at first seem unfortunate to find that the paradigm that works so well in culture cannot be successfully extrapolated to nature. But this really is not so, because what we are really protecting is wildness, where the category of rights does not exist. We are forced to a more adequate concept of these wild values that we do wish, and ought, to protect.

People who love animals often belong to organizations such as a humane society, which is laudable. Where humans have taken animals into their care, as pets, raising for food, laboratory research, and work, we should be "humane." Yet that is a revealing choice of words. We are treating humanely something that is not human, extending the compassion that is appropriate for humans to nonhumans. Where we have adopted them, adapted them to inhabit our culture, house-broken them, tamed them, domesticated them, we do generate responsibilities for their care. Yet to exactly this same degree they have lost their wildness. We have taken their wildness away, and we still have to wonder whether we should be humane toward those other animals in which wildness remains.

Moving across the spectrum (the species) of wild animal being, the concept of rights extrapolates less and less well: rights for sheep, bats, eagles, mussels. The problem only grows as we plunge further into radically different orders of being. We might at first think that there are "rights" behind each of the pairs of eyes that we confront. But that is not so; what is there is a fierce "wildness." The value of that is indisputable, even though it is a value that is not carried adequately by the concept of rights. There is an independent integrity in the wild life, and humans ought not to violate this without justification.

3. ANIMAL WELFARE AND MANAGED WILDLIFE

In the fall of 1988 the world cheered when we rescued two gray whales off Point Barrow, Alaska. The whales were stranded several miles from open water, rising to breathe through small—and shrinking—holes in the ice. Chainsaws cut pathways through the ice and a Russian icebreaker broke open a path to the sea. We spent more than a million dollars to save them; they drew the sympathy of millions of people. A polar bear, coming in to eat the whales, was chased away. Television confronted the nation with the plight of the suffering whales. Seeing them sticking their heads out of the ice and trying to breathe, everybody soon wanted to help. We saved the whales and people felt good about it.

Was that really the right thing to do? The bumper stickers say: "Save the whales!" But maybe our compassion overwhelmed us, and we let these two whales become a symbol of survival, but they do not really symbolize our duties in animal welfare.

Let us consider a less expensive case, no big media event. One February morning in 1983 a bison fell through the ice into the Yellowstone River in Yellowstone National Park, and, struggling to escape, succeeded only in enlarging the hole. In mid-afternoon a party of snowmobilers looped a rope around the animal's horns and, pulling, nearly saved it, but not quite. It grew dark and the rescuers abandoned their attempt. Temperatures fell to twenty below that night; in the morning the bison was dead. Coyotes and ravens ate the exposed part of the carcass. After the spring thaw, a grizzly bear was seen feeding on the rest.

The snowmobilers were disobeying park authorities who had ordered them not to rescue it. One of the snowmobilers was troubled by the callous attitude. A drowning human would have been saved at once; so would a drowning horse. The Bible commends getting an ox out of a ditch, even if this means breaking the Sabbath. It was as vital to the struggling bison to get out; the poor thing was freezing to death. A park ranger replied that the incident was natural and the bison should be left to its fate. A snowmobiler protested, "If you're not going to help it, then why don't you put it out of its misery?" But mercy killing, too, was contrary to the park ethic, which was, in effect, "Let it suffer!"

That seems so inhumane, contrary to everything we are taught about being kind, or doing to others as we would have them do to us. Isn't it cruel to let nature take its course? Isn't there somebody there, behind those bison's eyes, with a right to life? One of the snowmobilers contacted radio commentator Paul Harvey, who made three national broadcasts attacking park service indifference to animal welfare.

But is the park policy indifferent to animal welfare? Might not intervening, with misguided compassion, sever the animals from their wild worlds? Consider the coyotes, ravens, grizzly bear, and other scavengers whose lives depend on just such winterkill. Intervening would have hurt the others. Now we begin to see that a simple compassion extended from human or humane society ethics to wildlife is too indiscriminate. It does not take into account how their welfare is entwined with their wildness, how their integrity is ecological.

In April 1989 in Glacier National Park a wolverine attacked a deer in deep snow but did not kill the deer. The injured deer struggled out onto the ice of Lake McDonald, but, hamstrung, could move no further. Park officials declined to end its suffering, and the lame deer suffered throughout the day, the night, and died the following morning. Critics said that park officials were blinded by a philosophy of false respect for cruel nature. Park officials, however, can sometimes be compassionate. That spring a bear was injured when hit by a truck, and they killed the bear so that it would not suffer needlessly.

Different rules can apply. Treating whales, bison, deer, with compassion at first seems kind, but, on reflection, it elevates them unnaturally, unable to value them for what they are in the wild. There is something insufficiently discriminating in such judgments—species blind in a bad sense, blind to the real differences between species, valuational differences that do count morally. The rescue of individual animals—a couple of whales, a bison, a deer—is humane enough and might not seem to have any detrimental effects, but that might not be the end of moral considerations, which ought to act on principles that can be universalized, analyzing what kind of values are at stake. We do not want to do what makes us feel good if this is not really for the best conserving of all the values present.

We can make this clearer if we consider populations. The bighorn sheep of Yellowstone caught pinkeye (conjunctivitis) in the winter of 1981–82. On craggy slopes, partial blindness can be fatal. If a sheep misses a jump or feeds poorly, it is likely to be soon injured and starving as a result. In fact, more than three hundred bighorns, over 60 percent of the herd, perished. Wildlife veterinarians wanted to treat the disease, as they would have in any domestic herd, but Yellowstone officials left the sheep to suffer, seemingly not respecting their life. The disease was natural and should be left to run its course.

In other words, the ethic of compassion must be set in a larger context, recognizing the function of pain in the wild. While intrinsic pain is a bad thing whether in humans or in sheep, pain in ecosystems is instrumental pain, through which the sheep are naturally selected for a more satisfactory adaptive fit. Pain in a medically skilled culture is pointless, once the alarm to health is sounded, but pain operates functionally in bighorns in their niche, even after it becomes no longer in the interests of the pained individual. To have interfered in the interests of the blinded sheep would have weakened the species. The larger question must be whether they suffer with a beneficial effect on the wild population as a whole. As a result of the park ethic, only those sheep that were genetically more able to cope with the disease survived; and, as a result, this coping is now coded in the survivors and their offspring.

Now we see why the lame deer should not be euthanized but why the bear hit by a truck was. The encounter with a truck (an artifact) is not part of the forces of natural selection. Where humans cause the pain, they are therefore under obligation to minimize it. A human being in a frozen river would be rescued at once; a human attacked by a wolverine would be flown by helicopter to the hospital. When we happen upon an opportunity to rescue an animal with the pull of a rope, or to kill it lest it suffer, why not? That seems to be what human nature urges, and why not let human nature take its course? *But compassion is not the only consideration in an ethic.* To intervene artificially in the processes of natural selection is not to do wild animals any benefit at the level of the kind. Human beings, by contrast, are no longer subject to the forces of natural selection. The integrity of *Homo sapiens* does not depend on wild nature.

Do we then never manage wildlife? In the spring of 1984 a sow grizzly and her three cubs walked across the ice of Yellowstone Lake to Frank Island, two miles from shore. They stayed several days to feast on two elk carcasses, when the ice bridge melted. Soon afterward, they were starving on an island too small to support them. The mother could swim to the mainland, but she would not without her cubs. On this occasion park authorities rescued the mother and her cubs. The relevant difference was a consideration for an endangered species within an ecosystem.

It might seem now that, inconsistently, we refuse to let nature take its course. The Yellowstone ethicists let the bison drown and the blinded bighorns die. But this time the Yellowstone ethicists promptly rescued the grizzlies in order to protect an endangered species. They were not rescuing individual bears so much as saving the species. They thought that humans had already and elsewhere imperiled the grizzly and that they ought to save this form of life. Duties to wildlife are not simply at the level of individuals; they are also to species.

Sometimes this can even mean that the good of individuals ought to be sacrificed for the good of the species. The handsome Siberian tiger is almost extinct in the wild, shot for its skins. But international agreements now prevent the sale of such skins, and the Chinese are interested in restoring the tigers. They therefore need animals to release into the wild. While there are cats in zoos, all the Siberian tigers in North American zoos are descendants of seven animals; they have been through a genetic bottleneck and thus only a few tigers are available that are genetically competent. If the defective tigers were replaced by others nearer to the wild type and with more genetic variability, bred, and released, the species could be saved in the wild. Some have raised the possibility of killing the genetically inbred, inferior cats, presently held in zoos, to make space available for such breeding.

At present this is not being done, partly out of misgivings over whether it ought to be done, and partly because the zoos fear adverse public relations. But, following the logic here, this ought to be done, assuming that no other alternative can be found. A top predator free in the wild is of more value than defective tigers imprisoned in zoos. When we move to the level of species, we may kill individuals for the good of their kind.

In every state, wildlife officials set aside conservation areas, restock species, plant food, and cover. They sometimes do this to grow an annual crop of deer for hunters to shoot; but they are also concerned with wildlife for what they are in themselves. They manage in order to compensate for human interruptions, really a form of restoration biology. This promotes animal welfare, only if, after restoration, their wildness returns. Humans must remain at a distance, or, if at times coming close to intervene, they then back off to leave wild animals alone in their autonomy. In the end, managed wild life really is a contradiction in terms. Wildlife is life that can manage itself, even if human wildlife managers have to arrange so that this can happen.

4. FERAL AND EXOTIC "WILDLIFE"

Europeans introduced both horses and burros to the American West, which sometimes were abandoned and yet managed to survive over the years on their own. Two decades ago there were about two thousand mustangs on public lands, their populations kept down because they were hunted for dog food, or shot as a nuisance. Concern for the mustangs and burros led the U.S. Congress, in the Wild and Free Roaming Horses and Burros Act of 1971, to declare that there should remain, on public lands, a limited population as "living symbols of the historic and pioneer spirit of the West." Congress's primary intent, then, is to maintain mustangs as *cultural* symbols.

But Congress goes on to claim that these horses "contribute to the diversity of life forms within the Nation," and that "they are to be considered in the area where presently found, as an integral part of the natural system of the public lands." The Secretary of the Interior "shall manage wild free-roaming horses and burros in a manner that is designed to achieve and maintain a thriving natural ecological balance on the public lands." (U.S. Congress 1971, Preamble, sec. 3). Few legislators have studied ecology. These horses, more accurately speaking, are feral and not wild. They are not native to the landscape; they are escapes from introduced domestic animals. Nevertheless, to Congress, and many others, they seemed to belong on the western landscape. When so protected, their populations began to explode. By the 1990s the mustang population had increased twenty-five times to about fifty thousand horses (U.S. Congress 1990).

The Bureau of Land Management spent over $50 million rounding the mustangs up and offering them for adoption. But there were not enough takers, and the bureau proposed killing 10,000 of them. Many animal activists, and westerners who identified with these symbols of the Old West, objected. The real problem is that not even an act of Congress can declare and thereby make it happen that an exotic species, introduced to a landscape, is "an integral part of the natural system of the public lands." Nature decides that, not Congress. True, many thousands of years ago horses once roamed over what is now the American western landscape. But they went naturally extinct in the New World, presumably no longer fit for an altering landscape. In the historical dynamism of ecosystems, since the Pleistocene period, the western ranges in this hemisphere developed without them. Introduced (or "reintroduced," as it were) to the present landscape, they can survive. But this does not make them good adapted fits on today's landscape, where there have been dramatic changes in climate, predation pressures, disease and parasite vectors, and so on.

The mustangs are mostly in arid Nevada and Utah, and Bureau of Land Management ecologists and environmentalists agree that the quality of public lands is in serious decline because of overgrazing. So far as that overgrazing is due to the mustangs, then conserving natural values will prefer the integrity of ecosystems to the welfare of feral animals. The mustangs ought to be removed, preferably by adoption or sterilizing, if necessary by killing. The exploding population does show that there is a problem otherwise.* It will also be possible, in

---

* A complicating factor is crucial, however. The overgrazing problem is more often a result of too many cattle, sheep, and goats, which outnumber the mustangs fifty to one on public lands.

selected localities, carefully to manage a few souvenir populations of mustangs, for those who want to remember the Old West.

We cited earlier the case where tens of thousands of feral goats were shot to save three endangered plant species in an endangered ecosystem on San Clemente Island (chapter 2, sec. 7.6). Is it inhumane to count plant species more than mammal lives, a few plants more than thousands of goats? Those who advocate animal rights say that the goats can enjoy life and suffer when shot but that the plants are insentient and do not feel anything at all. But pain and pleasure felt is not the sole consideration. The goats do not have a welfare compatible with the wild ecosystem of the island. Conserving natural value thus requires removing the goats.

Are there cases where introducing exotic animals might increase natural values? Possibly, though first appearances can be deceiving. On the Hawaiian islands, before humans arrived there were no terrestrial reptiles, amphibians, or mammals. (There was one species of small bat.) Where these higher species do occur, nearly everywhere else on Earth, we count them among the major evolutionary achievements that enrich the landscape, the charismatic megafauna. We would think it catastrophically tragic on any continental landscape to lose all the warm- and cold-blooded land animals.

Why were there none on Hawaii? The explanation, simple enough, is that there was no way for them to get there. But surely they would be a good thing on Hawaii too. So, both the Polynesian and European settlers introduced first domestic animals but also, later, wild ones, such as deer. The mongoose (*Herpestes auropunctatus*) was introduced to control rats, which had been accidentally introduced; it is well-established as a feral animal. In India the mongoose is a handsome animal, quick and alert. It can outsmart a cobra. Why is it not also admirable in Hawaii, as well as useful? True, the mongoose was, at the time of introduction, an artifact, but its wildness has long since returned. Cannot a good thing in India be a good thing in Hawaii? Perhaps we should move the endangered lemurs from Madagascar, where they will probably not survive, to Hawaii, where they might. A colony of four hundred rhesus macaques was moved by Columbia University scientists to the Caribbean island of Cayo Santiago, off Puerto Rico, in 1938, and they have flourished since.

This line of argument runs as follows: amphibians, reptiles, and mammals are missing from Hawaii by an accident of oceanic geography and plate tectonics. If we set aside that contingency and introduce the mongoose artificially, it does quite well. There is, we might say, no particular reason to respect sheer contingency in environmental ethics. We respect the genius of life, ecosystemic integrity and beauty, and so on, but there is no reason to think that all the accidental outcomes of nature are significant or valuable. To the contrary, the accidental results here make impossible what we elsewhere think are the most significant achievements in ecosystems. So introduce them, or else we are rejecting the higher animals. We value them on one landscape but not on another, where they happen not to be.

But ought we to view this as sheer contingency? Perhaps the differences between Indian and Hawaiian natural history mean that the mongoose is an adapted fit in one place and not in another. Amphibians, reptiles, and mammals, for all their marvelous evolutionary achievements, lacked the capacity to get there. The higher land animals did not, oddly enough, have as much oceanic mobility as plants and insects. The skills of birds, who developed wings, proved superior to the skills of mammals, who did not (except for the bats). From this perspective, we do not view the colonization of Hawaii as a matter of contingency so much as of skills that could be deployed there in directions and degrees that was nowhere else possible. Hawaii is only a minute fraction of the land surface of the Earth, and, though we admire mammals, reptiles, and amphibians elsewhere, we might want to let Hawaii be an especially remote test of oceanic mobility.

Because mammal and reptile predators were absent, Hawaii's birds evolved in unusual ways, many as ground-nesting birds, often with reduced powers of flight. Birds took up the niches that might otherwise have been occupied by reptiles and mammals. Such birds have been especially vulnerable to introduced predators; this is one of the factors in the dramatic extinction rate of Hawaiian birds, of which the nene, or Hawaiian goose, is an example. The mongoose loves to eat nene chicks, as also do feral cats and rats (Stone 1985). Of sixty-eight species and subspecies of birds unique to the Hawaiian islands when the Europeans first arrived, forty-one are now extinct or virtually extinct. One entire family of birds, the Hawaiian honeycreepers, has suffered greatly (Halliday 1978). Likewise the plants of Hawaii evolved in dramatic ways but they did not evolve defenses against mammal grazers (such as thorns or chemical defenses) or against aggressive weedy species, and they are vulnerable to these introductions. More plants and birds are known to have gone extinct in Hawaii than in all of North America. Now the Hawaiian mammal introductions are beginning to look different. They are not really adding to the richness of the fauna and flora on Earth; they are subtracting from it.

There are places where wildlife are absent by sheer contingency and possibly nature has not generated alternative natural histories. In the western United States there are so-called barren waters, because fish could not get there—usually because there is a waterfall downstream too high to jump. The Columbia River is full of rainbow trout, native in the lower reaches, but some of the tributary headwaters are barren of trout. So the rainbow was helped upstream; and, once it gets there, it can flourish. That might seem to enhance natural values. Such upstream waters are often not barren of other fish, and this can be detrimental to the natives.

But what if the waters really were barren of fish, as were about forty percent of Yellowstone waters. Some thought it wise to introduce fish, and did so, from 1900 onward. But Yellowstone Park, where some barren waters still occur, has, since 1936, a policy that selected waters will be left barren. These may not be barren of the "lower" forms of life; the tiger salamander (*Ambystoma tigrinum*) flourishes there in a niche fish might otherwise occupy; the phantom midge (*Chaoborus*) becomes dominant in the aquatic ecosystem; and even dragonflies and diving beetles play different roles. Maybe there is richness in the barren waters after all (Varley and Schullery 1983). The charismatic species do not have all the grace of life, nor is the biodiversity all in the higher forms.

5. AESTHETIC APPRECIATION OF WILDLIFE

What are the values of wildlife for people? Three answers, examined next, are: we watch them, we hunt them, and we use them commercially.

Aesthetic experience of wildlife differs from aesthetic experience in culture. Animals can move. In the charismatic megafauna we enjoy spontaneous form in motion. In the art museum nothing moves; in the picturesque scene little moves. Wildflowers sway in the breeze, but *they* do not move; they *are moved* by the wind. At the cinema, the play, the symphony, there is movement, but for the most part programmed so that the audience response is carefully controlled. There is nothing of that kind in the field. The wildlife is organic form in locomotion, on the loose, without designs on the human beholder, indifferent to if not desiring to avoid persons. The animal cares not to come near, sit still, stay long, or please. It performs best at dawn, or twilight, or in the dark. Yet just that wild autonomy moves us aesthetically. I catch the animal excitement. Here is motion in defense of life, and I gain an admiring respect for it. Plants are rooted to the spot, move themselves in autotrophic metabolism, slowly, invisibly to my eye. But the animal must eat and not be eaten; its heterotrophic metabolism forces a never-ceasing hunt through the environment, an ever-alert hiding from its predators. If, as a carnivore, one's food moves as well, so much the more excitement. This requires sometimes stealth and sometimes speed.

Unlike plants, the animal's resources, though within its habitat, are at a distance and must be sought. That is the survival game. The aesthetic delight I, as an observer, take in animal motion reaches to participate in a defended life. We are invited to empathize with the somebody there behind the fur and feathers. We rejoice in the stimulus of spontaneous, alien, yet kindred life.

There is grace in the overtones of this motion. In a strange, fortunate mixing of the aesthetic with the pragmatic, the solving of these problems of motion routinely yields dynamics of rhythmic beauty—the gazelle on the run, the eagle in flight, the slithering blacksnake, the streamlined fish, the nimble chipmunk. Even where this grace seems to fail—in the lumbering moose calf or the fledgling fallen from the nest—the aesthetic experience remains. Here is motion, clamoring for life. Wild lives move themselves; and they move us.

Excitement lies in surprise. A principal difference between scenery and wildlife lies in how one knows that the mountain or the river cascades will be there, but the redtail hawk perched in the cottonwood, the fox running across the meadow, the grouse flushed at the creek? The latter add improbability, contingency. This puts adventurous openness into the scene. One can return to linger over the landscape, but not—with more or less uncertainty—over the bull elk just stepping from cover. See him now, or perhaps not at all. The scenes are frameless; you can stretch or shrink at option what properties of symmetry, form, color you will savor, now or after lunch. But the animal on the run or the bird in flight demand an intense focus; they set constraints of appreciation that one must catch as catch can, postponing reflection until later.

Time counts, not just space; time brings to the animal freedom in space, and the aesthetic experience of that freedom must delight in the spontaneity. Through the binoculars, one isolates that redpoll right now--Quick!--picking seed from that dried sunflower. "Did you see him when he turned just before he flew, almost the last of the flock? How the red cap and black chin flashed when the sun broke out! Had we come ten minutes earlier, or later, nothing!" The creeks and cliffs, the forests and open space, the turns of the trail are more or less on the map. But the wildlife encounters are entirely off the map. One needs proper habitat, of course, but habitat alone is not sufficient for encounter. You are likely to highlight the surprises, hoped for or not, and likely to take for granted the certainties of your trip.

Even places to which we later return remain haunted with events of the past. "Here, at the mouth of this hollow, a decade ago, I met the bobcat, so intent on chasing the ground squirrel that he almost ran over me. Once upon a time, but no more." And if I do not find wildlife at all? There is a thrill in knowing they are present and hiding.

This explains why television wildlife programs and wildlife art are poor substitutes for the real thing. The surprise is gone. This explains why zoos do little to preserve wildlife aesthetically. Their motion has been captured; a caged bobcat is aesthetically a bobcat no more. This explains why domestic pets can never substitute for wild lives aesthetically. The motion has been tamed; no dog is the equal of a coyote; a thousand housecats are less than a cougar. This explains why the rural landscape offers a different and in this respect poorer pleasure than does the wildlife refuge. A cow is never as exciting as a deer. The pariah species, which prosper as parasites and outcasts of civilization, lose their glory. We are disappointed when the bird on the telephone wire is a pigeon and not a kestrel, when the flutter in the bush is an English sparrow, not a warbler. A walk across the fields is twice as exciting if there are rabbits and bobwhites, ten times as exciting with a fox or a great horned owl. Wild lives raise the excitement level; the untrammeled quality of their lives raises the quality of human life.

Behind the motion and sentience there is struggle. The animal freedom brings with it the possibility of success and failure. The scenery cannot fail, because nothing is attempted; but living things can be better or worse of their kind, they have prime seasons and plain ones, and we have to evaluate achievement. Looking over the herd of elk, we spot the bull with the biggest rack. The big bull does not have more merit than the yearling but it does have more strength and wisdom of its kind. An adult eagle better than an immature exemplifies the glory of its species. The more commanding token of its type has made the ideal real. Each is a display of animal excellence, and, who knows, perhaps displays praiseworthy animal virtue as well.

The critic will say that admirers of wildlife overlook as much as they see. The bison are shaggy, shedding, and dirty. That hawk has lost several flight feathers. That marmot is diseased and scarred. The elk look like the tag end of a rough winter. Every wild life is marred by the rips and tears of time and eventually destroyed by them. But none of the losers and seldom even the blemished show up on the covers of *National Wildlife*. Doesn't the aesthetician repair nature before admiring it? Can we pick the quality out of the quantity, praise the rare ideals and discard the rest, who are statistically more real? Wildlife artists select the accidental best and discard the rest, broken by accidents.

But the matter is not so simple when we couple aesthetics with genetics and evolutionary ecology. The aesthetician sees that ideal toward which a wild life is striving and which is rarely reached in nature. The observer zooms in with her scope on the full-curl ram, or the artist paints warblers ornamented in their breeding prime and perfection. The artist portrays and the admirer enjoys that phenotype produceable by the normal genotype in a congenial environment, although that ideal has only partly been executed, owing to environmental constraints. Such an ideal is, in a way, still nature's project. In a distinction going back to Aristotle, the ideal is true to the poetry of a thing, though not its history, and yet the poetry directs its history (*Poetics* 1451b). The form, though not wholly executed, is as natural as is the matter. Some will insist that all this is not true to the plain facts; others will realize that this is not so much fiction as a way of getting at a natural essence only partly expressed in any individual existence.

We can enjoy conflict and resolution. The weatherbeaten elk are not ugly, not unless endurance is incompetence; nor is the spike ram displeasing, not unless potential is uninspiring. The warblers in spring are indeed in prime dress, but the warblers in fall plumage are equally fitted to their environment, neither less ideal, less real, nor less beautiful, only requiring more subtlety to appreciate, now that the expenditure of energy and motion is not in color and reproduction but in camouflage and survival toward winter. If we take the natural kind on its own terms, "intentions" coded in the animal nature are "carried out" in the struggle for life, and this is heroic even in its failures. The struggle between ideal and real adds to the aesthetic experience. Repeatedly, the more we know the more there is to see, and the more there is to be admired. Seeing becomes both wisdom and art.

6. USING WILDLIFE: ANIMAL SPORTS

Humans choose to leave wildlife on their landscapes for sport hunting. After the aesthetic experience of wildlife, it can seem philistine to shoot and eat them. And only a few of the many wild animals are desired as food. In fact, whether even those shot are primarily desired as food is a principal issue in recreational hunting. Environmental ethics is far more complex than first appears, both theoretically and operationally, and this is true of ethics and values in hunting as well (Loftin 1984; Causey 1989; Vitali 1990; King 1991; Bekoff and Jamieson 1991). Hunting takes us out of the onlooker mode and plunges us into participation. It can return us to our origins; it can educate us into the way the world is created, where it then can become more re-creational than recreational. But it can also be recreational killing.

Hunting is no one single thing but a complex of biological and cultural factors. We need to see how hunting is both natural, bringing the hunter, though a human in culture, into identification with the wild world, and also how hunting can be unnatural, a blood sport that spills out life gratuitously, just for pleasure and pride of this "game," a machismo killing for thrills. Few human relationships to nature have the ambiguity of hunting.

Some behaviors are natural for humans, even though humans have emerged from nature to enter culture. Humans are biological beings, and they too need to eat. It is biologically natural for humans to capture animals to meet their basic, animal-level requirements. It is, of course, just as natural to eat vegetables; humans are omnivores. But there is little doubt that humans evolved as meat eaters (Bunn 1981). We were first gatherer-hunters, and the hand and brain evolved in that context. The earliest tools were hunting tools; the hand held a spear.

Capable of culture, humans devised novel, artifactual ways of such capture, weapons of various kinds. But that does not make such capture unnatural, as humans resided in nature. Later, in agriculture they domesticated animals, largely replacing the hunt, and crops, largely replacing the gathering. In their culture, humans have a distinctive nature. A unique dimension of this is that only humans are ethical. There are hunters throughout nature; only humans are moral hunters. Critics of hunting will say that the only moral animals should refuse to participate in the meat-eating phase of their ecology, just as they refuse to play the game merely by the rules of natural selection. Humans do not look to the behavior of wild animals as an ethical guide in other matters (marriage, truth-telling, promise-keeping, justice, charity). Why should they justify their dietary habits by watching what animals do?

But these other matters are affairs of culture. Eating is an event in nature before, during, and after it takes place as an event in culture—in a way that cultural rites such as marriage, promise-keeping, courts of law, and fashion shows are not. The latter are person-to-person events. By contrast, eating is omnipresent in spontaneous nature; humans eat because they are in nature, not because they are in culture. Eating animals is not an event between persons, but is a human-to-animal event, and the rules for this come from the ecosystems in which humans evolved and have no duty to remake. Humans, then, can model their dietary habits from their ecosystems, but they cannot and should not so model their interpersonal justice or charity.

For this reason we can accept hunting where the taken animal is eaten. Participating in food chains in this earthy way can educate the hunter in philosophical ecology. We learn where humans live in nature as this lies in, with, and under culture. Eating an animal implies no disrespect for animal life as set in a trophic pyramid; to the contrary, it respects the ecology. Nothing is more natural than hunting for food. The fact that the hunter is a moral agent does not prohibit him from occupying a place in the ecosystemic food chain.

But with the success of domestication, hunting for food has become steadily less important, replaced by sport hunting, where morally relevant differences do appear. The question is not whether traditional hunting is natural, but whether hunting today is of the natural kind. There is little analog to sport hunting in nature, even if predators sometimes enjoy their hunts. Contemporary hunters are out for the sport; they do not need the meat; they may be trophy hunters.

Still, a characteristic injunction in the sportsman's ethic is that meat must not be wasted. Its waste is indecent, if not morally wrong. The quarry should not be sacrificed outside the paradigm of meat-hunting. In the nineteenth century, hundreds of thousands of buffalo were shot by sportsmen from the windows of trains; the now-extinct passenger pigeons were used like clay pigeons today. Most hunters disapprove of such killing. A trophy hunter may claim that he culls the herd. Such reasons are rationalizations and reflect the ethical ambivalence toward recreational killing.

The exhilaration of the hunt, kept in the context of ecological predation, would seem to justify the sport because it keeps up the illusion that it is not (mere) sport, since the hunt ends in a meal. So while there may be some marginal truth to it, not one hunter in several hundred needs the game in his diet. In other words, they eat what they kill, but they do not hunt to eat. Sport hunting uses nature as a playground on which there is killing. Field and stream recreationally re-create an illusion of the primordial hunt. Such a hunt was once necessary to life but has long since been made unnecessary by domestication of food animals, the latter requiring killing as well. The old, honorable context regained remains genuinely, though symbolically, present where a dominant animal stalks his prey. This is play, but reenacts a manly, dead serious game, the archetypal hunt.

The best case that can be made for sport hunting is that it is not merely recreational but is a vicarious, character-building, *re-creational* event, where a visceral urge is vented in the hunt, carried forth in its ecological setting. From this perspective, we can understand José Ortega y Gasset's dictum that death is a "sign of reality" in hunting, where "one does not hunt in order to kill, on the contrary, one kills in order to have hunted" (1972:110–111). In this sense, hunting is not *sport*; it is a *sacrament* of the fundamental, mandatory seeking and taking possession of value that characterizes an ecosystem and from which no culture ever escapes.

Is hunting blood lust, covered over with some ecological philosophy? Or does it have an ecological/moral rationale that accepts the facts of a world humans did not make and have no duty to remake? Is it hardened hearts versus bleeding hearts? Or is it taking the world to heart? The ecological ethic, which kills in place, is really more advanced, harmonious with nature, than the animal-rights ethic, which kills no animals at all, in utter disharmony with the way the world is made. Those who go out and kill for fun may have failed to grow up morally; sometimes those who wish no killing in nature and in human encounter with nature have not matured biologically or morally either. There is a necessary element of tragedy in the drama of creation, the blood sacrifice on which sentient life is founded, which both *is* and *ought* to be. In ways that mere watchers of nature can never know, the hunter knows his ecology. Though the hunter succeeds, this is not conquest, but submission to his ecology. It is an acceptance of the way the world is made. Hence the ambivalence toward a nature we need to slay and to love surfaces in the contradictions of the hunt. The unease with which the good hunter inflicts death is an unease not merely with his conscience but with affirming his "animality" in the midst of his struggles toward humanity and charity, an unease about the dialectic of death with life.

The satisfactions of skill at the hunt must run deep; they sometimes flatter male vanities but we cannot always interpret them so. And the fact that some men enjoy skilled hunting, mixed with unease about killing, is no embarrassment. Presumably, the tigress enjoys her kill, necessary though this is; and, if she does, this will only add to its survival value, since she enjoys what she must do to survive.

Our ethics here takes its cues from our animal roots. Animals eat and are eaten. We have made exodus from that natural order in forming culture; we transcend nature asking whether animals are morally considerable. Wild animals still remain in nature (unlike humans, whom we do

not eat, since they are with us in culture). But we humans are still natural enough to eat animals. We follow nature, accepting ourselves, animals, and ecosystems for what they are and the continuity we have with
them. Human hunters share no ethics with animal predators. An ethical
hunter is, in his or her ethics, discontinuous with anything found in nonhuman nature, at the same time that he or she, as a hunter, is continu-
ous with nature. Meat hunting is natural, shared with animals; trophy
hunting is unnatural—no wolves hunt for trophies. Sport hunting is
hybrid; kept in a meat-hunting matrix, if hunters eat what they kill, it is
acceptable. Animal hunters enjoy their kill. Pushed toward the mere-
killing-for-sport syndrome, it becomes evil. All this is complex, but it is
better to get the theory right, even if the theory resists simple applications, than to have simple applications based on bad theory.

7. USING WILDLIFE: ANIMAL COMMERCE

Another reason for keeping wildlife on the landscape is because they
have value in commerce. In the United States, we increasingly resist
this value for two reasons: bad experience overexploiting wildlife in
the past, and philosophical doubt whether wildlife ought to be so used
in a society that today has readily available substitutes. We prohibit,
for instance, the sale of game. But in other nations, commerce may be
a principal value of wildlife. This can sometimes involve tourism for
watchable wildlife, but it can often involve animal products for trade,
such as skins and hides, tusks and horns. Some say that, given the
pressures of escalating human population and natural-resource needs,
unless wildlife can produce some cash to them, people will not leave
wildlife on the landscape. They are an unaffordable luxury.

This may be cast in the language of a "harvest" of wildlife, which,
rather awkwardly, employs an agricultural metaphor to describe the
values obtained from wild animals. Even more awkwardly, it forces
wildlife into the value framework of the marketplace, which commits
a category mistake: thinking that wildlife has value only when humans
can take possession of it for some marketable commodity. Wildness is
useless, unless it can pass this commercial filter. But even within culture there are many domains of value: moral, religious, aesthetic,
political, legal, social, historical, as well as economic. Nature is not

culture, and it is difficult enough to get nature valued adequately using all these domains of value; it is impossible if one insists that wildlife must have cash value on the bottom line.

What good are elephants? Well, we can shoot them and make ivory piano keys, we can make ashtrays out of their feet. That will produce dollars needed for foreign exchange, and some of the money can go to support poor indigenous peoples in the areas where the elephants live. That seems a good thing for humans, but rather obviously there is no appropriate respect for the lives of wild elephants. That issue isn't even raised in such an argument. What good are snow leopards? We can make fur coats to wear. What good are alligators? We can use their hides to make ultra-chic purses and high-fashion shoes. The women will be well dressed; they can go to fancy piano concerts; if they smoke, they will have exotic ash trays.

The case of elephants is especially difficult. Elephants are wide-ranging and, from the viewpoint of native farmers, often destructive and dangerous animals. Their ivory also is, or was, quite valuable. The poaching of elephants, rising rural human populations moving onto elephant habitat, combined with severe drought, has dramatically reduced the elephant populations of Africa. Increasingly, elephants are no longer free-ranging but live in large fenced preserves, where they are semi-natural and managed. An international ban on the sale of ivory has caused market prices to plummet and this has reduced poaching, benefiting the elephants. But it also means that legitimate ivory, taken from animals culled by managers, cannot be sold (since, with present technology, it is impossible to separate legal and illegal ivory once it enters the market). African wildlife managers complain that this prevents their sale of ivory and results in the loss of revenue that could be used for the benefit of the local peoples, and could also be used to further elephant conservation. So the question is whether the ivory ban is, on balance, conserving natural values or resulting in a net loss of such value.

A detailed decision will involve economic, ecological, and other technical data, beyond our scope here. But we can sketch some principles. First, wildlife ought not to be put on the market for frivolous purposes—for fashion, for artistic uses, where these destroy the animal and involve no respect for what the animal is in itself, especially not where substitutes are available (feathered hats, anaconda boots, kangaroo jogging shoes). Carved ivory no doubt exhibits worthy craft skills, and perhaps it generates positive aesthetic experiences, but that alone does not justify using ivory for this purpose, since such skills can be otherwise directed, and such aesthetic experience is otherwise available.

Even if there is a market for such products, what is being furthered in such markets is a misperception of wildlife values. When all that counts is what a wildlife body part will bring on the market, all we can expect is exploitation, which, at best, can be regulated for sustainable exploitation, and it will, more than likely, perpetuate abuses of animals. This is especially true where the market for such products is based on folklore and superstition, not infrequently the case. Rhinoceroses are killed for their horns, which are ground into a powder and used as an aphrodisiac, or carved into a dagger to flatter the vanities of an Arabian prince. Gorillas are killed so that their testicles can be used as charms. All this is bad in principle and so the practice is to be lamented. There is no trade in ivory that is in principle desirable. The value that elephants carry is not as a resource for commerce.

The second principle, in tension with the first, is operational compromise to protect the integrity of the species. This is really a pragmatic compromise of principle. Earlier, we warned against the kinds of compromise that think half a loaf is better than none when what is at stake is half a horse. Half an elephant is not better than none either. But elephants that we save from extinction by tolerating an undesirable trade are better than no elephants at all, elephants extinct with our purist ideals victorious. One needs to do what is in the best interests of the species, even when this may not be in the best interests of the people who misuse wildlife, if this gains ground and time for eventually doing what is in the best interests of both. People need to be educated to respect wildlife for what such life is in itself. Society needs to be reformed so that human population levels are controlled and resources adequately distributed, preventing exploitation of wildlife to relieve poverty. Meanwhile, en route to putting better principles in place, one has to find a pragmatic route from here to there. Sometimes the end does justify the means.

But only sometimes. Often the commercial exploitation of wildlife is simply deplorable, especially when done by persons well enough off to prosper by other means. The towns of Nucla and Naturita, Colorado have recently initiated an annual prairie dog shoot to boost tourist business. Each sharpshooter is issued fifty rounds, and, in the two-day festival, kills as many as he or she can. Over one hundred hunters killed nearly three thousand prairie dogs in the first annual shoot. The chambers of commerce make the double claim that this does not adversely affect the population, at the same time that they claim these are "varmints" and need to be controlled. But the prairie dogs have been on the landscape in the region for centuries, and otherwise controlled by ranchers where they have been locally a problem. The real reason is to use animals as targets for a contest that amuses the contestants and puts some cash into the local economy, hardly an adequate justification for the killing.

The Sweetwater, Texas, Jaycees sponsor the "World's Largest Rattlesnake Round-Up" each spring for the past thirty-five years, a spectacular event that draws up to 35,000 people and has resulted in the capture and killing of up to 18,000 snakes in a single weekend (Weir 1992). In addition to the boost for tourism, the Jaycees make about $30,000 profit, of which 90 percent goes to charity. They also claim to further the balance of nature by ridding the landscape of dangerous pests. They claim to have educational events and to teach snake safety, and to supply venom and snakes for scientific research, as well as skins for boots and belts.

Hunters use garden sprayers with long tubes to spray gasoline into dens, and the snakes, unable to breathe in the fumes, emerge from their dens and are captured. The rattlesnake populations have managed to survive over the decades, though reduced, which has driven hunters to cover a larger area. Many other animals that also den are inadvertently killed—other snakes, toads, lizards, insects. Residual chemicals from the gasoline remain as soil and water contaminants. Rattlesnakes seldom bite cattle, and when they do, the bite is rarely fatal. County agricultural agents do not consider this a problem. Furthermore, humans are rarely bitten. The rattlesnakes play a considerable role in the regulation of rodent populations, and this benefit is reduced by their capture.

The annual event is an extravaganza that is in principle unjustified on any serious account of wildlife values. Perhaps it can be modified in practice to limit the senseless killing. The people of Sweetwater no doubt think that the event is a winner, the world's largest such event, but in truth, they do not win either, to say nothing of the loss of value in the wild lives of the snakes. For they only cheapen themselves by misperceiving the natural values on their landscape, exploiting the snakes for a boost in their economy, justified by the benefits to charity at about $2 per snake. That is doubtful enough an interhuman altruism, and it is no interspecific altruism at all.

8. WILDLIFE IN CULTURE

Wild lives become symbols of characteristics we value in ourselves. They carry associations that enrich the cultures we superimpose on landscapes. The bald eagle perches on top of American flagpoles and is portrayed in the seal behind the president, expressing freedom, power, grace, lofty alertness. The British prefer the lion; the Russians the bear. States have chosen their animals; Colorado has selected the bighorn sheep—stately, powerful, nimble, free, loving the hills. Tennessee has the raccoon, Kansas the buffalo, Oregon the beaver. Sports teams are called the Wolf Pack, Panthers, Falcons, Gators, Razorbacks, Rams. We call our automobiles Cougars, Skylarks, Rabbits. Humans abstract the qualities they wish to express, intensifying (sometimes even imagining) the real to make of it an ideal. We elevate into symbolism something of the competence, the integrity, the character of the wild life.

Wild lives as easily become images of grace and beauty. They decorate and lighten our homes. So we enjoy an Audubon calendar on the kitchen wall, or we pattern curtains with butterflies, or steal feathers for fashionable hats (an objectionable practice). The birds are colorful; they can sing and fly; and would that human life be like that too.

The flair, beauty, and activity of wild animals can express qualities that penetrate the culture. We want a yard with cardinals and squirrels; we want picnics, hikes, vacations where wild lives play around us; we pause to admire the geese overhead in flight or welcome the swallows as they return in spring. We regret that the river through town is polluted and dead; the city is poorer because the fish with their jump and sparkle can be found there no more. Wild lives elevate the quality of human life with the vitality they express; their presence in culture reveals and symbolizes the sensitivity of that culture, even where no particular human virtues correspond to the animal achievements. So the alligator enters the Florida lifestyle, even though Floridians make no anthropomorphic use of its competence in the swamps.

Wild lives diversify cultures. A culture is more aesthetically appealing if it includes not only artifacts but also fauna and flora. A painting on an executive's office wall is as likely to be of a stag or a hunt as of his factory or granddaughter. Wild lives are part of our environmental quality, the most threatened part of it. Especially in a culture with a tendency toward increasing sameness, diversity in wild lives will be something that our grandchildren will be glad we left them, or complain that we took away. The grizzly in the Yellowstone ecosystem is a challenge to human integrity because it calls us to discipline ourselves for quality over quantity of human society. Our children will be ashamed if we lose the grizzly, just as we are ashamed for what our fathers did to the passenger pigeon.

Wild lives give what our too-readily-mobile, rootless culture especially needs, an attachment to landscape, locale, habitat, place. We name a street Mockingbird Lane, or a summer home is more romantic if it lies up Fox Hollow, and such places even in their culture are more exciting if there are still mockingbirds and foxes about. Wildlife comes to have its social values, but the social values spin off from— because they make symbolic use of—values intrinsic to the animals themselves.

The Wildlife Society, the principal organization of professional wildlife biologists, states in its policy and ethical code "that wildlife, in its myriad forms, is basic to the maintenance of a human culture that provides quality living." The society seeks "to develop and promote sound stewardship of wildlife resources and . . . to increase awareness and appreciation of wildlife values," and it urges "ethical restraints in the use of living natural resources" (1988). What a culture does to its wildlife reveals something of the character of that society, and a society fails itself if it fails to conserve its wildlife. When we really learn how to measure richness, the wildlife will figure in on their own terms, not simply for what they are worth on the market or in the skillet.

After seeing the mating dance of the woodcock, Leopold concluded, "the woodcock is a living refutation of the theory that the utility of a game bird is to serve as a target, or to pose gracefully on a slice of toast. No one would rather hunt woodcock in October than I, but since learning of the sky dance I find myself calling one or two birds enough. I must be sure that, come April, there will be no dearth of dancers in the sunset sky" (1968 [1949]:4). Grouse or warblers, buffalo or bear, rabbits or deer, eagles, and even mussels—animal lives enrich culture with the age-old dance of life. The American society and economy is surely rich enough that we can afford to keep them; it is not so rich that we can afford to lose them.

The top carnivore is missing from most of our American landscapes, and we are wondering whether we ought to restore the gray wolf. One place the wolf does remain is in Minnesota where there are about 1,200 wolves. That respects the integrity of this species in that ecosystem. Yet there are also 12,000 livestock ranches scattered through the wolves' territory, or, to phrase it the other way, the wolves are scattered through the properties of thousands of ranchers. That works surprisingly well, but each year problem wolves begin to kill livestock on forty to fifty of these ranches. A controller inspects the kill, and if a wolf is guilty, it is trapped and killed. About thirty to forty wolves each year are so killed.

In this mix of nature and culture, if we are to have wolves, we must kill wolves. We ought to do both. We have to consider the interests of the ranchers and the value of the cattle. But the integrity of the wolf population is also served by removing those animals who turn from their natural prey to domestic animals. Aldo Leopold remembered from his trigger-happy youth the "fierce green fire" in the eyes of the dying wolf. Here in order to keep that fire going in the species, we have, sadly, to put it out in individuals who lose that wildness and turn to killing cattle. We ought to restore that fierce green gaze on our landscape, where and as we can, even if in the resulting confrontation of people and wildlife, we sometimes have to kill. Sometimes in environmental ethics, there are no easy choices.

5

Anthropocentric Values

██

"Human beings are at the centre of concerns." So the Rio Declaration begins, the Earth Summit creed that once was to be an Earth Charter, signed by almost every nation on the planet. That is anthropocentrism, loud and clear. So humans gathering at the world's biggest summit put themselves in the center. The claim is, in many respects, quite true. The human species is causing all the concern. Environmental problems are people problems, created by people and needing to be solved by people. The problem is to get people into "a healthy and productive life in harmony with nature" (recall chapter 1, sec. 8). And yet those who put themselves "at the center of concerns" are liable to the fallacy of misplaced values.

Does this make nature peripheral or marginal? The center of a circle is circumscribed by, embedded in, the larger area. Being located at the center may highlight, rather than reduce, ties and responsibilities. Those who are located on top may be more dependent, not less so, on those who support them; they may have duties as great as their privileges. We need to get humans properly in their place by assessing the human values that require natural values, asking also what human values may override or yield to natural values.

1. HUMAN VALUES CARRIED BY NATURE

What human values are *carried* by natural systems? As we make a list, notice that some values (the nutrition in a potato) seem objectively there, while others (the eagle as a national symbol) are merely assigned. Either way, certain experiences that humans value require natural things. This will force us to ask about intrinsic values in nature (Rolston 1988).

1. *Life support value.* All culture remains tethered to the biosystem and the options within built environments, though they free us by shifting our dependencies around, provide no final release from nature. Humans depend on air flow, water cycles, sunshine, photosynthesis, nitrogen fixation, decomposition bacteria, fungi, the ozone layer, food chains, insect pollination, soils, earthworms, climates, oceans, and genetic materials. Humans live in a technosphere but remain residents in a biosphere. Forests and soil, sunshine and rain, rivers and sky, the cycling seasons—these are *resources*, but they are also the *sources*, the perennial natural givens that support everything else. Does this put humans at the center?

2. *Economic value.* Humans labor, rebuilding nature to their cultural needs. Any living thing uses its environment as a resource. A squirrel hides a cache of acorns. But these activities take place in ecologies, hardly yet economies. Economic value involves deliberately redoing spontaneous natural things, coupled with a commerce in such remade things. Animals do not exchange in markets; by contrast, markets are basic to every culture. Human labor so dramatically adds value that we may devalue raw nature. But nature has economic value because it has an instrumental capacity. Nature has a rich utilitarian pliability, due both to the plurality of natural sorts and to their multifaceted powers.

Nature is a fertile field for human labor, but that metaphor praises not only the laborer but his environment. Such economic value is partly a function of the state of science, of supply and demand, but it is also a function of available natural properties. When humans conserve nature, we hope in the genius of the mind, but we reveal our expectations regarding the as yet undiscovered wealth of natural properties that we may someday convert into economic value. That partly decenters the human genius and recouples it with natural properties.

3. *Recreational value*. For some recreators, nature is a place to *show what they can do*, they want a mountain to conquer; for other recreators, values are reached as they are *let in on nature's show*, they watch hummingbirds. These two sorts of value—the gymnasium and the theater—can often be combined. People like to recreate in the great outdoors because they are surrounded by something greater than anything they find indoors. The focus is on nature as a wonderland. Sometimes this is an escape value, getting away from it all. Sometimes this is a getting back to it all, to pristine nature beside which culture can seem ephemeral.

Recreation rejuvenates humans. At a deeper analysis, when such re-creation takes place in the natural environment, the creation is the context of human recreation. Preserved by humans, a park or a wildlife refuge preserves human life—by re-creating it. Recreating in natural systems, they touch base with something missing on baseball diamonds. Sometimes what they seem to be valuing is *creation* more than *recreation*. This is not exactly putting humans at the center.

4. *Scientific value*. Natural science is perhaps our most sophisticated cultural achievement, but we should not forget that its focus is primitive nature. Although much recent science requires elaborate analytical equipment (electron microscopes and ultracentrifuges), the subject matter of natural science lies first and fundamentally in natural systems—mitochondria or a feldspar crystal. We admire scientists with their theories and instrumented intelligence, but valuing science does not devalue nature; rather, we learn something about the absorbing complexity of the natural environment when it serves as the object of such noble studies.

Natural science per se cannot be worthwhile unless its primary object, nature, is interesting enough to justify being known. To praise cognitive science is also to praise its object, for no study of a worthless thing can be intrinsically valuable. Deciphering the story of natural history cannot be worthless, not only because human roots lie in it, but because we find it a delightful intellectual pursuit that has enlisted the greatest human genius. Applied science may put humans at the center, using nature resourcefully; but pure natural science keeps nature at the center. Biology, the science, is something that goes on in the human mind, but biology, the logic of life, goes on in the natural world.

5. *Aesthetic value*. Nature presents beauty in life and landscape—an eagle soaring, the fiddleheads of ferns, purple mountains' majesties, the roar of cataracts. Sensitivities in both pure science and in natural aesthetics help us see further than required by our pragmatic necessities. In both, one gets purity of vision. And, sooner or later, we know an authentic sense of awe. The sense of abyss overlooking a gorge is sublime, as is the eerie chill when, nearing a stormy summit, one's hair stands on end in the charged air. A climber admires the mist that floats about an alpine cliff, spitting out lacy snowflakes, tiny exquisite crystals, at the same time that the gathering storm is dangerous to him. All these experiences are unlikely to be had sitting in a Chippendale chair. We seldom gets goose pimples before human artistry.

We may think that, since animals and wildflowers have no sense of beauty, aesthetic experience of nature is something that centers on humans, the only species that can really enjoy it. Yet people who undergo the experience of the sublime are not exactly putting themselves at the center.

6. *Biodiversity value*. Endangered species ought to have their place on the landscape, mixed with the values of citizens. It is true that such species are being preserved, in part, as economic, scientific, recreational resources, and yet there is more. The deepest goods being preserved are these wild species of life itself. Humans are awakening to new duties of preservation. When humans extinguish species, they stop the story of natural history. They bring death without survivors into Earth's prolific exuberance of life.

In the Convention on Biological Diversity, we recall, most of the nations on Earth are conscious of "the intrinsic value of biological diversity" and "of the importance of biological diversity for evolution and for maintaining life sustaining systems of the biosphere," if also "of the ecological, genetic, social, economic, scientific, educational, cultural, recreational and aesthetic values of biological diversity" (recall chapter 2, sec. 1). Is that putting humans at the center or not?

7. *Historical value.* Wildlands provide the profoundest historical

museum of all, a relic of processes that moved the world through 99.99 percent of past time. Humans are relics of that world, and that world as a tangible relic in our midst contributes to our sense of duration, antiquity, and identity. An immense stream of life has flowed over these lands humans so lately inhabit and humans need places to experience what the world was like for almost forever, before we so recently came. Science teaches us this natural history, although science cannot teach us all we need to know about nature, especially not how to value this natural history, or what meaning it has, if any. For that we will need to become philosophical or religious.

Wildlands further provide historical value for the cultures superimposed on natural history. New World Americans have a recent heritage of self-development against a diverse and challenging environment, seen in pioneer, frontiersman, cowboy, and gaucho motifs. Nor should we forget the pre-Columbian years, before the Europeans came, nor that every nation, Old World as well, has historical memories associated with nature: for example, the British with the moors; the Russians with the steppes. We want forests and prairies conserved as souvenir places for each generation to learn (however secondarily or critically) their forefather's moods. Such places provide a lingering echo of what we once were, of a way we once passed. Without these memories we cannot know who and where we are. The second of these historical values may be anthropocentric, but the first is not.

8. *Cultural symbolization value.* We noted earlier how wildlife become cultural symbols: the bald eagle and the bighorn sheep. That is also true with the flora: the pasqueflower is the state flower of South Dakota; the maple leaf for Canada; the trillium for Ontario; the arbutus for Nova Scotia. Nature comes to express the values of the culture superimposed on it. What would be the impact on American hopes if the bald eagle became extinct? What are the psychological connections between the Mississippi River and the state of Mississippi? Between the Scots and Loch Lomond? Would not the death of the last bighorn lower the perceived quality of life in Colorado?

9. *Character-building value.* Wildlands are used by organizations that educate character—Boy and Girl Scouts, Outward Bound, and church camps. Similar growth also occurs in individuals independently of formal organizations. The challenge of self-competence, in teamwork or alone, is valued, together with reflection over skills

acquired and one's place in the world. Wildlands provide a place to sweat, to push oneself more than usual, to learn the luck of the weather, to lose and find one's way, to reminisce over success and failure. They teach one to care about his or her physical condition.

Wildlands provide a sense of proportion. While the virtues of humility, simplicity, frugality, serenity, and independence can also be learned in town, they are nowhere better taught than in encounter with nature. Wildlands help us achieve self-identity. So far as humans have been selected over the evolutionary epic to need challenge, adventure, exertion, and risk, society needs to provide avenues for such archetypal emotions, or expect deviant behavior. There are alternative routes for such expression—sports, for instance, or alas, the military. Humans are remarkably unspecialized. But perhaps wild and rural areas provide a "niche" that matches some deep-seated psychosomatic needs. We do not know, but can suspect that encounter with nature is often related to our mental health. If so, does that put humans at the center?

10. *Diversity-unity values.* The physical sciences reveal the astronomical extent of matter while reducing it into a few kinds of elements and particles. The taxonomist enlarges the array of natural kinds, while the biochemist finds only the materials of physics organized in basic chemistries, such as the citric acid cycle or DNA and RNA. Evolution has traced every life form back to monophyletic or a few polyphyletic origins, while ecology has interwoven these myriad forms into interdependence. The story of science is the discovery of a bigger universe with more things in it, and the finding of laws and structures to explain their common composition and kinship.

We find it agreeable to live in a nature that is at once plural and yet with connectedness. Both this diversity and unity feed the human mind. A complex mind evolves in order to deal with a diverse world, yet one through which unifying relationships run. Do we then say that these features are of no value until thickened by the addition of human interest? Or do we wonder that just this system, evolving so, did thicken to form the interested mind prehistorically and that it continues to do so now? There is even a sense in which the mind, founded on the cerebral complexity and integrating capacity, is a product of nature's inclination both to diversify and to unify. That may put humans at the apex of it all, but it hardly makes the system that spins diversity out of unity valueless. We humans, at the center, have to notice what we are at the center of.

11. *Stability and spontaneity values.* A pair of complementary values mixes counterparts that are descriptive and also valuational. That natural processes are regular—gravity holds, oaks breed in kind, and succession is repeated—yields laws and trends rooted in the causal principle, and means that natural systems are dependable. The polar value, really a sort of freedom, is hardly known to science by any such name. Still, nature sometimes provides contingency, or openness. Neither landscapes, nor aspen leaves, nor ecological successions are ever twice the same. What happens in field and forest is always something of an adventure, as the way the cottontail evades the coyote, or just when the last leaf is tossed from this maple and where the gusting wind lands it.

We do not value rigid order at the expense of spontaneous novelty—too much system and too little story. We value constancy with contingency. The regularity is valuable but so is the openness. Just this wildness in natural systems, which might threaten to make nature chaotic, in fact adds novelty. By making each location different, wildness makes a favorable difference. It makes each ecosystem historic, the more excellent because no two are alike. The Darwinian revolution revised the Newtonian view to find nature sometimes a jungle and not a clock, and many have disliked this. Contingencies do put a bit of chaos into the cosmos. But you can have a sort of adventure in Darwin's jungle that you cannot have in Newton's clock. This openness brings risk and often misfortune, but it sometimes adds excitement.

Humans are here deciding what they like, a mixture of stability and spontaneity, and are pleased with what they find; but it is the system that is providing this mix of which they approve. So where is the center of value?

12. *Dialectical value.* We humans are not really bounded by our skin, but life proceeds in environmental dialectic. Culture is carved out *against* nature, but also out *of* nature, and this is not simple to handle valuationally. Superficially, we first say that so far as nature is antagonistic and discomforting, it has disvalue. With deeper insight, we do not always count environmental conductance as good and resistance as bad, but the currents of life flow in their interplay. An environment that was entirely hostile would slay us; life could never have appeared within it. An environment that was entirely irenic

would stagnate us; human life could never have appeared there either.

Nature insists that we work, even struggle. The pioneer, pilgrim, explorer, and settler loved the frontier for the challenge and discipline that put fiber into the American soul. We do not want entirely to tame this aboriginal element in which our genius was forged. But this is of a piece with the larger natural process of conflict and resolution. Half the beauty of life comes out of it—flowers, fruits, shells, scales, muscles, hair, locomotion, perception, endurance. The coming of Darwin's theories is also thought to have ruined our perceptions of nature's "harmonious architectures," but the struggles he posits, if sometimes overwhelming, are not always valueless. None of life's heroic quality is possible without this dialectical stress.

We might say that humans only wrest values instrumentally from intrinsically valueless nature. That would put humans at the center of an otherwise valueless world. But this ignores the dialectical context of life. We owe all culture to the mixed support and hostility of nature; the one is the warp, the other the woof in the weaving of what we have become. A person who knows his ecology finds it difficult to say that all value is at his center, or even anthropocentric, because value has become relational and systemic. If nature is the thesis, human life arises in antithesis, and the resolution is a synthesis.

13. *Life value.* The first lesson learned in evolution is perhaps one of conflict, but a subsequent one is of kinship, for the life we value in persons is advanced from, but allied with, the life in monkeys and wildflowers. We humans share in such life. Animals and plants are already engaged in the biological conservation of their identity and kind, long before conservation biologists come on the scene. Humans may and do value such animals and plants instrumentally, as game to shoot, or a resource for making medicine, or even as a wildflower that enriches their experience on a hike. But they also realize that a life defended is a center of value for itself.

There is a parity of reasoning based on kinship. If I, as a human, value my life, and if that wild life, with eyes, values its life, and if our lives share much in common, then how can I value my own life without conceding value in this other life like my own? Humans ought to respect plants for what they are in themselves—natural systems of conservation biology, for I myself am one, too. Does that place my life at the center?

14. *Philosophical and religious value.* Nature inspires poetry,

philosophy, and religion. Mountaintop experiences, sunsets, canyon strata, or a meadow of dogstooth violets can generate experiences of "a motion and spirit that impels . . . and rolls through all things"(Wordsworth 1798). A wilderness works on a traveler's soul as much as it does his muscles. We might say, overworking the term, that nature is a philosophical or religious "resource." Using a better word, we want a wilderness "sanctuary," a sacrosanct, holy place, where we draw near to ultimacy.

Nature as a school for character is an instrumental use, but what shall we say when nature is used as a church? An instrument for generating human religious experiences? Will we discover God's creation, or some ultimate reality, or a Nature sacred in itself? How profound are the psychological forces stirred within us by the gray and misty sky, the balmy spring day, the quiet of a snowfall, the calling of loons! How the height of mountains "elevates" us, and the depths of the sea stimulate "deep" thoughts within! Only humans can do metaphysics, and that puts them at the center of philosophical and religious experiences. But, once again, we have to remember what we are at the center of. Neither metaphysics nor religion are usually self-centered activities.

2. WINNING OR LOSING IN ENVIRONMENTAL ETHICS?

Can and ought humans ever to lose in favor of nature? Ought nature ever to lose in favor of humans? Let us begin with a philosophical approach; an ecological one will follow. Socrates made a famous claim that "no evil can come to a good man" (*Apology*, 41d). In environmental ethics, will humans lose when they do the right thing? The entwined destinies view teaches us that there are often win-win situations. A bumper sticker reads: *Recycling: Everyone wins*. Is that the model for the whole human-nature relationship? If we are in harmony with nature, everyone wins. But this is evidently not always so. If we decide in favor of wolves, restoring them, ought the ranchers to lose some sheep?

Socrates' claim is about "evil" befalling people, more than their losing sheep, however. He claims that the only true harm befalls one's character—he calls this the "soul." If doing wrong ruins the soul, doing the right is ipso facto such a great benefit that even if considerable other harms come in result, the just person never loses. For no accumulation of resulting harms from doing right can outweigh negatively the *arete*, excellence, we gain, which more than compensates for other losses, such as one might have in business or political affairs. While the wolves win their survival, the ranchers gain in virtue more than they lose in sheep.

Is this a shell game? Or is it the truth? Suppose that humans reside in an excellent natural world, which they have too much devalued in favor of cultural goods. In a particular decision context, a person can lose. The loser will be worse off by his lights, but his lights are wrong, and if he or she gets things in the right light, there is no loss. It doesn't do any good to win if you're wrong; the win isn't a win. We are corrected from a misperception. We win because we get our values right.

Consider abolishing slavery. Although slave-owners lost in the short term, they and their society really gained. When the right thing was done, the result was win-win in the long term. Similarly with the liberation of women. Some men lost job opportunities; others have to do housework. Males lost their dominance, they lost power. But relationships are now more just and humane; interpersonal relationships male to female, white to black, are more genuine. The talents and skills of women and blacks, formerly often wasted, now are more likely to be utilized in the work force; family incomes are higher, marriages are richer. In environmental ethics, there is a parallel. The person reforms, re-forms his or her values, and becomes a winner because now living in a richer and more harmonious relationship with nature.

Some will protest that we insist that humans can win, but then redefine winning. We win by moving the goal posts. And that's cheating, like showing a net positive balance in your checkbook by revising the multiplication tables. You will win, by losing at the old game and playing a new game. Some persons did lose, in the sense that losing had when our argument started. They lost timber, or opportunities for development, or jobs, or sheep. But now you redefine winning, and they do not lose.

Yes, moving the goal posts might be cheating if the game were football. But in environmental ethics, there is a disanalogy. You move the goal posts because you discover that they are in the wrong place. And that is really to win, because getting to the wrong goal is not winning. With the new goalposts in the right place, people find more values in the natural world than before. We stop exploiting nature and become a member of a human and a biotic community, residing on a richer, more meaningful Earth.

The person who is doing the wrong thing will, quite likely, not think this is wrong. Or even if, in more honest moments, one knows it is wrong, one expects to win. If such a person is wrong, the goal posts, misperceived, will have to be moved. That is facing up to the truth: what was before thought to be winning is losing.

Consider the Pacific Northwest. There will be some losers, in the sense that some will have to change jobs. They will, meanwhile, come to reside in a community that is stable in its relationship to the forests; that makes them winners. They once lived in a community with a world-view that saw the great forests only as a resource to be mined, exploit-ed. But that is not an appropriate worldview; it sees nature as com-modity for human gratification, and nothing else. This idea of winning is to consume, the more the better, and those who satisfy consumers get the profit. Moving the goal posts, these "losers" at the exploitation game will come to live in a community with a new worldview, a sus-tainable relationship with the forested landscape; and that is a new idea of winning. What they really lose is what it is a good thing to lose: an exploitative attitude toward forests. What they gain is a good thing to gain: a land ethic. All this is what the entwined destinies view teaches.

But is that the whole truth? Can the good of nature and that of cul-ture ever be at odds? Is there some peculiar human excellence that requires that nature be harmed? When culture wins, must nature lose? That question has a time-bound answer; and the first answer to this question has to be: yes. Culture is the peculiar human excellence, and advanced agricultural and technological culture is not possible except as it is superimposed on nature so as to capture natural values and redirect them to cultural use.

Take forestry as an example. Civilization on Earth over the past twenty centuries is almost unthinkable without the use of wood for structure and fuel. Such an extractive resource use can ideally be put on a sustainable basis. Yet when a forest is harnessed as a resource for cul-ture, the integrity of the primeval forest ecosystem is sacrificed, more or less. Or consider agriculture. Plowed soil will disturb the native forest or grassland that preceded it. The ecosystem can perhaps retain its health; an agriculture can be intelligently fitted into the ecological process of a landscape. Nevertheless, agriculture proportionate to its extent harms the pristine integrity of the landscape. It rebuilds the landscape to meet the needs of the farmers and those they feed. The farmers win; the pristine grasslands and forest are sacrificed to their benefit.

Consider animals reared for food. Where animals are domesticated, the cows, sheep, and goats must be tended. The welfare of the cows is entwined with the welfare of the cowboy, that of the sheep with the shepherd, but the animals are bred for the qualities humans desire, tender meat or soft wool; their reproduction is manipulated by breeders; they are traded in markets, and so on. They are often not particularly unhappy animals; the chickens that I remember on my grandfather's farm in Alabama rather liked it where they were. Nevertheless, we butchered, sheared sheep, and ate chicken every Sunday.

Consider beasts of burden. It is difficult to think that civilization could have developed to its advanced state without them. Humans would not have figured out how to build motor cars and trucks without ever having built buggies and wagons, or if no human had ever ridden a beast nor laid a load on its back. It is true that a horseman attends to the welfare of his horse, and that most of these animals would never have existed without their breeders; nevertheless they became artifacts of culture.

When Columbus set foot in the Americas in 1492, there is no way that modern America could have been built without damage to the integrity of the then-existing ecosystems. America could, however, have been built with much less damage; we might have preserved ecosystem health where we could not preserve pristine integrity. But that is hindsight.

What now? Must we further harm nature to develop culture? No. A satisfactory culture is quite possible without further degrading nature, and indeed degrading nature is likely to make culture less satisfactory. We do not need increased development at cost to fauna, flora, endangered species, or ecosystem health. Nor will humans be harmed if we do not get it. We still win even when there is no more such development. And our win is simultaneously nature's win. While it is a sad truth that life preys on life—culture does have to eat nature—but that is not the only truth; there is a glad truth that culture can be satisfied, can only be satisfactory, in entwined destiny with nature.

In the relations between humans and nature, we cannot always have a win-win outcome. But we can always look for harmony, optimizing values, and conserving nature, more or less. We can find paths of cultural development to enjoy, even though (and indeed because) they are constrained out of respect for nature. Some things in nature will be sacrificed, but some things in culture will be left undone. In the latter case, there will be compensations that are enriching: living on a more diverse landscape, with its integrity and biodiversity preserved. We will have some (but not all) of nature. We will have enough (but not maximum) cultural development. Such culture is really a better culture because it is harmonious with nature.

In one sense, culture is triumphant on Earth; pristine nature ought to be sacrificed to it; we live in a postevolutionary phase of Earth's history (see chapter 7, sec. 5). But we also live in a postmodern phase of culture; the exploitative attitude has gone past extremes. Nature is overconquered, and further sacrifice of it will not benefit humans. Culture cannot profit by moving to some imagined postecological stage.

3. RICH AND POOR, POPULATION AND CONSUMPTION

We can put these issues into graphic form by considering the human population growth curve. The realm of culture has exploded relative to the realm of nature, both in the developing and the developed countries. Not only have the numbers of people grown, their expectations have grown, so that, to get the true picture, we will have to superimpose one exploding curve on top of another one. A superficial reading of such a graph is that humans really start winning big in the second half of the twentieth century. There are lots of them, and they want and many of them get lots of things.

But when we come to our senses, we realize that this kind of "winning," if it keeps on escalating, is really losing. When we get the goal posts in the right place, we see that we are headed in the wrong direction. Humans, competing for fewer resources, will eventually lose, and nature will be destroyed as well. Cultures have become all-consumptive, with an ever-escalating growth of insatiable desires, overlaid on an ever-escalating population growth. Culture does not know how to say "Enough!" and that is not satisfactory. Starkly put, the growth of culture has become cancerous. That is not strictly a metaphor, for a cancer is essentially an explosion of unregulated growth.

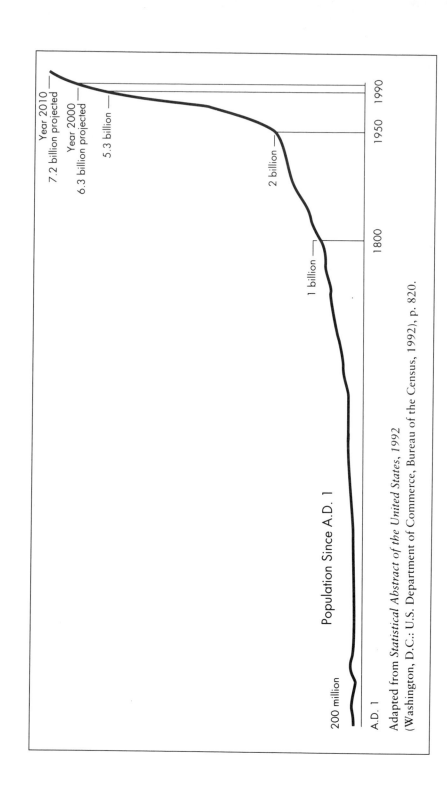

Population Since A.D. 1

Adapted from *Statistical Abstract of the United States, 1992*
(Washington, D.C.: U.S. Department of Commerce, Bureau of the Census, 1992), p. 820.

If, in this picture, we look at individuals, caught up in this cancerous growth, some can and will be harmed in terms of their immediate, perceived personal goals, perhaps even of their bodily needs. Surely that is a bad thing. And would anyone want to say that such persons ought not to sacrifice nature, if need be, to alleviate such harm as best they can? From their perspective, they are only doing what humans have always done, making a resourceful use of nature to meet their own needs. Isn't that a good thing anymore? Such persons, often poor, are doomed to perpetual poverty, unless they can capture natural values. They need to exploit their natural resources, and rise out of their poverty.

Again, we face a time-bound truth, for too much of a good thing becomes a bad thing. We have to figure in where such persons are located on the population curve, and realize that a good thing when human numbers are manageable is no longer a good thing when such a person is really another cell of cancerous growth. That sounds cruel, and it is tragic, but it does not cease to be true for these reasons. For a couple to have two children may be a blessing; but the tenth child is a tragedy. When the child comes, one has to be as humane as possible, but one will only be making the best of a tragic situation, and if the tenth child is reared, and has ten children in turn, that will only multiply the tragedy. The quality of all human life deteriorates; the poor get poorer. Meanwhile natural resources are stressed even further, and ecosystem health and integrity degenerate, and this only compounds the losses again, leading into a vicious cycle. Human and natural values are lost—surely a lose-lose situation. An individual human is who he is where he is, and if he is in a social system misfitted to its landscape, his wins can only be temporary in a losing human ecology.

But there is a way to relieve this tragedy, if there would be a just distribution of the goods of culture, now so inequitably distributed. Few would need to go without enough if we could distribute the produce of the already domesticated landscape justly and charitably. If such redistribution does not take place, people can and will get hurt. But it is better to try to fix this problem where it arises, within society, than to try to enlarge the sphere of society by the sacrifice of remnant natural values. Indeed, the problem really cannot be fixed the latter way; it can only be postponed.

Peoples of the South (the lesser developed countries) complain about the overconsumption of peoples in the industrial North, often legitimately so. But Brazil, for instance, has the most skewed income distribution in the world. The U.S. ratio between personal income for the top 20 percent of people to the bottom 20 percent is 9 to 1, while the ratio in Brazil is 26 to 1. Just 1 percent of Brazilians control 45 percent of the agricultural land. The largest twenty landowners own more land between them than the 3.3 million smallest farmers. There is already more arable land per person in Brazil than in the United States, much of which is held for speculation. In fact, an area of 330 million hectares of farm land, larger than India, is lying idle. Furthermore, the top 10 percent of Brazilians spend 51 percent of the national income (Power 1992). This inequity between human beings is what really ought to be "at the center of concern," if we are ever to optimize natural and cultural values.

South Africa is seeking an ethic of ecojustice enabling five million privileged whites and twenty-nine million exploited blacks (as well as several million underprivileged mixed-race "coloureds") to live in harmony on their marvelously rich but often fragile landscape.[*] Whites earn nearly ten times the per capita income of blacks. White farmers— 50,000 of them—own 70 percent of farmland; 700,000 black farmers own 13 percent of the land (17 percent other). Black land ownership has long been severely restricted by law. Forced relocations of blacks coupled with high black birth rates give the so-called homelands, small areas carved out within the South African nation, an extremely high average population density. When ownership patterns in the homelands are combined with those in the rest of the nation, land ownership is as skewed as anywhere on Earth. Compounding the problem, the black population is growing, and is now more than ten times what it was before the Europeans came.

The land health of South Africa is poor, to say nothing of the integrity in the magnificent wildlife populations. South African water resources are running out; the limited wetlands in an essentially arid nation are exploited for development and water is polluted by unregulated industry. Natal, one of the nation's greenest and most glorious areas, is especially troubled with polluted winds. Everywhere herbi-

---

[*] All of the following data can be found in Huntley, Siegfried, and Sunter 1989; Preston-Whyte and House 1990; and Durning 1990.

cides float downwind with adverse effects on human, vegetative, and wildlife nontarget organisms; there is acid rain over Cape Town, sometimes worse than in Tokyo or London. With an abundance of coal, South Africa generates 60 percent of the electricity on the African continent, sold at some of the cheapest rates in the world (although less than a third of South Africans have electricity). The Eskom coal-burning power plants in the Transvaal are the worst offenders in air pollution, leaving the highveld of eastern Transvaal as polluted as was eastern Germany, and threatening an area that produces 50 percent of South Africa's timber industry and 50 percent of the nation's high-potential agricultural soils. On a per person basis, white South Africans are the world's worst greenhouse offenders. South African farmers lose twenty tons of topsoil to produce one ton of crops. Soil erosion and vegetative degradation on the homelands, contrasting with the white-owned areas, is so bad that the outline of the homeland boundaries can be seen in satellite photographs.

What is the solution? Laissez-faire capitalists, often prominent in government, propose growth so that every one can become more prosperous, oblivious to the fact that even the present South African relationship to the landscape is neither sustainable nor healthy. They want "growth" because this will avoid redistribution of wealth. In an industry-financed study of strategies for the next century, Brian Huntley, Roy Siegfried, and Clem Sunter conclude: "What is needed is a much larger cake, not a sudden change in the way it is cut" (1989:85). But more pie, just as unequally cut, is not the right solution in a nation that already stresses the carrying capacity of its landscape.

What is happening is that an unjust lack of sharing between whites and blacks is destroying the green. And it would be foolish for all, even for white South Africans acting in their own self-interest, to jeopardize environmental health further, rather than to look first and resolutely to solving their social problems. Fortunately, many South Africans have realized the deeper imperative, and recent efforts toward constitutional change promise deep social changes there. This, in turn, will make possible a more intelligent conservation of natural values.

We make a serious mistake, however, if we conclude from the problem of the inequitable distribution of wealth that there is not also a population problem. Even if there were an equitable distribution of wealth, the human population cannot go on escalating without people becoming all equally poor. Of the 90 million new people who will come on board planet Earth this year, 85 million will appear in the Third World, the countries least able to support such population growth.

We make a final serious mistake if we conclude that there is no consumption problem. Compared with the Third World, each North American, for example, will consume two hundred times as much energy. The five million new people in the industrial countries will put as much strain on the environment as the 85 million new poor. Uncontrolled consumption is as cancerous as uncontrolled growth. In essence, there are three problems: overpopulation, overconsumption, and underdistribution.

4. HUMAN RIGHTS TO DEVELOPMENT

Still, critics may object that when it comes to dealing with individuals caught up in these social forces, we should factor out all three, none of which are the fault of the particular individuals who may wish to develop their lands. "I did not ask to be born; I am poor, not overconsuming; I am not the cause but rather the victim of the inequitable distribution of wealth." Surely there still remains for such a person a right to use whatever natural resources one has available, as best one can, under the exigencies of one's particular life, set though this is in these unfortunate circumstances. "I only want enough to eat; is that not my right?"

We have already recommended a human right to an environment with integrity (chapter 1, sec. 5). Human rights must include, if anything at all, the right to subsistence, to basic needs of food, clothing, and shelter. So even if particular persons are located at the wrong point on the global growth graph, even if they are willy-nilly part of a cancerous and consumptive society, even if there is some better social solution than the wrong one that is in fact happening, have they not a right that will override the conservation of natural value? Granted that culture is unhealthy, will it not just be a further wrong to these same people to deprive them of their right to what little they have? Can human rights ever be overridden by a society that wants to do better by conserving natural value? Should nature win, while such unlucky persons lose?

Answering such questions requires the serious weighing of values. Consider the tropical forests. There is more richness there than in other regions of the planet—half of all known species. On the one continent of South America, for example, there are one-fifth of the planet's species of terrestrial mammals (800 species); there are one-third of the planet's flowering plants (Mares 1988). Given the ecology of the tropical forests, which does not respond well to fragmentation, these species can be preserved only if large Amazonian rainforest and other wetland regions of South America are left relatively undeveloped and at low population densities, areas that in any case are not well suited to agriculture. The peak of global plant diversity is the combined flora of the three Andean countries of Colombia, Ecuador, and Peru. There over 40,000 species live on just 2 percent of the world's land surface (Wilson 1992:197). But population growth in South America has been as high as anywhere in the world (Coale 1983), and people are flowing into the forests, often crowded off other lands.

What about people? Consider first people who are not now there but might move there. This is not good agricultural soil, and such would-be settlers are likely to find only a short-term bargain, a long-term loss. Consider the people who already live there. If they are indigenous peoples, and wish to continue to live as they have already for hundreds and even thousands of years, there will be no threat to the forest. If they are *cabaclos* (of mixed European and native races), they can also continue their traditional lifestyles, without serious destruction of the forests. Such peoples may continue the opportunities that they have long had. Nothing is taken away from them.

Can these cabaclos and indigenous peoples modernize? Can they multiply? The two questions are connected, since it is modern medicine and technology that enables them to multiply. These are problematic questions for, in a sense, a modernized, overpopulated indigenous people is not an indigenous people any more. The cabaclos' lifestyle modernized has really been transformed into something else. Have they the right to develop into modern peoples, if this requires an exploitation of their resources that destroys the rainforests? The first answer is that they do, but with the qualification that all rights are not absolute, some are weaker, some stronger, and the exercise of any right has to be balanced against values destroyed in the exercise of that right.

The qualification brings a second answer. If one concludes that the natural values at stake are quite high (perhaps higher than anywhere else in the world), and that the opportunities for development are low, because the envisioned development is inadvisable, then a possible answer is: No, there will be no development of these reserved areas. There will be development elsewhere, to which those who choose so can move. If they stay, they must stay under the traditional lifestyle of their present and past circumstances. So they must pay, if you like, an opportunity cost if they remain. They do have the right to develop, but such a right can be exercised only if such persons move elsewhere.

Anywhere that there is legal zoning, persons are told what they may and may not do on the lands on which they reside, in order to protect various social and natural values. Land ownership is limited ("imperfect," as lawyers term it) when the rights of use conflict with the rights of others. One's rights are always constrained by the harm one does to others, who have a right not to be harmed, and we legislate to enforce this (under what lawyers call "police power"). Environmental policy ought to regulate ("police") the harms that people do on the lands on which they live, and it is perfectly appropriate to set aside conservation reserves to protect natural values, because of the ecological, scientific, economic, historical, aesthetic, religious, and other cultural values people have at stake here, as well as for values that the fauna and flora intrinsically possess. Indeed, unless there is such reserving (and policing) of natural areas throughout the world, counterbalancing the high pressures for development, there will be almost no conservation at all. Every person on Earth is told that there are some areas that he or she cannot develop.

So people are told that they may develop there but not here. If one is already residing in a location where development is forbidden, or constrained, this may seem to be unfair, forced relocation. Does that not violate human rights? Consider relocation in general, and start on the development side. Every large dam ever built has forced people to move out of the way. Kariba Dam, on the Zambezi River between Zambia and Zimbabwe, supplies water, electricity, fish, and benefits wildlife in both nations, but forced 50,000 Tonga people to move from their ancestral homelands. Typically we think this a justifiable overriding of their rights; we may also think that due compensation is required for the taking. General Motors is closing twenty-one manufacturing plants, affecting 76,000 jobs between 1990 and 1995, in favor of subcontracting for parts, production overseas, and efficiency. From 1920 to 1960, most of the textile mills in Lowell, Massachusetts, moved south, in search of cheaper, nonunion labor, lower taxes, to get closer to the cotton, to modernize plants, and, no longer needing water power, to take advantage of cheaper electricity provided by the Tennessee Valley Authority, and other government incentives to develop the South. The U.S. government closes military bases and tens of thousands have to move.

We may not think these decisions are always right, but we think that they are often right. We have never said that social decisions could not require people to relocate; to the contrary we regularly make decisions that require them to do so. We have done this in the interests of various better and worse goods; market efficiency, cheaper labor, aging plants, shifting demands, and so on. On a parity with this, but on the conservation side, we may also ask people to relocate. When national parks have been established, we have asked people to move. What is so amiss about asking people to relocate in the interest of protecting nature, where the stakes are especially high? No more human rights are being "violated" for the conservation of nature than have regularly been "violated" in the name of development.

This will be especially permissible where we ask persons to relocate only if they are revising their lifestyles in ways that put new threats on the environment. It is they who are proposing to introduce changes, and the burden of proof should be on them to say why they should introduce those changes there to the jeopardy of nature, rather than move to less sensitive areas. One way of putting this is that the people have options; the forests do not. People can move; forests cannot, nor can the animals they contain. Saving the natural values present, optimizing the mix of values in nature and culture can require limiting the options of people in order to save the nonoptional forest values.

Significant social decisions do affect whether people prosper. Making decisions on national or global scales, setting policies, a great deal is at stake. We ought to be as humane as possible about this, but we deceive ourselves if we pretend that any and all human rights are, in some absolute way, nonnegotiable checks on such decisions. We regularly make policy decisions that even result in more people dying, where other decisions would result in fewer dying. This was the case, for instance, when the United States increased the national highway speed limit from fifty-five to sixy-five miles per hour. We do that when we decide to go to war, or to put fewer police on the streets. Or to spend money on art shows or space research that could be spent on AIDS research, or on highway, industrial, or environmental safety.

The point is that human rights to development, even by those who are poor, though they are to be taken quite seriously, are not always and everywhere absolute, but have to be weighed against all the other values at stake. A person may be doing what would be, taken individually, a perfectly good thing, a thing he has a right to do, were he alone, but which, taken in collection with thousands of others doing the same thing, becomes a harmful thing, which he has no right to do because it destroys the commons and irreversibly destroys natural values. These poor may not have so much a right to develop in any way they please, as a right to a more equitable distribution of the goods of the Earth that we, the wealthy, think we absolutely own.

5. DEMOCRACY, ECONOMICS, AND ENVIRONMENT

Government and business provide and protect many human values, and both dramatically affect the possibilities for the conservation of natural value. Animals neither form governments nor trade in markets, but humans cannot escape doing both. Government and business have vast power to influence our behavior toward the environment for better or worse. School and church are no less important, for these also critically help us to form a concept of natural value. Politics and business are value enterprises especially likely to put "humans at the center of concerns" (sometimes enlisting the school and church to help do so).

We have long kept many important social decisions off the market. We do not, for example consult an economic cost-benefit analysis when we decide who should vote (women? 18-year olds?), or whether to abolish capital punishment or abortion, whether and whom to draft into the military, or what counts as free speech or the free exercise of religion. Natural-resource decisions, however, have been long considered to be primarily economic decisions. Lands under private ownership are bought and sold in markets and cared for under economic incentives. Even public lands, in the commons, could best be managed with a cost-benefit approach if we were interested in what goods we could collectively harvest from them. That leads many to think that conserving nature is largely a matter of getting the appropriate market incentives into place.

Shifting concepts of natural value, however, now mean that many, even most, of the values carried by natural systems cannot be safely left to unregulated capitalist markets. Recalling the taxonomy of values above, economics is only one among over a dozen others and we have little reason to think that economics alone will guarantee the preservation of, or sensitize us appropriately to, any of these other domains of value. Hence we look to democracy to regulate economics, by removing some natural values from economic access, or, where we do consume resources, by creating incentives or prohibitions to obtain the balance of other natural and social goods we value as citizens (Costanza 1991). One cannot look to the market to produce or protect the multiple values that citizens enjoy in general on public lands, much less in wilderness areas, since many of the values sought here are not, or not simply, economic. A nation needs collective choices to produce a public land ethic.

In some ways a market is rather like an ecosystem (Anderson and Leal 1991:5). The spontaneous generation of order arises when many individuals, each jostling with their own self-interest, are forced into mutual coactions and cooperations. There are diverse levels of specialization, niches to be occupied and exploited, pressures toward efficiency, networks of nutrient, resource, and energy cycling and recycling. Both are equilibrating systems. But there are also more important disanalogies. In ecosystems, there is no management and labor, no hiring and firing, no capital acquisition, no loans, no money exchange, no taxes. Information may be patented or production require machinery that only the wealthy can afford. Property is inherited, disposed of by will, or mortgaged by corporations. All the critical differences between nature and culture separate the two. Perhaps we often wish to "let nature take its course" in the wild, but nothing follows from this about any "invisible hand" by which capitalism can be left unregulated.

Therefore, in order to conserve natural value, we must regulate capitalism. One purpose of regulation is to internalize costs, to create a more perfect market. We want to make the playing field level, so that the market game can continue with full cognizance of the costs. But ideally we also want regulation to permit values other than market ones to enter into our decisions. In that sense, the purpose of regulation is not to perfect the market, but to ensure that nonmarket values are also included. The purpose is to open up new options in what business can afford to do.

In the market per se, people operate in self-interest. There it is rational to be efficient, get the most for your money, make the most profit. Within economics, that is the meaning of rationality. But people are motivated by many different concerns; these may be economic, but they may also be aesthetic, moral, religious, psychological, sociological, political, scientific, ecological. People may be self-interested, but the self can have lots of interests, often not economic, and often not immediately pertaining to the personal self. The self makes investments in whatever it identifies with. This can be nation, company, church, club, community. Or it can be countryside and landscape. The self identifies with the community in which it resides, and we sum up by saying that people, in their self-interest, enlarge their interests into communities in which they are member citizens.

Call this enlightened self-interest, if you wish, but if the self has thousands of interconnections, we might just as well call it an entwined self, or a communal self. This is an ecological view of the self. Regulation polices these interconnections to see that the economic ones stay in their legitimate domain. Environmental regulation arises to protect by national will environmental values whose protection cannot be left to economic interests alone.

In that sense, for those in business regulation brings freedom. By the government's insisting on specifying, considering, and testing of alternatives in the full view of environmental and social impacts (as does the National Environmental Policy Act), or by seeking a no-jeopardy-to-species solution (as the Endangered Species Act does), environmental policy enlarges the context of consideration. In this sense, regulation should not be viewed as prohibitive policy, but liberating policy. It pushes back economic constraints and permits sensitivity to environmental and cultural values. It lets businesspersons operate within a larger worldview, think about optimizing satisfactory development as culture is set within nature, and not simply submit to criteria of economic efficiency.

Policy and regulation enable citizens to act in concert. And unless such an ethic is enforced, as well as merely encouraged, it is largely useless. There can be no effective private, voluntary environmental ethics. Of course, minority rights and the right to dissent have also to be considered—and enforced! But no one has the right to harm others, without justified cause. Where breaking an environmental ethic—especially one that has a democratic consensus behind it—harms others by destroying a public good, enforcement can be justified.

Democracy, though more admired than capitalism, is no more perfect. The humans who gather to do business together are the same humans who gather to form government. This means that human nature will be the same in both places, even though the values at stake differ. If human nature is sometimes flawed, these flaws will as soon turn up at the courthouse as in the marketplace. We have largely thought that democracy is the form of government best able to combine individual freedoms and mutual cooperation with checks on these flaws in human nature. Democracy, with its more comprehensive sense of the public good, with all the citizens crosschecking each other, can put checks on the flaws in human nature that will make the market inhumane.

But we have also to realize that democracy can itself be a flawed institution. One tough question is whether democracy can regulate capitalism for the protection of the more comprehensive set of natural values; a still tougher question is whether democracy can discipline itself enough to be environmentally rational (Wenz 1989). A test of a democracy is whether its citizens can learn to practice enlightened constraint. One thing that democracy can produce is debate, discussion about values (though, alas, it does not always do so), and we do believe that we are more likely to act correctly about issues that have been well debated. Such debate is our best hope for uncovering and conserving all the natural values at stake.

But if, for instance, citizens insist on shortsighted, immediate, humanistic values, then congressional representation, which has to be reelected every two years, and senators, who have to be elected every six, will not be in all that much better position than corporate executives whose stockholders insist on maximum dividends every quarter, without regard for the long-range health of the business. We may be tempted to vote for the legislator who promises rewards now; if he/she does not produce, then the legislator will be out of office next election. But that can mean short-term decisions that are not really sustainable over generations, the generations of our children and grandchildren. Conserving political careers is not the same as conserving natural values. The half-life of a politician is four years, plus or minus one or two; the half life of a corporate director is twice that. The half-life of a species is several million years.

In the next century we will learn whether democracy and capitalism can establish themselves in harmony with the natural world, on which they both depend. Those who are poor and unliberated face one kind of crisis; those who are rich and liberated face another.

6. ANTHROPOGENIC AND ANTHROPOCENTRIC VALUES

Humans may not place themselves at the focus of every evaluation, but they are certainly the central evaluators. So we are concerned, are we not, with human virtues and valuations, even when the values are carried by nature? Any science or recreation or aesthetic or religious or philosophical experience or character formation is in people, not in trees or rocks. The way to put this in value theory is to say that natural values are not always anthropocentric (centered on humans) but that they are always anthropogenic (generated by humans).

All value in nature is by human interaction and projection. Sometimes humans value nature instrumentally, as when they use soil to grow crops. Sometimes humans value nature intrinsically, as when they save endangered lemurs, refusing to convert a lemur forest sanctuary into cropland. But this is always humans doing the valuation: anthropocentric if the decision is for croplands, but still anthropogenic if the decision is for lemurs. Wild nature is value-free, and only becomes valuable when humans evaluate it. Is this a plausible account?

We need to clarify concepts. The language of valuing nature in itself may be used, but it is misleading. Value is always and only relational, with humans one of the relata. Nature in itself (a wilderness) is without value. This is something like the way in which trees in nature are not really green, but only become green when humans behold them. It doesn't seem to us that we hang the green on the tree, but, in truth, we do.

All so-called intrinsic value in nature, claims J. Baird Callicott, is "grounded in human feelings" and "projected" onto the natural object that "excites" the value. "Intrinsic value ultimately depends upon human valuers." "Value depends upon human sentiments" (1984:305). "There can be no value apart from an evaluator, . . . all value is as it were in the eye of the beholder" (1980:325).

> The *source* of all value is human consciousness, but it by no means follows that the *locus* of all value is consciousness itself. . . . An intrinsically valuable thing on this reading is valuable *for* its own sake, *for* itself, but it is not valuable *in* itself, i.e., completely independently of any consciousness, since no value can in principle . . . be altogether independent of a valuing consciousness. . . . Value is, as it were, projected onto natural objects or events by the subjective feelings of observers. If all consciousness were annihilated at a stroke, there would be no good and evil, no beauty and ugliness, no right and wrong; only impassive phenomena would remain. (1986:142–43)

This, Callicott says, is a "truncated sense" of value where " 'intrinsic value' retains only half its traditional meaning" (1986:143). Only human beings value (evaluate) natural things; but it does not follow that they conclude that only humans have value. Man is the only measurer of things, but man does not have to make himself the only measure he uses. If he does, he will miss much richness in natural values.

Without humans, all that nature has is the potential to be evaluated by humans, who, if and when they appear, may incline, sometimes, to value nature in noninstrumental ways. "Nonhuman species . . . may not be valuable *in* themselves, but they may certainly be valued *for* themselves. . . . Value is, to be sure, humanly conferred, but not necessary homocentric" (Callicott 1986:160). The value-generating event is something like the light in the refrigerator—only on when the door is opened. Values in flora and fauna are only "on" when humans are perceiving them, and otherwise "off." Actual value is an event in human consciousness, though of course natural items while still in the dark have potential intrinsic value. Perhaps even when humans leave, having turned these values "on," the values still stay on (like leaving the refrigerator door open).

No doubt the lemurs will take a dim view of such a theory, since lemurs, when they value their own lives intrinsically for what they are in themselves and value fruits instrumentally as food to eat do not behave as if these were anthropogenic values. They were doing these things before any humans came to Madagascar, about 1,500 years ago. The value of the food they eat is not "humanly conferred." Lemurs cannot self-consciously evaluate their value theory, but they can behaviorally demonstrate what they value. And humans, who can reflect on value theory, ought to be able to see that the lemurs are not valuing anthropogenically at all. They do not have to wait for humans to come around for their lives to be valuable to them. They have their own ends. There is autonomous, not just anthropogenic, intrinsic value.

A powerful emotion is the sense of entrance into a place flourishing independently. The forces by which natural systems run are not human forces; they are the biological and physical forces that have generated the world. The wilderness is a complex tapestry of values, with each living thing defending itself, and the whole system a network in which goods are circulated round and integrated into other goods through both conflict and complementarity. Contemplating it all, there come moments of truth when we can value life's storied achievements. The natural history that envelops us is of value because value is there regardless of whether or not we value it.

Anthropogenic value leaves us uneasy. For all this seemingly generous talk about caring for others, about *our* placing value *there*, since it is only *we* who can place value anywhere, humans really do remain at the center of concern; their concern is central to having any value at all. Their concern is all that matters, and it is not always going to be easy to get up concern for animals or plants, or species or ecosystems that really don't matter in themselves. We are likely to express concern for other species only if they matter to us, and that places humans right back at the center.

What can be confusing is the question of value ownership. When humans do come around to valuing lemurs, humans get let in on what is going on with regard to lemur values in the forest. So no human is ever going to be able to value lemurs without relating to what the lemurs themselves value. There will always be anthropogenic value, value generated by humans, and this value will sometimes not be anthropocentric at all. Humans will be enriched by this relationship. If humans are to talk about natural values, we must be actively "in on" them, that is, share those values in personal experiences adequate to judge them.

Humans are rather more "turned on" by making evaluative judgments than by straightforward empirical ones, but that can mean that we are rather more "tuned in" with what is so. That does add a dimension of human biography to every report about nature, but it would be valuational solipsism to conclude that in those values that natural things seem to carry we are getting back nothing but our projections. We do not want to commit the fallacy of misplaced location, and ascribe to the viewer what he or she is in fact seeing out there in nature.

We must not beg the question of nonanthropogenic objectivity. We want rather to examine it. Humans must come to own any values about which they deliberate. Humans participate in them and we realize that we are enjoying them. But it would be fatal to further analysis to conclude that since humans experientially own these values under analysis, values are found only in felt existence, and projected onto nature, nothing more. Trees may not be green if humans are not looking, but trees are photosynthesizing whether humans are looking or not, and this photosynthesis has survival value both to the tree and to everything dependent on it.

Value is not received as the conclusion of an argument, or by the indifferent observation of a causal series. A value or disvalue recognized has got some bite to it. That can confuse us into thinking that values lie entirely in the human experiences that nature generates, no matter how greatly features in the wilderness contribute to it. But life support and genetic information operate regardless of whether humans are aware of these things. Perhaps the human valuing of nature generates new values, a kind that are experiential by logical necessity, but these are superimposed on spontaneous natural values, some kinds of which do not require human experiences to generate them.

Well, it may be replied, perhaps the anthropogenic claim is too strong. But the felt experience claim is not. Lemurs can value themselves, on their own, but what they value is their own experiences of pain and pleasure. For them value is "lemur-centric." And so on for all other subjects of a life, down to about spiders, whose value is arachno-centric. But no further, because there are no subjects lower down. Value is always subjective, felt experience in subjects, though some subjects are not humans, a question to which we shall return.

We might first think that the phrase "experienced value" is a tautology and the phrase "unexperienced value" a contradiction in terms, somewhat like the phrases "experienced thought" and "unexperienced thought," a "felt tickle" and an "unfelt tickle." But the existence of unexperienced value (undiscovered vitamins, genes anciently beneficial to dinosaurs, cougar predation keeping the deer herd healthy) is not a contradiction in terms, unless one builds into the meaning of value that it must be experienced.

If natural things have values, we cannot conceivably learn this without experiences by which we are let in on them. With every such sharing there comes a caring, and this may seem to proscribe objective neutrality. In fact, it only prescribes circumspect inquiry. All natural science is built on the experience of nature, but this does not entail that its descriptions, its "facts," just are those experiences. All valuing of nature is built on experience, too, but that does not entail that its descriptions, its "values," are just those experiences. Valuing could be a further, nonneutral way of knowing about the world, an advanced kind of experiencing where a more sophisticated, living organism/instrument is required to register natural properties. Value must be lived through, *experienced*, but so as to discern the character of the surroundings one is living through.

7. HUMAN EXCELLENCES AND NATURAL VALUES

"Now I see the secret of the making of the best persons. / It is to grow in the open air, and to eat and sleep with the earth" (Whitman 1961 [1860]:319). Whitman has taken some poetic license, since quite excellent people also grow in urban settings. But there is a lot of truth in it, first in terms of character formation, and also in the sense that humans can appreciate where they are. On top of the benefits of a wise use of resources, there come still higher excellences, an appreciation of the richness of nature that the person enjoys, and personal satisfactions in having done the right thing. An admirable trait in persons is their capacity to appreciate things outside themselves, things that have no economic, medical, or industrial uses, perhaps even no ordinary recreational, aesthetic, or scientific value.

An interest in natural history ennobles persons. It stretches us out into bigger persons. Humans ought sometimes be admirers of nature, and that redounds to their excellence. A condition of human flourishing is that humans enjoy natural things in as much diversity as possible—and enjoy them at times because such creatures flourish in themselves. Humans can always gain excellence of character from acts of conservation. We have a duty to our higher selves to respect nature. We have already said that humans who do the right thing in environmental ethics can really never lose. They get more Socratic soul.

Bryan Norton calls this a "weak anthropocentrism" (1984). Weak anthropocentrism makes strong characters. Getting enlightened about saving nature transforms us into the richest kinds of persons that we can be. Nature has "transformative value" (Norton 1987:185–213). Rather paradoxically, humans do not become their highest selves until they stretch out of themselves by this higher sense of valuing others. We know that is true in interpersonal relations. But it is also true for humans valuing nonhumans. Only by so doing can they become most genuinely human. The noblest character can best be gained by appreciating nature. That is what Whitman meant. So environmental ethics is really self-actualizing; it is the pursuit of human excellence, if we get our goal posts right. There will be only excellent winners.

Now we begin to get confused about our motivations, however. Are we valuing our excellent selves, or are we valuing excellent others? An environmentally virtuous person seems to be valuing natural things for what they are in themselves, but then the primary value on which the system is based is human virtue. That virtue no doubt includes an appropriate respect for nonhuman creatures. But the ultimate value is really in the experiences of human excellence that are triggered by an appropriate response to it. "Excellence" is still a domain of human welfare.

If human excellence really is the motivation, then this high-souled person is not especially seeking the good of nature, but rather seeking his or her own good—the real payoff. If ever it were the case that such a person could increase soul and harm nature, or win-lose, there would be no restraint. That is beginning to sound environmentally shallow, not a deep view at all. Nature is only good as a transformer of persons, and transformers aren't any good unless they are working to transform one kind of human value into another kind. Maybe we are committing a fallacy of misplaced value. If the virtue of human character really comes from appreciating another, nonhuman form of life, then why not attach intrinsic value to this alien life? Let the human virtue be a corollary to that. Why praise only the virtue in the human beholder?

How can it be virtuous for humans to treasure for what it is in itself something that has no value in itself? Why take a wildflower into account unless there is some value there to take into account? Human virtue is intrinsically a good state for the self, but there are various intrinsic goods that the self pursues in relation to others that are not self-states of the person who is desiring. The preservation of the whales is not covertly the cultivation of human excellences; the life of the whales is the overt value defended. An enriched humanity results, with values in the whales and values in persons compounded—but only if the loci of value are not confounded.

The Roman Catholic bishops urge us: "The web of life is one. Our mistreatment of the natural world diminishes our own dignity and sacredness . . . because we are engaging in actions that contradict what it means to be human" (1991:426) Yes, that seems right, it seems humane. But wait a minute! I make a large donation to the Fund for the Whales, and, being asked what motivated my charity, I answer: "I wish to augment my dignity! I am affirming what it means to be human!" Doesn't that still put humans "at the center of concern"? Christians, caring for creation, ought to be able to do better! They might, instead, have concern for the integrity of creation, and forget their self-image and dignity. Those who give only to cultivate their excellence of character are really yet small of spirit, with a long way to go.

How about just affirming the whales for what they are in themselves? The humans are, of course, not going to lose any dignity by their concern for the whales. We never lose soul by doing the right thing. But there are some right things we ought to do, regardless of soul and our dignity. Let's be frank. It seems unexcellent—cheap and philistine—to say that excellence of human character is what we are after when we conserve whales. We may say that the destruction of whales is "uncalled for," but why so? Shall I answer that the whales have "transformative value," they can make me a nobler person by enlarging my soul? Is that what they are good for? Or does not the person with a genuine noble soul say: "They are good in themselves. If this excellence of character really comes from appreciating otherness, then why not value that otherness in wild nature first?"

It is hard to gain much excellence of character from appreciating an otherwise worthless thing. Worthless things don't transform or dignify us much. To prohibit needless destruction of wild species seems to depend on some value in the species as such, for there need be no prohibition against destroying a valueless thing. The excellence of human character, a value in my life as a dignified subject, depends on a sensitivity to excellence in the objective natural world. The human mind grows toward the realization of its excellences by appropriate respect for nature, but that respect is the end and the growth the byproduct. It is even true that realizing this excellent humanity in *Homo sapiens* is a greater value than the flourishing of lemur life in *Lemur catta*, but the realizing of excellent humanity here is exactly the *expansion* of human life into a concern for lemur life for what it is in itself, past concern for self-dignity. Here humans are higher than lemurs only as and because humans, moving outside their own immediate sector of interest, can and ought to be morally concerned for lemurs, while lemurs have no moral capacities at all and can neither cognitively entertain a concept of humans nor evaluate the worth of humans. What "higher" means here is having the capacity to be concerned for the "lower."

Ethics is not merely about what humans love, enjoy, find rewarding, nor about what they find wonderful, ennobling, or transforming. It is sometimes a matter of what humans *ought* to do, like it or not, and these *oughts* may not always rest on the likes of other humans or on what ennobles character. Sometimes we ought to consider worth beyond that within our selves. If one insists on putting it this way—emphasizing a paradox in responsibility—concern for nonhumans can ennoble humans (although this concern shortcircuits if the concern is explicitly or tacitly just for noble humans). Genuine concern for nonhumans could humanize our species all the more. That is what the argument about human excellence and dignity is trying to say, only it confuses a desirable result with the primary locus of value.

> Self-actualizing people are more able to perceive the world as if it were independent not only of them but also of human beings in general. This also tends to be true of the average human being in his highest moments, i.e., in his peak experiences. He can then more readily look upon nature as if it were there in itself and for itself, and not simply as if it were a human playground put there for human purposes. He can more easily refrain from projecting human purposes upon it. In a word, he can see it in its own Being ("endness") rather than as something to be used, or something to be afraid of, or to be reacted to in some other human way. (Maslow 1968:76)

Both anthropocentric and anthropogenic values have to come to an end before we can become the best persons. We have to discover intrinsic natural values.

6

Intrinsic Natural Values

⚏

"Every form of life is unique, warranting respect regardless of its worth to man." So begins the United Nations World Charter for Nature, as nonanthropocentric as the Rio Declaration's preamble is anthropocentric (UN General Assembly 1982). One hundred and twelve nations endorsed the charter, including China, France, the United Kingdom, and the Soviet Union. The United States was the only nation vigorously opposed. It is possible for humans to be "at the center of concerns" and also for every form of life to have its worth regardless of humans. Both can be true.

Fortunately, some officials in the United States also vigorously defend intrinsic values in nature. William Reilly, head of the Environmental Protection Agency under the Bush administration, insists, "Natural ecosystems . . . have intrinsic values independent of human use that are worthy of protection" (Reilly 1990). The Society of American Foresters has adopted overwhelmingly by referendum a land ethic canon that "demonstrates our respect for the land." This means, says Raymond S. Craig, chair of their Land Ethic Committee, that foresters, in addition to anthropocentric values on forests, also "value all components of ecosystems, without regard to their usefulness to humans, because all components have intrinsic value" (Craig 1992). We have steadily been building toward the concept of objective natural value.

1. LIFE AS CONSERVATION

Biological conservation did not begin when the United Nations promulgated its World Charter for Nature, nor when the United States Congress passed the Endangered Species Act, nor even when Teddy Roosevelt withdrew forest reserves, nor even when Noah built the ark to save endangered species. Biological conservation began when life began, three and a half billion years ago. Those who do not conserve natural value are soon dead. Biological conservation in the deepest sense is not something that originates in the human mind, is modeled by Forplan programs on national forests, or written into acts of Congress. Biological conservation is innate as every organism conserves, values its life.

A merely physical object has nothing to conserve. Though conservation of mass and energy takes place during the various events that happen to a rock—heated by the noonday sun, eroded by the rains—the rock conserves no identity. It changes without conservation goals. An inert rock exists on its own, making no assertions over the environment and not needing it. When high waters run into a lake, the lake level rises and later subsides to its former level. But the lake is conserving nothing. Biological organisms, by contrast, conserve an identity—a metabolism maintains itself and an anatomy over time. Organisms have a life, as physical objects do not.

Organisms are self-maintaining systems; they grow and are irritable in response to stimuli. They resist dying. They reproduce. They can be healthy or diseased. They post a careful, semipermeable boundary between themselves and the rest of nature; they assimilate environmental materials to their own needs. They gain and maintain internal order against the disordering tendencies of external nature. They keep rewinding, recomposing themselves, while inanimate objects run down, erode, and decompose. Life is a countercurrent to entropy, an energetic fight uphill in a world that overall moves thermodynamically downhill. Organisms suck order out of their environment; they pump out disorder. In physics, entropy is not conserved; it increases. In biology, organisms must locally fight this increase, a conservation of negentropy.

The constellation of these life characteristics is nowhere found outside organisms. A crystal reproduces a pattern and may restore a damaged surface; a planetary system maintains an equilibrium; a volcano may grow in countercurrent to entropy. A lenticular altocumulus cloud, formed as a standing wave over a mountain range, is steadily recomposed by input and output of air flow. But any mechanical precursors of life fail to integrate into the pattern that we call an organism. Or perhaps we should say that over evolutionary time they did, and that there emerged something vitally greater than the physical precedents: organismic life.

The "genius" of life is coded into genetic sets, which are missing from minerals, volcanoes, or clouds. An organism is thus a spontaneous cybernetic system, self-maintaining, sustaining and reproducing itself on the basis of information about how to make a way through the world. There is an internal representation symbolically mediated in the coded "program" held forth, motion toward the execution of this goal, and checking against performance in the world, using some sentient, perceptive, or other responsive capacities by which to compare match and mismatch. The cybernetic controlling program can reckon with vicissitudes, opportunities, and adversities that the world presents.

Causes are pervasive in physics; conservation persists through causal chains. There is conservation of spin, or baryon number, and we do not worry about it; it cannot be otherwise with deterministic causation. But something more than causes, if (sometimes) less than sentience, is operating within every organism. There is *information* superintending the causes; and without this information the organism would collapse into a sand heap. This information is a modern equivalent of what Aristotle called formal and final causes; it gives the organism a *telos*, "end," a kind of (nonfelt) purpose. Organisms have ends, although not always ends-in-view.

All this cargo is carried by the DNA, essentially a set of linguistic molecules. Humans artificially impose an alphabet on ink and paper, but living things long before were employing a natural alphabet, imposing a code on four nucleotide bases strung as cross-links on a double helix. A triplet of bases stands for one of the twenty amino acids, and by a serial reading of the DNA, translated by messenger RNA, a long polypeptide chain is synthesized, such that its sequential structure predetermines the bioform into which it will fold. Ever-lengthening chains, logical lines, like ever-longer sentences, are organized into genes, like paragraphs and chapters, and so the story of life is written into the genetic library. The DNA is really a set of *conservation molecules.*

That story is perpetuated generation to generation, and each living thing is constantly required to conserve its life. The genetic program is played out in the drama of life. The defense of a somatic "self" is vital to an organism's integrity. Life requires an inside and an outside, an organism that has separated itself from its environment. There must be some kind of a cell, some defining envelope. In multicellular organisms there is a skin or shell or bark. After that an organism can take in nutrients from the environment and sequester them for its own uses. Biology requires preserving the identity of selves, articulated from other selves, in an environment with which the self must be in constant exchange. Self-identity means self-defense, self-stability, self-integrity. This self-impulse just is the life impulse, the principal carrier of biological value. That, above all, has to be conserved.

The ecosystem evolves organisms that attend to their immediate somatic needs (food, shelter, metabolism) and that reproduce themselves in the very next generation. In the birth-death-birth-death system a series of replacements is required. The organism must do this, it has no options; it is "proper" for the organism to do this (Latin *proprium*, one's own proper characteristic). Somatic defense and genetic transmission are the only conservation activities possible to most organisms; they are necessary for all, and they must be efficient about it.

Conservation in biology both is and is not a natural law. Conservation is required for survival; but, unlike physics, conservation may fail. Conservation in physics pervades the universe as natural law. A group of concerned physicists, gathered to guarantee conservation goals, would be confused. But conservation in biology is both natural law and moral duty. The law of life is do or die, and that never fails to be true. Yet conservation often fails; in the end, when organisms die, it always fails, although life in the species lineage overleaps death and continues generation to generation. Even species go extinct, so that conservation fails in the species line; but many species are conserved by passing over into something else. That carries on, unfailingly, the story of life over the millennia.

Biology can mean two different things. On the one hand, it can refer to the science that humans have produced; this appears in textbooks, as in theories of kin selection. Such biology goes on during laboratory exercises and field trips. This is a subjective affair in human heads. Take away humans, and biology, like the other sciences, disappears. On the other hand, biology can also refer to the life metabolisms that appeared on Earth long before humans. Such biology is an objective affair out there in the world. Take away humans, and this nonhuman biology remains. Biology in the latter sense is primary, and on it biology in the former, secondary sense depends. In the primary sense, biology without conservation is impossible, a contradiction in terms, a condition that can exist in the actual world only temporarily, since it will be self-defeating and selected against. Biology without conservation is death.

Unlike physics, where conservation is true willy-nilly all over the universe, conservation in biology has to defend a local, Earthbound self-organization. This difference introduces alternatives into biology. When humans appear, this further introduces options and moral decisions. Now biologists, and other residents on Earth as well, who study and appreciate the objective story of life, can and ought to become conservation biologists. The life conservation process took place independently of humans for billions of years, but today we know that this ancient life process can be lost by human misdoing, and we would be wise to worry about it.

2. INTRINSIC, INSTRUMENTAL, SYSTEMIC VALUES

"What good is at stake here?" Broadly, two different philosophical perspectives are possible when a valuing agent (a valuer) encounters an x in the world: (a) what is x good for? and (b) what is x's own good? The first is a question about instrumental value, the second about intrinsic value (Callicott 1992a). That is true when we confront persons. What is Sally good for? She can serve as a cook or legislator. What is Sally's good? Her well-being of body and mind, the meaning she finds in life. This is true, in comparative ways, when we encounter animals and plants, and even species and ecosystems, though we shall need to add, interpreting the latter, a concept of systemic value as well.

Beyond dispute, animals and plants defend a good of their own, and use resources to do so. Warblers preserve their own lives, and make more warblers; they consume (and regulate) insects and avoid raptors. They have connections in their ecosystems that go on "over their heads," but what is "in their heads" (and in their genes) is that being a warbler is a good thing. Organisms have their standards. They promote their own realization, at the same time that they track an environment. They have a technique, know-how. Every organism has a *good-of-its-own*; it defends its kind as a *good kind*. To know what a kind is is also to know what a good-of-that-kind is. As soon as one knows what a yellow-rumped warbler is, one knows what a good yellow-rumped warbler is. One knows the biological identity sought and conserved.

A genetic set is a sort of language that urges a defense of life: a *propositional set*, to choose a deliberately provocative term, mixing biology and philosophy, and recalling how the Latin *propositum* is an assertion, a set task, a theme, a plan, a proposal, a project, as well as a cognitive statement. From this it is also a *motivational set*, unlike human written material, since these life motifs are set to drive the movement from genotypic potential to phenotypic expression. No book is self-actualizing. But, given a chance, these molecules seek organic self-expression. They project a life way and claim the other as needs may be, an assertive claim. Unlike the physical rock, existing on its own and making no claims on its environment, coyotes must eat. The biological organism must claim the environment as source and sink, from which to abstract energy and materials and into which to excrete them. It "takes advantage" of its environment. Life thus arises out of earthen sources (as do rocks), but life turns back on its sources to make resources out of them (unlike rocks).

DNA is thus a *logical set*, not less than a *bio-logical* set. Coding the logic of a life that is carried on not only at the molecular, genetic level but equally at the native-range, environmental, phenotypic level, organisms by a sort of symbolic logic make these molecular positions and shapes into symbols of life. The novel resourcefulness lies in the epistemic content conserved, developed, and thrown forward to make biological resources out of the physicochemical sources. An open cybernetic system, with an executive steering core, is partly a special kind of cause-and-effect system, and partly something more: a historical information system discovering ends so as to make a way through the world, a system of significances valuing operations, pursuits, resources.

Even stronger still, the genetic set is a *normative set*; it distinguishes between what *is* and what *ought to be*. The organism has a biological obligation thrust upon it. This does not mean that the organism is a moral system, or has options, preferences among which it may choose. Those are levels of value reached only much later, dramatically in humans. Nevertheless, the organism is an axiological, evaluative system. So the organism grows, reproduces, repairs its wounds, and resists death. The physical state that the organism seeks, idealized as its programmatic form, is a valued state. The living individual, taken as a "point experience" in the interconnecting web of an ecosystem, is per se an intrinsic value.

A life is defended for what it is in itself, without necessary further contributory reference—although, given the structure of all ecosystems, such lives invariably do have further contributory reference. There is intrinsic value when a life is so defended. That is ipso facto value in both the biological and the philosophical senses, intrinsic because it inheres in, has its focus within, the organism itself. Even those who think that nature has only instrumental value (deer are valuable only to be hunted, eaten, watched) think that matters can be better or worse for the living "instrument" (the deer), and this amounts to saying that the alleged nothing-but-an-instrument (the deer) has value on its own.

All such intrinsic value has its place ecosystemically; intrinsic value couples with instrumental value, and this will lead us on, presently, to systemic value. Things do not have their separate natures merely in and for themselves, but they face outward and co-fit into broader natures. Value-in-itself is smeared out to become value-in-togetherness. Value seeps out into the system, and we lose our capacity to identify the individual as the sole locus of value. Intrinsic value, that of an individual "for what it is in itself," becomes problematic in a holistic web. True, the system increasingly produces such values with its evolution of individuality and freedom. Yet to decouple this from the biotic, communal system is to make value too internal and elementary; this neglects relatedness and externality. Every intrinsic value has leading and trailing *ands* pointing to value from which it comes and toward which it moves. Adapted fitness makes individualistic value too system-independent. Intrinsic value is a part in a whole, not to be fragmented by valuing it in isolation. Everything is good in a role, in a whole, although we can speak of objective intrinsic goodness wherever a point event—a trillium—defends a good (its life) in itself.

When eaten by foragers or in death resorbed into humus, the trillium has its value destroyed, transformed into instrumentality. The system is a value transformer where form and being, process and reality, fact and value are inseparably joined. Intrinsic and instrumental values shuttle back and forth, parts-in-wholes and wholes-in-parts, local details of value embedded in global structures, gems in their settings, and their setting-situation a corporation where value cannot stand alone. Every good is in community. So we have to keep intrinsic values networked; they are not absolute but exist as points of focus within relation. The "for what it is in itself" emphasis, the self-actualizing character of such value cannot forget relatedness.

Intrinsic value, unchecked, wants to be independent; but environmental values are interdependent. Intrinsic value tells us to look at the thing itself, as we ought to do; environmental value tells us to always look further afield, as we also must do. Intrinsic values cannot be supposed to possess and retain their value without reference to anything else. We may say that a tiger has intrinsic value for what it is in itself, but if we were to transport a tiger to the moon, would this intrinsic value remain? No, because the tiger does not have any intrinsic value that it can, all by itself, take to the moon; the tiger is what it is where it is, in the jungle, and that means that the question of intrinsic value has to stay located in its appropriate place. It belongs with the storied achievement and the site integrity, in the wilderness, to which we come in the next sections. It belongs on the home planet (see chapter 7).

So there are no intrinsic values without contributory instrumentality, beneath, above, behind, and before. Every biological intrinsic value must figure into the picture of a satisfactory fit. Biological intrinsic value requires ownership, but it cannot survive isolation. A tiger is what it is in the jungle; a tiger relocated on the moon (or in a zoo) is a tiger no more. Intrinsic value is always in a web that connects with others; value explanations never stop but keep on moving. The tiger, valued for what it is in itself, is at the top of a trophic food pyramid that moves downward through gazelles, grass, microbes, and which requires the rainfall, meteorological, geomorphic, and erosional cycles that produce the soil, and so on. The inquiry about value connections never stops.

Holism and self-sufficiency are thesis and antithesis that form a synthesis. Holism is plural enough both to permit and to require selves that have to be defended, knots in the network, organismic lives in the community, and these selves defend their own lives for what they are in themselves and not for the sake of the other lives to which they contribute. A warbler does not eat insects in order to regulate them, although she serves that role. A warbler neither eats insects, maintaining itself, nor makes other warblers in order to make food for raptors, even though she and some of her offspring may be so eaten. The value of the whole does not wash out the value of the individual. That the selves have to be integrated into community does not mean that they cease to be selves. A concept of intrinsic value insists on being discriminating about individuals. Every organism is a bounded particular, with skin, membranes, bark; even colonial and clonal organisms have edges and boundaries. The biological conservation that goes on in the world is vitally of individual lives.

So we insist on both instrumental and intrinsic natural values. But we also need to form a proper evaluation of the system in which individuals and species are embedded. The traditional concepts of instrumental and intrinsic value are incomplete, not false, but truths that need to be set in a more comprehensive picture, that of ecosystems and of the home planet Earth.

Ecosystems generate and support life, keep selection pressures high, enrich situated fitness, evolve congruent kinds in their places with sufficient containment. Can an ecosystem be a valuer? Is an ecosystem valuable, value-able? Is it able to value? Of course the system is valuable instrumentally to other valuers able to find their life support within it. It is valuable for the roles and relations it sustains. In that sense, ecosystems are as important, and as valuable, as organisms. How are we to insist on the value of these relationships? Simply as an equilibrating system of instrumental and intrinsic values? Predator and prey, parasite and host, grazer and grazed are contending forces in dynamic process where the well-being of each is bound up with the other—coordinated (orders that couple together) as much as heart and liver are coordinated organically. The ecosystem supplies the coordinates through which each organism moves, outside which the species cannot really be located.

To look at one level for what is appropriate at another makes a category mistake. So we cannot look for a single center or program in ecosystems, much less for subjective experiences, that might form the center of value. We do not look for a valuer, but rather for the ability to form value. We look for a matrix, for interconnections between centers of value (individual plants and animals, dynamic lines of speciation), for creative stimulus and open-ended potential. We look for a system able to produce and support value, and ask whether that ability is a value in itself, and also a value for those it produces and supports.

Organisms value and defend only their selves, with species increasing their numbers. But the evolutionary ecosystem spins a bigger story, limiting each kind, locking it into the welfare of others, promoting new arrivals, increasing kinds and the integration of kinds. Species increase their kind; but ecosystems increase kinds, superposing the latter increase onto the former. Ecosystems are selective systems, as surely as organisms are selective systems. The natural selection comes out of the system and is imposed on the individual. The individual is programmed to make more of its kind, but more is going on systemically than that; the system is making more kinds.

Communal processes—the competition between organisms, more or less probable events, plant and animal successions, speciation over historical time—generate an ever-richer community. Hence the evolutionary toil, elaborating and diversifying the biota, that once began with no species and results today in five to ten million species, increasing over time the quality of lives in the upper rungs of the tropic pyramids. Ecosystems have been the fountain of the diversity, the complexity, the richness, the integrity we have been celebrating.

Instrumental value uses something as a means to an end; *intrinsic value* is worthwhile in itself. A warbler eats insects instrumentally as a food resource; the warbler defends her own life as an end in itself and makes more warblers as she can. A life is defended intrinsically, without further contributory reference. But neither of these traditional terms is satisfactory at the level of the ecosystem. Though it has value *in* itself, the system does not have any value *for* itself. Though a value producer, it is not a value owner. We are no longer confronting instrumental value, as though the system were of value instrumentally as a fountain of life. Nor is the question one of intrinsic value, as though the system defended some unified form of life for itself. We have reached something for which we need a third term: *systemic value*. Duties arise in encounter with the system that projects and protects these member components in biotic community.

Ethical conservatives, in the humanist sense, will say that ecosystems are of value only because they contribute to human experiences. They will put humans at the center of concerns. But that mistakes the last chapter, perhaps the climaxing concern, for the concerns of the whole story, as though there were no concerns except those in center focus. Humans count enough to have the right to flourish here on Earth, but not so much that we have the right to degrade or shut down ecosystems, not at least without a burden of proof that there is an overriding cultural gain. Ethical conservatives, in the biocentric sense, will say that ecosystems are of value because they contribute to animal experiences or to organismic life. But the really conservative ecological view sees that the stability, integrity, and beauty of biotic communities is what is most fundamentally to be conserved. That is, in fact, where the real value-ability—the ability to produce value—arises, and not as we in our anthropocentric or anthropogenic arrogance might say, when we arrive on the scene to assign and project value there. Making the fallacy of misplaced values, that is like dipping water at a fountain of life, watering a lush land, and, then, valuing the water and the fountain instrumentally, and commenting that nothing was of value until I came. Valuing the products but not the system able to produce these products is like finding a goose that lays golden eggs and valuing the eggs but not the goose.

3. STORIED ACHIEVEMENT

The value is flowing from the storied system. Though there is no *Nature* in the singular, and not some one valuer, the system has a nature, a loading that pluralizes, putting *natures* into diverse kinds, $nature_1$, $nature_2$, $nature_3$ . . . $nature_n$. Some natural kinds are inorganic, such as minerals or geomorphic features. Some are biological species. The natural system constructs these diverse kinds on the basis of possibilities inherent within it. This creation requires natural laws, giving stability, which are mingled with random elements, giving spontaneity, thus spinning diversity with its unity. An ecosystem has no head, but it has a "heading" for species diversification, support, and richness.

Astronomical nature and micronature, profound as they are, are nature-in-the-simple. At both ends of the spectrum of size, nature lacks the complexity that it demonstrates at the meso-levels, found in earthbound ecosystems. We encounter advanced forms of natural organization only at the middle ranges. On a gross cosmic scale, Earth's fauna and flora, including humans, are minuscule. The universe is staggeringly lavish in its size and within it matter is very rarefied. But matter also condenses into fascinating formations, the rarest, most impressive, and most complex of which are life and mind.

Dynamic form is the magic of the universe, and on Earth this dynamism takes historical form. On other planets, so far as we know, there is little story, although they too have their astronomical records—events in their physics and chemistries. Earth adds biology and natural history; there is a cumulative historical evolution, coded in genes, lived out in each new generation, with novel mutants, producing new chapters in the history. Earth adds cultural history, and now the story is stored in cumulative transmissible cultures, within which persons choose their careers and have their adventures, form their nations and cultures, live out their biographies, and write new chapters in the story.

The logic of life on Earth, in that sense, is biography emplaced in geography. The etymology of "bio-graphy" is to graph a life, the etymology of "geo-graphy" is to graph that life on Earth. "Biology" is the logic of life; and, in that sense, the idea of "graphing," drawing out a world line, biography, is more historical, better catching the logic of biology. Life is not a timeless syllogism; all life, including human life, on Earth has to be distributed some place on Earth. *Geology* is the logic of the Earth; *geomorphology* is the dynamism of form on Earth, especially its landscapes. Even the latter is historical, although often repetitive; mountain-building followed by erosion, orogeny, and degradation, cycles after cycles. Superimposed on Earth's nomothetic features is a unique, one-way, irreversible history, the idiographic story of natural history. The logic of Earth, comprehensively, includes biology, biography, human psychology, sociology, and history. Life is always taking a journey through time and place.

Nature generates; that is the root meaning of "nature," "to give birth." Nature launches life, which is embodied in individuals who are embedded in ecologies, which in turn undergo evolutionary history. Prehuman nature is already historical in form. At long ranges, over millennia, evolutionary ecosystems have been dramatically eventful in spinning stories on Earth that are never twice the same. Only in short-range perception is there seasonal recurrence, recycling, homeostasis, dependable patterns, repeated order. In that sense, words such as *homeostasis, conservation, preservation, stability* are only penultimate in a metaphysics and an ethics of nature, although they are the words with which environmental philosophy was launched. Conservation can only be the conservation of dynamic identity developing through space and time. The ultimate word is "history."

Humans awaken to their historical subjectivity in an already historically objective world. The genome is a historical genetic set. Plants and animals are historical beings objectively, although they do not know this subjectively. Plants and animals do not know their own stories. Some animals have memories; so that animal life may have precursors of historical consciousness, but animals make no reflection on their historical character. Humans are the only species that can become self-conscious historians, or biologists, or geographers, who can reflect over the history of life on Earth.

The story of applied science has been one of learning to remake the world in human interests, to use it resourcefully; but the story of pure science has been one of discovering the nature of nature, learning the natural history of our sources. Early science thought this nature to be lawlike and repetitive but recent science has learned the evolutionary Earth history. And life is still arriving. Earth is not so much a syllogism with premises and conclusions, as it is a text to be interpreted. Like the books in our libraries, the landscapes are to be read, palimpsests of the past. We have become aware of the deep time and deep history that lie behind and around us. Biological science has cleverly deciphered much of the past; it reads the historically produced landscape, as well as the records left in the biomolecular genetic coding.

But bioscience can present little theoretical argument explaining this history—little logic (tracking causes) by which there came to be a primeval Earth, Precambrian protozoans, Cambrian trilobites, Triassic dinosaurs, Eocene mammals, Pliocene primates, eventuating in Pleistocene *Homo sapiens*. No theory exists, with initial conditions, from which these follow as conclusions. And bioscience can predict little of future natural history. To the contrary, from the viewpoint of the best available theory—that of natural selection with its descriptions how, and demands that, the fittest survive—the whole odyssey seems some hybrid between a random walk and a tautology. Evolutionary theory neither predicts outcomes, nor, looking back after the outcomes are known, retrodicts why this course of events occurred rather than thousands of others equally consistent with the theory.

Likewise, passing from science to ethics, philosophy can present no argument why these stories ought to have taken place. The most that we can discover is good stories, and that is what we have to learn to value. We may even come to love the epic, and prefer narrative over argument, over some theory by which natural history would follow as an inevitable conclusion, or even a statistically probable one. In that sense, neither science nor philosophy can present an argument that either necessitates or justifies the existence of each (or any!) of the five million species with which we coinhabit Earth. Nor is there any argument that, given the existence of each (or any!) of these species, conclusively necessitates or justifies their value. But we can begin to sketch nesting sets of marvelous tales. There is no logical calculus with which to defend the existence of elephants or lotus flowers, squids or lemurs; but each in its niche enriches Earth's story. That alone is enough to justify their existence.

If we now ask what is the value of nature, the answer must lie in these systemic powers. We perhaps do not want to say that nature is a valuer, for that is too individualistic. We might incline to say that the system cannot be of value to itself, or for itself, because it does not have any norms. It does not have any concerns. Not even plants, much less places, much less planets can be concerned for themselves. Meanwhile, the system does have fecundity, creativity. The system has no self, but it is nevertheless self-organizing. Spontaneously, of itself, it organizes natural history, and it fills that natural history with organismic selves, each also self-organizing. That is certainly the most impressive feature of Earth; it would be the main plot in any report on Earth that space visitors might write. This is what we call its systemic value.

In practice the ultimate challenge of environmental ethics is the conservation of life on Earth. In principle, the challenge is a value theory profound enough to support that ethic. In nature there is negentropic construction in dialectic with entropic teardown, a process for which we hardly yet have an adequate scientific, much less valuational theory. Yet this is nature's most striking feature, one that ultimately must be valued and of value. In one sense nature is indifferent to mountains, rivers, fauna, flora, forests, and grasslands. But in another sense nature has bent toward making and remaking these projects, millions of kinds, for several billion years. These performances are worth noticing—remarkable, memorable—and not just because of their tendencies to produce a noticing in certain recent subjects—our human selves. The splendors of Earth do not simply lie in their roles as human resources, supports of culture, or stimulators of experience The most plausible account will find some programmatic evolution toward value.

How do we humans come to be charged up with values, if there was and is nothing in nature charging us up so? A systematic environmental ethics does not wish to believe in the special creation of values, nor in their dumbfounding epigenesis—at the moment that humans appear on the scene. It discovers that values have evolved out of a systemically valuable nature.

4. INTEGRITY OF PLACE

Life is not the only criterion of value. Those who framed the 1959 Antarctic Treaty were concerned with preserving Antarctica's scientific value, with preserving its hardy fauna and flora, even though the Antarctic is rather lifeless. They were not at all concerned with tourism. The negotiators of the treaty, however, felt an awe for the physiographic region, for the fact that, on the entire Earth, it was the area least touched by human intervention, and they wanted it to stay that way (Stone 1987:95–96). There is something about the place that they did not want to spoil.

President Theodore Roosevelt exclaimed before the Grand Canyon: "Leave it as it is. You cannot improve on it. The ages have been at work on it, and man can only mar it." He no doubt wanted to conserve the plants and animals there, but his concern also was for the Grand Canyon as a remarkable place. In Mammoth Cave, in a section named Turner Avenue, there are rooms laden with gypsum crystals spun as fine threads, a rare formation known as "angel hair." So fragile are these needles that humans passing through and disturbing the air can destroy the hair-thin filaments. This part of the cave is closed to tourists, and only on exceptional occasions open to speleologists for scientific study. A nonbiotic work of nature is here protected at the cost of depriving humans of access to it. This park policy is partly for humanistic reasons (to preserve angel hair for scientific research). But it also involves an appreciation of angel hair as a phenomenon of systemic nature. Angel hair has objective value in the sense that it here lays a claim on human behavior.

We do not really want to say that the only value in the system is its production of life, although this is of greatest moment within it. Nature is not inert and passive until acted upon resourcefully by life and mind. Neither sentience nor consciousness, nor even life, is necessary for inventive processes to occur. Nonbiotic things have no information in them, no genome, much less sentience or experience. There are no cells, no organs, no skin, no metabolisms. Impressed with the display of life and personality on Earth, we correctly attach most of our ethical concern to persons and to organisms; but we may incorrectly assume that mere things are beyond appropriate and inappropriate consideration for conservation, for what they are in themselves.

A "mere thing" can, however, be something to be respected, the project of a creative nature. Crystals, volcanoes, geysers, headlands, rivers, springs, moons, cirques, paternoster lakes, buttes, mesas, canyons—these also are among the natural kinds. They do not have organic integrity or individuality. They are constantly being built, altered, and their identity in flux. But they are recognizably different from their background and surroundings. They may have striking particularity, symmetry, harmony, grace, spatiotemporal unity and continuity, even though they are also diffuse, partial, broken. They do not have wills or interests, but rather headings, trajectories, traits, successions, beginnings, endings, cycles, which give them a tectonic integrity. The question now is not whether these things can suffer, nor whether they have lives they defend, nor whether they have interests or concerns. The question is: what deserves appreciation?

Natural places can be loci of value so far as they are products of systemic nature in its formative processes. The opening movements of a symphony contribute to the power of the finale, but they are not merely of instrumental value; they are of value for what they are in themselves. The splendors of the heavens and the marvels of Earth do not simply lie in their roles as a fertilizer for life, or a stimulator of experience. There is value wherever there is creativity.

It was once the practice in Yellowstone National Park to put soap into certain geysers (altering the surface tension of the water) in order to time the eruptions conveniently for tourists. For almost a century, the Park Service at Yosemite built an enormous fire on the lip of Glacier Point at dusk. "Indian Love Call" was played and the fire pushed over the cliff to the "ahs!" of spectators. But the spectacle has now been discontinued as inappropriate. Bridges, simply for amusement, have been built defacing Royal Gorge in Colorado and Grandfather Mountain in North Carolina. Highways were built to the 14,000-foot summits of Colorado's Mount Evans and Pike's Peak. George Washington carved his initials in rock on Virginia's Natural Bridge and left his signature in Madison's Cave at Grand Caverns, as did hundreds of others, including Thomas Jefferson and James Madison.

Walter De Maria used a bulldozer to cut *The Circumflex*, a shallow trench over a mile long in a desert wilderness (privately owned), cut in the shape of a loop in a rope. Michael Heizer built *Complex One*, a rectangular mound 23 feet high, 140 feet long, of concrete and earth in an otherwise untouched, extremely remote, high desert plateau. Mount Rushmore, South Dakota, has been carved into a monument to national pride (with Washington's and Jefferson's faces), and has provoked a response at nearby Crazy Horse, a (partially completed) mountain-sized Indian on his horse. Stone Mountain, Georgia, is a monument to the old South.

But we may not want any more summit roads up fourteeners, or fun bridges over gorges, or carved-up mountains, firefalls, soap in geysers, names written over rock cliffs or stalagmites, or circumflexes bulldozed into the desert wilderness, because a developing environmental ethics insists that there is a better way to behave at these places, one that recognizes their site integrity. We will leave the pyramids on the sands of Egypt for historic reasons but oppose carving President Reagan's face on Yosemite's Half Dome. We will say that humans can have no duties to clouds or dust devils, even though these are temporary aggregations with enough identity for us to say where they start and stop. They have little integrated process in them. But then again, toward other projects in nature there is inappropriately responsive behavior.

There are no valuers here, until humans arrive, or until some animal or plant arrives. But is there value? It is as reasonable to say that such objective achievements of the natural system are of value in themselves as to say that the only value is subjective human excellence generated in the presence of nature's wonders. We might think of these places as a kind of wonderland. But does the value in a wonderland arise only when the wonderer arrives? Can there be a wonderland without a wonderer? If so, we might want to reappraise whether there can be value without a valuer.

5. WILDERNESS

Wilderness combines the integrity of physiographic place with the natural history of such place, in counterpoint to the presence of human beings.

> A wilderness, in contrast with those areas where man and his own works dominate the landscape, is hereby recognized as an area where the earth and its community of life are untrammeled by man, where man himself is a visitor who does not remain. An area of wilderness is further defined to mean . . . [an area] retaining its primeval character and influence, without permanent improvements or human habitation, which is . . . primarily affected by the

forces of nature, with the imprint of man's work substantially unnoticeable. (U.S. Congress 1964, sec. 2[c])

Congress has designated nearly five hundred such wilderness areas, totaling some ninety-one million acres in forty-four states. Similarly, five other nations have so legislated wilderness areas: Canada, Zimbabwe, South Africa, Australia, and New Zealand. Further, over half the nations in the world have protected areas that they regard, more or less, as wildlands (Hendee, Stankey, and Lucas 1990).

In a way, the "wilderness movement" is a particularly twentieth-century idea and ideal, which began in such nations as the United States, South Africa, and Australia, and developed impressively during the century. John Muir founded the Sierra Club in 1892. Aldo Leopold persuaded the U.S. Forest Service to set aside the Gila Wilderness in New Mexico as a "primitive area" in 1924; in 1935 he founded the Wilderness Society. Congress began enacting legislation in 1964. At the same time, the "wilderness" that this recent movement seeks to preserve is primeval wildland, as it was and is without humans at all. Wilderness is, on the one hand, a cultural ideal; yet on the other, primitive nature is spontaneous nature that runs itself.

Wilderness is an exclusive word, holding nature apart from any reconstruction by human hands, outside the human orbit and control. An often-given reason for saving it, politically and scientifically important, is as a baseline from which to understand human interruptions of nature elsewhere on the landscape—a control for studying ecosystem health. "Paleontology offers abundant evidence that wilderness maintained itself for immensely long periods; that its component species were rarely lost, neither did they get out of hand; that weather and water built soil as fast or faster than it was carried away." That is why "wilderness . . . assumes unexpected importance as a laboratory for the study of land health" (Leopold 1968 [1949]:196). Wilderness is watershed, game refuge, gene pool, sink for CO_2, escape from civilization, recreational theater or gymnasium, scientific laboratory, historical museum, place for solitude, tourism booster, and so on.

At more depth, the reasons become increasingly moral, philosophical, religious. "Wilderness was an adversary to the pioneer. But to the laborer in repose, able for the moment to cast a philosophical eye on his world, that same raw stuff is something to be loved and cherished, because it gives definition and meaning to his life" (Leopold 1968 [1949]:188). Leopold does not mean that wilderness is only a resource for personal development. He means that we humans never know who we are or where we are until we respect our wild origins and our wild neighbors on this home planet. We never get our human values straight until we also value wilderness appropriately.

Those who value wilderness, when they gain this sense of proportion and perspective, insist that there are intrinsic wild values that are not human values. These ought to be preserved for whatever they can contribute to human values, but they ought to be preserved because they are valuable in and for themselves. Just because the human presence is so radically different, humans ought to draw back and let nature be. Humans can and ought to see outside their own sector and affirm nonanthropogenic, noncultural values. Only humans have the cognitive power to erect cultures that destroy wilderness. Humans must, and ought, destroy wilderness when they build culture; neither agricultural nor urban lands can be wilderness. At the same time, only humans have a conscience. That conscience emerges for the building of culture, to relate humans to other humans with justice and love, but it also emerges for the relating of humans to nature, to the larger community of life on the planet. That relationship, governed by conscience (and also by pragmatic self-interest), requires a harmonious blending of nature and culture, where this is possible. And conscience also generates a duty to respect wild nature at some times and places enough to leave it untrammeled.

In that sense the so-called American concept of wilderness is not an ideal or duty at national option. Actually it is not even peculiarly American because the same ideal arose in other places, such as South Africa. Whatever its origins, the ideal must be a global one, which some Americans were able to carry out politically in sparsely settled parts of their continent. Wilderness may no longer be possible in highly settled countries (France or Holland), but it is nevertheless there too an ideal because, in retrospect, it would have been better for such countries had they set aside wilderness areas. "Ought" implies "can," so that one cannot now urge wilderness on those who have none to conserve; but also what one might once have done, but failed to do, is relevant in assessing duties and values. Wilderness is not nation-specific as an ideal, though it is nation-specific as to feasibility.

Well-settled countries ought even yet, so far as they can, set aside wilderness remnants and restore remaining semi-wild lands. Wilderness can return (in senses examined in chapter 3, sec. 5). Wilderness is not an ethnocentric ideal (an option peculiar to American culture); it is a universal ideal, even when the opportunity to do so has already been lost. Wilderness conservation is a good thing to do in any culture; it would be good to do so even if all cultures thought otherwise. And many nations in the world can and ought to set aside wilderness.*

Wilderness, when set aside, has to be managed, and that idea requires some philosophical examination. Wilderness management, on the face of it, appears to be a contradiction in terms. A scientifically managed wilderness is conceptually as impossible as wildlife in a zoo. Does not any attempt at management intent spoil the wildness? Yet there needs to be management—or at least education and monitoring—of the humans who visit the wilderness. There needs to be trail building, maintenance, restorative practices, monitoring of the processes protected. If the wilderness is too small to be a viable ecosystem, there will need to be management at the boundaries and buffers.

What of the claim that true wilderness is impossible, because there are no landscapes unaffected by humans? The definition of wilderness, we recall, uses rather the term "untrammeled," and so effects of humans do not make wilderness impossible, provided that the land yet "retains its primeval character and influence, without permanent improvements or human habitation." That makes wilderness impossible over most of the landscape, but does it make this everywhere impossible? Some say that there is no real wilderness left today in the New World, subsequently to the last five hundred years of European cultural invasion, none now. An even stronger claim is that the aboriginals had already extinguished wilderness, that wherever there has been human habitation true wilderness is not possible. Therefore,

---

* For an attack on the idea(l) of wilderness, see Callicott 1991. According to him, the wilderness concept is triply flawed. It metaphysically and unscientifically dichotomizes humans and nature. Further, it is ethnocentric, because it does not realize that practically all the world's ecosystems were modified by aboriginal peoples. It is static, ignoring change through time. Humans, themselves entirely natural, ought to reside in and improve wild nature, conserving wilderness as refugia for this enhancement. For a reply see Rolston 1991.

there was no wilderness remaining even when Columbus arrived in 1492 (Thompson and Smith 1971; Gómez-Pompa and Kaus 1992).

How much did native Americans modify the landscape? That is an empirical question, and philosophers have no particular competence at answering it.[*] This is partly an ecological question, whether ecosystems were thrown out of balance. But it is also in part an anthropological question, about what were the practices of pre-Columbian native peoples. Indian cultures altered the locales in which they resided, more so in Central America, less so in portions of North America, variously in South America. In that respect, Indian culture was not different in kind from the European culture. They too had areas that were urban, rural, and wild (chapter 1, sec. 4), their villages, some lands they planted or otherwise managed, and lands that they left wild, making little impact on such areas. But the proportion of human space and influence to the world space and natural processes was low, when they had only the muscles of arm and foot to employ, as well as less knowledge and perhaps desire than we for the radical alteration of landscapes. What is important to know is the degree to which the landscape was altered and the difference in approach between native and European cultures. Did the Indians transform the pre-Indian wilderness (beginning perhaps as early as 15,000 B.C.) on regional scales beyond the range of its spontaneous self-restoration?

Most of what has been designated as U.S. wilderness was infrequently used by the aborigines, since it is high, cold, arid, and often difficult to traverse on foot. The Indians, too, were visitors who did not remain—for the same reasons that the whites after them left those regions sparsely settled. We have little reason to think that in such areas the aboriginal modifications are irreversible. What about the more temperate areas? Were they modified so extensively and irreversibly that wilderness designation would be an illusion? The North American Indians on forested lands had no horses or cattle; what agriculture they had tended to reset succession; and, when agriculture ceases, the subsequent forest regeneration will not be particularly unnatural. Otherwise they were hunters and gatherers, without irreversible adverse effects.

---

[*] For an excellent summary of wilderness and Indian fires, see Lotan et al. 1985, especially section 3.

The Indian technology for larger landscape modification was bow and arrow, spear, and fire. The only one of these that extensively modifies landscapes is fire. Fire is—we have by now learned—also quite natural. Forests in the Americas have been fire-adapted for at least thirteen million years, since the Miocene epoch of the Tertiary Period, as evidenced by fossil charcoal deposits. The fire process involves fuel build-up over decades, ignition, and subsequent burning for days or weeks; any or all of the three may be natural or unnatural. Fire suppression is therefore unnatural, and can result in unnatural fuel build-up, but no one argues that the Indians used that as a management tool, nor did they have much capacity for suppression. The argument is that they deliberately set fires. Does this make their fires radically different from natural fires? It does in terms of the source of ignition; the one is a result of environmental policy deliberation, the other of a lightning bolt.

But students of fire behavior realize that in dealing with forest ecosystems on regional scales the source of ignition is not a particularly critical factor. Once the fire has burned a hundred yards, the vegetation cannot tell what the source of ignition was. The question is whether the forest is *ready* to burn, whether there is sufficient ground fuel to sustain the fire, whether the trees are diseased, how much duff there is, and so on. If conditions are not right, it will be difficult to get a big fire going; it will soon burn out. If conditions are right, a human can start a regional fire this year. If not, lightning will start it next year, or the year after that.* On a typical summer day, the states of Arizona and New Mexico are each hit by several thousand bolts of lightning, mostly in the higher, forested regions. On average, the U.S. landscape is hit by 50 million bolts a year, or ten strikes for each square mile (Krider 1986). Lightning ignites about 10,000 fires each year. Doubtless the Indians started some fires too, but it is hard to think that their fires, centuries ago, so dramatically and irreversibly altered the natural fire regime that meaningful wilderness designation is today impossible. Natural ignition sources are available on an order of magnitude (a few years) that greatly exceeds the order of magnitude of fuel build-up for burning (several decades).

---

* "If the area is ready to burn, it makes little difference...whether the fire is set by lightning, by an Indian, or by [a park scientist],...so long as the result approximates the goal of perpetuating a natural community" (A. Starker Leopold, as quoted in Lotan et al. 1985:65).

Grasslands differ in that fuel becomes available annually for a burn. Fires can retain grasslands that, unburnt, would revert first to shrubland and then to forests. The frequent fires prevent the shrubs and trees from getting started. This happens naturally in the Midwest where the forests transpose to grasslands and lightning is frequent. In some grasslands situations, the Indians might have augmented ignition relative to fuel availability, and burned unnaturally often. There is good reason to think that the Indians could sustain some grassland openings on a modest scale. This merely shifts succession toward earlier stages, and, released from Indian burning, such lands resume their natural succession. Meanwhile, there is no reason to think that the Indians by deliberate fire policy really modified the regional grasslands ecology of the vast American West. Also, of course, few grasslands have been designated as wilderness.

In short, though the Indians lived on the landscape, there was much of it that they too only visited. Most of the land that they hunted over on was relatively untrammeled by them. And even the lands that they did manage were not managed outside their resilient capacity to return to natural landscapes, when the Indian interventions are removed.

When we designate wilderness, if humans are residents, must they leave? Since all wilderness in the United States lies on public lands, that question has seldom been faced. It has been faced, however, with the designation of national parks. When faced, the answer is yes, though such relocation can be assisted and can perhaps be over decades. Outside the United States, where wilderness designation is possible and where there is an exploding population, what should we do? Constraining an explosion takes some strong measures.

Here again indigenous peoples, transient in their residence, may only visit such areas themselves, or leave them relatively untrammeled, without permanent improvements and with the works of humans substantially unnoticeable. There are various semi-wilderness designations (such as extractive or game reserves) that may be more appropriate than wilderness in any pristine sense. Nevertheless, wilderness is an ideal, and, where possible, remains a duty in environmental ethics, subject always to the weights of other duties as well. We have already seen that society does ask persons to relocate or to restrain their development if they remain in certain protected locations. The peoples in such wildernesses need to be "wilderness peoples," nonagrarian, hunters, gatherers. They cannot be "developed." Any people who are developable are movable (see chapter 5, sec. 4).

Just those developed nations with little opportunity to preserve wilderness ought to be zealous about what opportunity they do have. Where there is not yet designated wilderness, people ought to be more, not less, disposed to inconvenience themselves. Otherwise a quite considerable opportunity will be lost. Those citizens will have no opportunity, inside their own national boundaries, for experiencing large-scale pristine nature, deep time, and regional wildness. Wilderness is sometimes said to be a luxury for the rich, although there is no particular evidence that the persons who visit it are among the wealthy. To the contrary, we will almost always find that the rich are those whose expansionist desires and whose inequitably large share of the produce of lands is forcing the poor onto wildlands, lands that these poor have no particular desire to lay waste.

Wilderness is said to be a "lock-up" use, contrasted with multiple use, the latter praised as a good thing, the former deplored because wilderness goes unused. But wilderness designation does not remove land from access for wilderness purposes, though it does prevent the multiple uses (often the multiple abuses) that make wilderness impossible. No one is locked out of wilderness, if they are prepared to come on wilderness terms. (Where there are crowds, wilderness sometimes has to be rationed to prevent its destruction.) Wilderness designations open up access; this permits access over many generations to come and to all comers. Designation prevents taking possession of property there (ores, wildlife, timber, forage, water) and removing private goods at public loss. Therefore, wilderness designation is not a lock-up use but prevents takeover, consumptive use. It makes the commons comprehensive in the fullest sense—not a commons for people only, but for squirrels and trilliums as well.

On Earth, man is not a visitor who does not remain; this is our home planet and we belong here. Humans too have an ecology, and we are permitted interference with, and rearrangement of, nature's spontaneous course; otherwise there is no culture. But there are, and should be, places on Earth where the nonhuman community of life is untrammeled by man, where we only visit. Leopold pleads, "I am asserting . . . that while the reduction of wilderness has been a good thing, its extermination would be a very bad one, and that the conservation of wilderness is the most urgent and difficult of all the tasks that confront us" (quoted in Meine 1988:245).

6. OBJECTIVE AND SUBJECTIVE NATURAL VALUE

There is no value without an evaluator. So runs a well-entrenched dogma. Humans are the obvious—some say the only—value holders. William James starkly portrays the utterly valueless world, suddenly transfigured as a gift of the human coming:

> Conceive yourself, if possible, suddenly stripped of all the emotions with which your world now inspires you, and try to imagine it *as it exists*, purely by itself, without your favorable or unfavorable, hopeful or apprehensive comment. It will be almost impossible for you to realize such a condition of negativity and deadness. No one portion of the universe would then have importance beyond another; and the whole collection of things and series of its events would be without significance, character, expression, or perspective. Whatever of value, interest, or meaning our respective worlds may appear imbued with are thus pure gifts of the spectator's mind. (1925:150)

Ralph Barton Perry, outlining a general theory of value, continues:

> Natural substances . . . are without value until a use is found for them, whereupon their value may increase to any desired degree of preciousness according to the eagerness with which they are coveted. . . . Any object, whatever it be, acquires value when any interest, whatever it be, is taken in it. (1954 [1926]:125, 115–116)

If value arrives only with consciousness, experiences where humans find value in nature have to be dealt with as appearances of various sorts. The value has to be relocated in the valuing subject's creativity as a person meets a valueless world, or even a valuable one—one *able* to be *valued*—but which before the human bringing of value ability contains only possibility and not any actual value. Value can only be extrinsic to nature, never intrinsic to it (recall chapter 5, sec. 6, and anthropogenic values).

That position seems almost a solipsism on the level of the human species of value. Solipsists (that only I exist) are notoriously hard to argue with, and notoriously unconvincing. Similarly with a solipsism of value (only I have value), including solipsism at the species level (only we humans have value). Surely a humanism of values is much too strong a claim, for evidently the higher animals can evaluate helps and hurts as they encounter them.

But, granting that, afterward one can—and now rather plausibly it first may seem—still hold on to subjectivism in value. Just as there are no thoughts without a thinker, no percepts without a perceiver, no deeds without a doer, no targets without an aimer, there are no values without a valuer. The mistake was to think that only human subjects can do such preferring; the correct view is that any subject-of-a-life can do so. Values are always subjective, though not always anthropocentric or anthropogenic. Animals too can value their world and their lives, at least the higher animals can.

Plants, by contrast, cannot evaluate their environment; they have no options and make no choices. The lower fauna are like the flora. A fortiori, species and ecosystems, rocks and rivers, wildernesses, Earth and nature cannot be bona fide evaluators. Values can be intrinsic to sentient natural things, but there are no values in insentient lives, because there are no valuers. Values are experienced in coyotes, but not in trees. Nothing matters to a rock. A subject must encounter an object.

The beholder perhaps may not assign the value, but he or she at least admits and receives it. Such value is not entirely at the beholder's option. Photosynthesis or rainfall is thus valuable without a beholder's will, but not yet without his, her, or its awareness. Before the valuer's coming, there are only precursors of value; value does not emerge until these are thickened by the addition of interests, human or animal. David W. Prall concludes: "The being liked or disliked of the object is its value. . . . Some sort of a subject is always requisite to there being value at all" (1921:227).

Can these axiological subjectivists be persuaded otherwise? Yes and no. One can always hang on to the claim that value, like a tickle or remorse, must be felt to be there. Its *esse* is *percipi*. Non-sensed value is nonsense. Such resolute subjectivists cannot be defeated by argument, although they can be driven toward analyticity. That theirs is a retreat to definition is difficult to expose because they seem to cling so closely to inner experience. They are reporting, on this hand, how values always excite us. They are giving, on that hand, a stipulative definition. That is how they choose to use the word *value*.

In contrast with these subjectivist, often anthropocentric or anthropogenic views, we have here been claiming that in an objective account value is already present in nonsentient organisms, which are normative evaluative systems, prior to the emergence of further dimensions of value with sentience. Biology has steadily demonstrated how subjective life is a consequence of objective life, the one always the necessary sponsor of the other. Why not value the whole process with all its product organisms, rather than restrict valuing to the upper level, subjective aspect? Certainly, the emergence of eyes, ears, and cognitive psychological experience is quite a miracle, but why is not the pursuit of vital, though nonconscious self-identity a value event objectively as well?

The tree is *benefiting* from the sunshine and the soil nutrients, and *benefit* is—everywhere else we encounter it—a value word. It seems foolish to say, "The tree is benefiting from the sun and the nutrients, but are those valuable to it?" It seems just as curious to worry, "The tree is defending its life, but is there any value that the tree has on its own?" If *defend* is too teleological a word, then shift the vocabulary: there is biological conservation in plants as well as animals. The DNA is a set of conservation molecules, a genome is a cognitive, propositional, axiological, normative set. Choose what vocabulary you will, each organism preserves its life as a good-of-its-kind.

These good kinds are webbed into ecosystems. Now it may be protested that even if there is objective natural value protected in organisms, the claim (which was doubtful enough before) becomes still more implausible because we have also been supposing an objective systemic value that transcends individual organisms. But the valuing individual, subjective or objective life, in an otherwise valueless system is an insufficient premise for life in an evolutionary ecosystem. Conversion to a biological view seems truer to world experience and more logically compelling. Here the order of knowing reverses—and also enhances—the order of being. This too is a perspective, but ecologically better informed.

Science has been steadily showing how the consequents (life, mind) are built on their precedents (energy, matter), however much they overleap them. Life and mind appear where they did not before exist, and with them levels of value emerge that did not before exist. Yet that gives no reason to say that all value is an irreducible emergent at the human (or upper animal) level. Value increases in the emergent climax, but is continuously present in the composing precedents. The system is value-able, able to produce value. Human evaluators are among its products. Some value depends on subjectivity, yet all value is generated within the geosystemic and ecosystemic pyramids. Systemically, value fades from subjective to objective value, but also fans out from the individual to its role and matrix.

There is value wherever there is creativity. The problem with the "no value without a valuer" axiom is that it is too individualistic; it looks for some center of value located at one focus—preferably evident in some subjective self, since we ourselves are, indisputably, such a valuing self, and, if not there, then arguably in an objective self, such as a plant with its integrating genome. And we here nowhere deny that there are values created by valuers. A valuer is sufficient for value.

But is that the whole account of value? Not in a more holistic, systemic, ecological account. Here the value is not localized but spread out through the entire creative system. Perhaps there can be no doing science without a scientist, no religion without a believer, no tickle without someone who feels the tickle. But there can be law without a lawgiver, history without a historian; there is biology without biologists, physics without physicists, creativity without creators, story without storytellers, achievement without achievers—and value without valuers. Value requires not so much individuals who value, as systems that create. One way for something to be valuable is for there to be a valuer able to evaluate; another way is for there to be a value-generating system able to generate value.

From this more objective viewpoint, there is something naive about living in a reference frame where one species takes itself as absolute and values everything else in nature relative to its utility, thereby placing itself at the center of all values. That, a biologist may insist, is just what goes on in the woods; warblers take a "warblocentric" point of view; spruce push only to make more spruce. Other biologists will also insist, however, that the system takes no such particular points of view but generates myriads of such kinds, the diversity, complexity, and richness that transcends the individuals who compose it.

Humans are the only species who can see an ecosystem for what it is in itself, objectively, a tapestry of interwoven values. Conservation biologists, in addition to saving fauna and flora, can save humans—philosophical subjectivists included—by daily rescue from this beguiling anthropocentrism through a perennial contact with the primeval biological and geomorphic givens. Conservation biology ought to liberate us from a narrow humanism—from putting ourselves at the center; conservation biology ought to help us gain a fuller humanity by transcending merely human interests. It reforms human character in encounter with a value-laden world.

Such values are, it is commonly said, "soft" beside the "hard" values of commerce. They are vague, philosophical, weak, impossible to quantify, argue for, or demonstrate. It may even be said, despite the argument here for their objectivity, that they are "subjective," meaning just a matter of some philosopher's (or romantic scientist's) doubtful opinion—as if economic values were not also matters of opinion, consumers' subjective estimates of what they are willing to pay for various goods. Some of these values are quite hard (the life support that ecosystems provide); some of them are quite scientific (the survival value of an adapted fit). All are quite real, and this means real human experience because also real in nature. Such values are not so much soft as do they lie deep.

A wild forest is something objectively there—without benefit of human subjectivity. Beside it, culture with its artifacts is a tissue of subjective preference satisfactions. Money, for example, counted among the hard values by the economist, is, in the wilderness, nothing at all. It is what it is only by the subjective preferences of humans. What is far more real is that there are natural values, in place before humans arrive, which humans cash in on, and spend. Do not humans sometimes value Earth's life-supporting systems because they are valuable, and not always the other way around?

Is this value just a matter of late-coming human interests? It seems parochial, uninformed ecologically, to say that our part alone in the drama establishes all its worth. Ecology is not something subjective that goes on in the human mind. In an ecological perspective, that Earth is *valuable* means that the evolutionary ecosystem is *able* to produce *value*, and has long been doing so. A late, remarkable product of the process is humans, who can claim to be of value in a unique way. When humans come, they find Earth often *valuable*, *able* to produce *valued experiences*. The subjective value events are a capstone subset super-posed on the global, objective *carrying* of value. This does not commit the naturalistic fallacy, because moving from an *is* to an *is of value, is valuable* and even to a (nonmoral) *ought-to-be* is what nature has done before us here. Humans are urged to move further to a moral *ought-to-be*. Otherwise we fall into the subjectivist, anthropocentrist fallacy.

7. THE END OF NATURE?

Perhaps there looms before us what some call, rather dramatically, "the end of nature" (McKibben 1989). Formerly, we could count on the natural givens. "A generation goes, and a generation comes, but the earth remains forever" (Ecclesiastes 1:4). But not any more. In this century, humans have stressed these natural systems to the breaking point. The water is polluted; the soil is degraded; the wildlife are gone or going; forests are cut down; deserts advance on overgrazed lands. Humans are upsetting, irreversibly, even the climate; the change will be disastrous because it will be so rapid that natural systems cannot track it. In the twenty-first century, there will only be nature that has been tampered with, no more spontaneous nature.

Indeed, already "we live in a postnatural world." We live hence-forth increasingly in "a world that is of our own making." "There's no such thing as nature any more" (McKibben 1989:60, 85, 89). Since the dawn of culture, humans have rebuilt their natural envi-ronments. No civilized humans can live in pure, pristine nature. But now there is a difference. Earlier, wild nature could also remain alongside culture. The natural givens stayed in place. There could not be wilderness everywhere, but there could be wilderness somewhere, lots of it, if we chose. There could be wildlands, more and less, all over the world. Wild creatures could coexist on their own in the reserves, the woodlots, the fencerows, the nooks, the crannies of civ-ilization. But with acid rain, with pollutants everywhere, with car-cinogens in the food chains, such coexistence is now impossible. With global warming accelerating climate change a hundred times over, "changing nature means changing everything" and this "seems infi-nitely sad" (McKibben 1989:78–79). Nothing, nowhere, can be wild and free any more.

We worry about what these momentous but still largely incalculable changes mean to humans, but our worries go deeper. That there is a greenhouse effect is bad, for we shall have to cope with it, and we do not yet know how. But even if we do cope, Earth has become a greenhouse, an artifact like a farmer's hothouse. The deeper tragedy is that cultural changes have now erased pristine nature forever. The problem is not just this or that species lost, this or that landscape developed or degraded, this or that resource exploited and gone. The whole Earth is whole no more; the global system is radically different. Everything, everywhere "bears the permanent stamp of man" (McKibben 1989:210).

Nature is therefore at an end. "Having lost its separateness, it loses its special power. Instead of being a category like God—something beyond our control—it is now a category like the defense budget or the minimum wage, a problem we must work out. This in itself changes its meaning, completely and changes our reaction to it. . . . There is no future in loving nature" (McKibben 1989:210–211). "We live at a radical, unrealistic moment. We live at the end of nature, the moment when the essential character of the world . . . is suddenly changing." There is no more nature *"for its own sake"* (McKibben 1989:174–175).

David Rothenberg, by contrast, a deep ecologist, is glad that wild nature is ending; he thinks it is a bad idea:

> The philosopher of ecology can only implore you to try to conceive of your self and your purpose not in opposition to an enviroment . . . but through the surrounding world which may support us forever. . . . It is the idea of nature independent of humanity which is fading, which needs to be replaced by a nature that includes us. . . . There is no such thing as a pure, wild nature, empty of human conception. . . . Wilderness is a consequence only of a a civilization that sees itself as detached from nature. . . . This is a romantic, exclusive and only-human concept of a nature pure and untrammeled by human presence. It is *this* idea of nature which is reaching the end of its useful life. (1992:2–3)

Has or might or ought nature come to an end? Partly the answers are matters of fact, but they are also matters of philosophical analysis. Is it the case, for instance, that, owing to human disturbances in the

Yellowstone Park ecosystem, we have lost any possibility of letting the park be natural? There will be an absolute sense in which this is true, since there is no square foot of the park in which humans have not disturbed the predation pressures. There is no square foot of the park on which rain fails without detectable pollutants.

But it does not follow that nature is absolutely ended, because it is not absolutely present. Answers come in degrees. Events in Yellowstone can remain 99.44 percent natural on many a square foot, indeed on hundreds of square miles, in the sense that they are substantially "untrammeled by man." We can put the predators back and clean up the air. Even where the system was once disturbed by humans and subsequently restored or left to recover on its own, wildness can return (chapter 3, sec. 5). Even if the original wildness does not return, nature having been irreversibly knocked into some alternative condition, we can thereafter at least let nature take what course it may.

Nor does it follow, contra Rothenberg, that, in wilderness areas, the idea of nature independent of humanity is fading. We examined wilderness earlier, to conclude that we do not want nature everywhere to include humans; sometimes we wish, as nearly as possible, to let wild nature be. There is such a thing as pure wild nature empty of human conception; that is what was on the planet for millennia before humans evolved, and it yet remains, more and less, in wilderness areas yet today. Wilderness is not a consequence of civilization; there was wilderness before there was civilization at all. It is true, of course, that there was no wilderness movement, a largely twentieth-century social and political effort to save wild nature that we sketched earlier in this chapter, until some humans got the idea that saving some pristine nature (as nearly as possible) was a good thing. But wilderness was and is there before and without people, and the idea of preserving some of that spontaneous nature has not at all reached the end of its useful life. The death of that idea, as McKibben laments, would be sad indeed.

On other lands, the natural and cultural will mix in differing degrees. Past certain thresholds, so far as land is managed for agriculture or industry, so far as it is fenced for pasture or mowed as lawns, wild nature has ended. This ending may be always, in its own way a sad thing; but it is an inevitable thing, and the culture that replaces nature can have compensating values. It would be a sadder thing still if culture had never appeared to grace the Earth, or if cultures had remained so modest that they had never substantially modified the landscape. We do not always lament our presence, even though we do want some lands where humans only visit. The human presence, permanently altering and improving the land, does make wilderness impossible, but there can still be more or less relatively natural environments where humans are in the picture.

Martin Murie, an ecologist, writes: "My main concern . . . is to suggest a rapproachment with nature in which nature is respected but we people are not required to hate our presence on the planet. I define 'natural environment' as any place where organisms exist in mutual relations that are free of direct management or other drastic human intervention; but presence or absence of people is not a criterion" (1972:43). That seems to be what Rothenberg was hoping to say: that humans belong on the planet, only he confused belonging somewhere on the planet with belonging everywhere on it.

Some rural environments can remain natural environments (portions of the Adirondacks of New York, for instance), although some agricultural environments (the wheat fields of eastern Washington state where every square inch of nature has been replaced with hybrid wheat) are neither natural nor even rural environments anymore, owing to the drastic intervention and management. The more drastic the intervention and management, the more nature has ended.

And we must be warned that the end of nature is a serious threat. If, for instance, global warming proves to introduce climatic changes so dramatic that natural environments cannot track these changes, then there will be no more nature. Again, this is not absolute, for some natural processes will remain, but the system will be unrecognizably natural. It will be an artifact. The five hundred wilderness areas will be about like city weedlots, with tatterdemalion scraps of nature. The epoch of spontaneously self-organizing systems, of wild nature with integrity, will be effectively over, and that will be a tragedy. Similarly, if other toxics or pollutants choke up the system, or if the extinction rate reaches the projected disastrous levels, or if deforestation or soil loss reaches levels that cause the system to crash, we will face the same fate. While the end of nature is not absolutely here, it is not absolutely possible, but it is relatively to be feared. Some end of nature is a good thing; but too much of any good thing is a bad thing (chapter 5, sec. 2).

We can and ought to see to it that nature does not come to further end. We depend on nature; and, now, nature depends on us. But we must be careful how we establish this interdependence, both on the ground and in our heads, because of the unusual character of the human-nature relationship. Steve Packard writes:

> Unprecedented numbers of people are becoming passionately involved with the environment. It's an honor to be among the first to have a nurturing relationship with wild nature. We know we're dependent on nature for replenishing the oxygen we breathe and for maintaining soil for the food we eat. If we are dependent on nature, what's so terrible about nature being dependent on us, too? We can help nature maintain its health. At least for the prairies, savannas, and oak woodlands of Illinois, we have to help those areas, or they'll be lost. Responsibilities can be enriching. Nature doesn't end as we become a part of it, any more than our parents cease to be our parents once they become older and we have to take care of them. (Packard 1990:72)

Yes and no. We become confused if we fail to distinguish between the architecture of culture and that of nature; managed wild nature really is a contradiction in terms. The parent-child analogy is misleading. Parents cease to operate as parents when they are dependent on us. Though, owing to the inevitable decline of individuals, parents will become dependent on their children, we do not want to cultivate those dependencies. Our parents are failing when these are required. Nature is not some failing parent that now needs to become dependent on us. What restoration biology does is put nature back to be on its own, and then pull back and let nature be—and that independent nature can continue forever.

In these latter years, we should be sad indeed if nature were always dependent on us, if the only "wild" animals were those in zoos, if the only "wild" flowers were those we had restored. Nature that remains dependent on us has not yet been rehabilitated—and a dependency relationship would bring nature too near an end. We cannot have enriched wild nature by clever management, because the management ultimately impoverishes rather than enriches. All that dependency should mean is that we resolve to protect, conserve, restore, and then to let nature take its course. Beyond, beneath, and around our culture, we do not want the *end of nature*. We value nature as an *end in itself*.

7

The Home Planet

::

Earth is the only planet, so far as we know, that is a home.[*] This is the biosphere, the planet known to have an ecology, etymologically "the logic of a home." Earth may not be the only planet where anything is valuable, but it is the only place where anything is vital. The astronaut Michael Collins recalled being earthstruck: "The more we see of other planets, the better this one looks. When I traveled to the Moon, it wasn't my proximity to that battered rockpile I remember so vividly, but rather what I saw when I looked back at my fragile home—a glistening, inviting beacon, delicate blue and white, a tiny outpost suspended in the black infinity. Earth is to be treasured and nurtured, something precious that *must* endure" (Collins 1980). Secretary-General Boutros Boutros-Ghali of the United Nations closed the Earth Summit with an imperative: "The Spirit of Rio must create a new mode of civic conduct. It is not enough for man to love his neighbour;

---

[*] Portions of this chapter appeared in Rolston 1993.

he must also learn to love his world" (1992a). "We must now conclude an ethical and political contract with nature, with this Earth to which we owe our very existence and which gives us life" (1992b).

That certainly seems to find value in Earth as a precious place, and to enjoin loving that place with the moral intensity with which we love neighbors, perhaps even God, for there is something almost religious about both injunctions. Neither the astronaut nor the secretary-general is thinking merely anthropocentrically, of Earth as a big resource to be exploited for human needs; rather, Earth is a precious thing in itself because it is home for us all; Earth is to be loved, as we do a neighbor, for an intrinsic integrity. In conserving natural value, our argument and our duty is not complete until we have moved to an Earth ethics. The center of focus is the planet. But valuing the whole Earth and responsibilities to it are unfamiliar and need philosophical analysis.

1. LAND ETHICS AND EARTH ETHICS

Views of Earth from space have given us an emerging vision of Earth and the place of human life upon it. "Once a photograph of the Earth, taken from *the outside* is available . . . a new idea as powerful as any in history will be let loose."[*] That idea is one world or none, the unity and community of the home planet, our global responsibility. Leaving home, we discover how precious a home is. The distance lends enchantment, brings us home again. The distance helps us to get real. We get put in our place. Viewing an Earthrise, Edgar Mitchell was entranced, "Suddenly from behind the rim of the moon, in long-slow motion moments of immense majesty, there emerges a sparkling blue and white jewel, a light, delicate sky-blue sphere laced with slowly swirling veils of white, rising gradually like a small pearl in a thick sea of black mystery. It takes more than a moment to fully realize this is Earth . . . home."[**]

That precious Earth, a pearl in a sea of mystery, is in crisis. The two great marvels of our planet are life and mind, both among the rarest things in the universe. Diverse combinations of nature and culture

---

[*] Astronomer Fred Hoyle, quoted in Kelley 1988, inside front cover.

[**] Edgar Mitchell, quoted in Kelley 1988, at photographs 42–45.

worked well enough over many millennia, but no more. In the past century, our modern cultures threaten the stability, beauty, and integrity of Earth. Behind the vision of one world is the shadow of none.

We need to form ethical and value judgments at the appropriate level. Earlier in our analysis, the object of ethical concern was persons, animals, individuals, species, ecosystems; but environmental ethics is not over until we have risen to the planetary level. Earth is really the relevant survival unit. In that sense, the term "land ethic," chosen by Aldo Leopold when he urged expanding ethics in the Wisconsin sand counties, is a little unfortunate when we further expand to global concerns. In the half-century since he wrote, we have had to enlarge ethics to include the Earth. Leopold's "land" is really the biotic community of life. He included the rivers, as well as the fauna and flora. Still, his vision is local.

A "land" ethic is not marine, for example. Yet Earth is mostly ocean. The planet could just as well have been named Aqua. Liquid water is what makes this Earth a gem, more than the rock crystals. An environmental ethic needs to include marine environments, too. A land ethic is not about the ozone layer, and Leopold had never heard of global warming. But the Earth's atmosphere is as vital as its water or dirt. "Earth" is the name of the whole system, the proper name of our planet, like Jupiter and Mars. A comprehensive environmental ethics must become an Earth ethics.

Ought implies can, and we do not construct an ethics for things that lie outside our powers. Ethics is sometimes a question of scale. The late-coming, moral species, *Homo sapiens*, has still more lately gained startling powers for the rebuilding and modification, including the degradation, of this home planet. There looms the "end of nature," an event not possible until recently. That does put ethics on a new scale. The value issues are so large-scale that the current events have to be interpreted as a fundamental contextual change altering the critical determinants of the history of the planet.

Only in the past century, Darwin's century more or less, have we learned the depth of historical change on this planet, life continuing over billions of years. Now, facing the next century, we humans have the understanding and the power to alter the history of the planet on global ecological scales. The future cannot be like the past, neither the next ten thousand years like the past ten thousand, nor even the next five hundred years like the last five hundred years. All this brings urgent new duties. We worried throughout most of this century, the first century of great world wars, that humans would destroy themselves in interhuman conflict. Fortunately, that fear has subsided. Unfortunately, it is rapidly being replaced by a new one. The worry for the next century is that humans may destroy their planet and themselves with it.

We are turning a millennium. The challenge of the past millennium has been to pass from the medieval to the modern world, building modern cultures and nations, an explosion of cultural development. The challenge of the next millennium is to contain those cultures within the carrying capacity of the larger community of life on our planet. On our present heading, much of the integrity of the natural world will be destroyed within the next century. To continue the development pace of the past century for another millennium will produce sure disaster. If we humans are true to our species epithet, "the wise species" needs to behave with appropriate respect for life. That will involve an interhuman ethics. It will involve an interspecific ethics, where the only moral species discovers that all the others, though not moral agents, are morally considerable. Ultimately, it will involve an Earth ethics, one that discovers a global sense of obligation to this whole inhabited biosphere.

Ethics in the modern West, has been almost entirely interhuman ethics. Ethics seeks to fit humans into their communities, so ethics has often dwelt on justice, fairness, love, rights, peace, troubled about personal relations. But ethics, too, is now anxious about the troubled planet. Can we have duties *concerning* the Earth, even duties *to* the Earth? Earth is, after all, just earth. Earth is, in a way, a big rockpile like the moon, only one on which the rocks are watered and illuminated in such way that they support life. Maybe it is really the life we value and not the Earth after all, except as instrumental to life. We do not have duties to rocks, air, ocean, dirt, or Earth; we have duties to people, or living things. We must not confuse duties to the home with duties to the inhabitants.

The belief that dirt could have intrinsic value is sometimes taken as a kind of ultimate foolishness, a *reductio ad absurdum* in environmental philosophy. Dirt is instrumentally valuable, but not the sort of thing that has value by itself; certainly not any value that could make a claim on humans. Put like that, we agree. An isolated clod defends no intrinsic value and it is difficult to say that it has much value in itself. But that is not the end of the matter, because a handful of dirt is integrated into an ecosystem; earth is a part, Earth the whole. Dirt is product and process in a systemic nature that we do respect. Maybe we should try next to get the global picture, and switch from a lump of dirt to the Earth system in which it has been created.

The elemental chemicals of life—carbon, oxygen, hydrogen, nitrogen—are common enough throughout the universe. They are made in the stars. But life, rare in the universe, is common on Earth, and the explanation lies in the ordinary elements in an extraordinary setting, the super special circumstances in which these common chemicals find themselves arranged on Earth. Any planet on which life finds a habitat must be large enough to retain an atmosphere; it must have cooled down to a temperature that accommodates life. It must be within a congenial range of the energy pouring out from the star it orbits, near enough for the supply of warmth to be adequate but not so close as to make the heat intolerable. The orbit needs to be approximately circular, or else the temperatures between perihelion and aphelion will be extreme. The orbit must be stable over long epochs, not disrupted by collisions with or near approaches to other planets or stars. The planet's rate of revolution must be such that there is not excessive heating in one hemisphere and excessive cooling in the other.

There must be fluid water, lots of it, which is driven to circulate. If there is to be terrestrial life, there must be land masses, adequately irrigated, and these masses need to be periodically rejuvenated from erosion. There needs to be a perpetual churning of the materials, irradiated with energy. Radioactivity deep within the Earth produces enough heat to keep its crust constantly mobile in counteraction with erosional forces, and the interplay of such forces generates and regenerates landscapes and seas. The atmosphere, waters, and lands must have the important precursors for the synthesis of organic materials. On Earth, what would otherwise be extremes of heat and cold, wet and dry, are moderated by the circulations of water. All this has been in place perhaps five billion years.

About three billion years ago, life evolved. Amino acids were constructed by energy radiated over inorganic materials, assembled into long polypeptide chains (with no previous templates, enzymes, or information to steer the process). These polypeptide chains folded into complex functional structures, or preproteins. Coincident with this, other molecules formed that, under the electrostatic pressures of water, organized into hollow microspheres, the empty prototypes of cells. These spheres came to envelop the preproteins, protecting the about-to-be-life chemistries from degradation by the outside environment and providing a semipermeable membrane across which the necessary nutrient inputs and waste outputs could take place. Metabolism and life were soon under way. What was before merely a landscape or seascape became an ecosystem. What was only a place became a home.

Life learned to replicate itself, with a genius for variation and development. Natural selection arose, with the differential survival of the better adapted. The pressures for survival proved to be pressures for complex development, not in all but in some lines of descent/ascent. Evolution has steadily introduced new forms, some replacements with newly acquired skills—metazoans with specialized cells, photosynthetic forms, sexuality, neurons, muscles, sentience, instincts, brains, behavior, the capacity to acquire information through experience, to live on land or fly through the air.

As a result, we have all the complexity and diversity, integrity, richness, natural history, and cultural history that we have been celebrating in previous chapters. The whole storied natural history is little short of a series of "miracles," wondrous, fortuitous events, unfolding of potential; and when Earth's most complex product, *Homo sapiens*, becomes intelligent enough to reflect over this cosmic wonderland, we are left stuttering about the mixtures of accident and necessity out of which we have come. But perhaps we do not have to have all the cosmological answers in order to be sure that this is a precious place, a pearl in a sea of black mystery. For some the black mystery will be numinous and signal transcendence; for others the black mystery may be impenetrable. Either way, Earth is what it is, a very special place.

We reach a scale question again. On an everyday scale, earth, dirt, seems to be passive, inert, an unsuitable object of moral concern. But on a global scale? The scale changes nothing, a critic may protest, the changes are only quantitative. Earth, too, is a big rockpile, only one that happens to support life. It is no doubt precious as a means of life support, but it is not precious in itself. To add a new imperative, loving Earth, to the classical one of loving neighbor (and God), is to make a category mistake. Neighbors (and God) are persons, ends in themselves, who respond to love. But Earth is just earth, dirt. Earth is not some proper-named person who can respond. There is nobody there in a planet, no subject of a life. There is not even the objective vitality of an organism, or the genetic transmission of a species line. Earth is not even an ecosystem, strictly speaking; it is a loose collection of myriads of ecosystems. So we must be talking loosely, perhaps poetically, or romantically of loving Earth. Earth is a "mere thing," a big thing, a special thing for those who happen to live on it, but still a thing, and not appropriate as an object of moral concern.

That argument, like the one about values being only in subjects-of-a-life, is not one its advocates can be argued out of, if they insist to stipulate such a meaning for Earth. But we can invite a paradigm shift, one that seems more systemically based and biologically sound. Humans ought to form an intelligible view of the whole and defend the creative system, collectively called Earth.

Dirt! Still, a skeptic may insist that we are going too far with an ethics about dirt. But we are trying to reply that dirt is earth, earth is Earth, and Earth is nature generating storied history. That is what dirt is really all about; it is the mother planet. Edward O. Wilson writes:

> Think of scooping up a handful of soil and leaf litter and placing it on a white cloth—as a field biologist would do—for closer examination. This unprepossessing lump contains more order and richness of structure, and particularity of history, than the entire surface of all the other (lifeless) planets. . . . Every species living there is the product of millions of years of history, having evolved under the harshest conditions of competition and survival. Each organism is the repository of an immense amount of genetic information.
>
> The abundance of the organisms increases downward, according to size, like layers in a pyramid. The handful of soil and liter is home for dozens of insects, mites, nematode worms, and other small invertebrates, most of which are just visible to the naked eye. There are also about a million fungi and ten billion bacteria, mostly microscopic. Each of the species has a distinct life cycle fitted to a portion of the micro-environment in which it thrives and reproduces. The individuality of each is programmed by an exact sequence of

nucleotides, the ultimate molecular units of the genes. These species have evolved as independent elements for thousands of generations. (Wilson 1983:4)

We might say that this is praising not so much the dirt as what is in the dirt. But another way of looking at this is that it is all dirt, only we find revealed in the humus what dirt can do when it is self-organizing under suitable conditions with water and solar illumination. That is pretty spectacular dirt. And if that is what is in a handful, think of what is in a planetful.

We can, if we insist on being anthropocentrists, say that it is all valueless except as our human resource, though quite valuable in that respect. But we will not be valuing Earth objectively until we appreciate this marvelous natural history. This really is a superb planet. In that light, moving from earth to Earth, duties to Earth do not seem misguided; to the contrary, a duty to Earth is the most important duty of all.

2. NATIONAL RESOURCES AND COMMON NATURAL HERITAGE

There is one Earth, and on it are one hundred and seventy-eight sovereign nations. Superimposed on this morally deep world, with its planetary wholeness, is the world of human culture, a politically fragmented world. "The Earth is one but the world is not" (UN World Commission on Environment and Development 1987b:27). True, the one Earth is plural in its landmasses and supports myriads of ecosystems, diverse species, diverse peoples. Still, the really divisive troubles arise among nation-states. The national sovereignties are not well adapted for harmonious relations with the Earth commons.* The rights of nations and rights as claimed by citizens of these political states are not well aligned with the ecology and geography of the home planet. In the twentieth century, the commons problem has

---

* International business organizations are another concern. Like sovereign nations, they too operate in their own sovereign interests, regulated by no one government, and, through exploiting conditions from nation to nation, are able to fragment international environmental standards (Donaldson 1989).

become transnational; at the turn of the millennium it is becoming global. Our citizenship is not synchronized with our residency.

Many of Earth's natural resources, unevenly and inequitably dis tributed, have to flow across national lines, if there is to be a stable community of nations. People have a right to water; that seems plausible and just. But then consider the nations in relation to the hydrology of the planet: at least 214 river basins are multinational. About 50 counties have 75 percent or more of their total area falling within international river basins. An estimated 35–40 percent of the global population lives in multinational river basins. In Africa and Europe most river basins are multinational. The word *rival* comes from the Latin word for river, *rivus*, those who share flowing waters. With escalating population and pollution levels, sharing water has become increasingly an international issue.

Nor is it any longer a matter of looking upstream and downstream. Water moves around the globe on air currents; there is meteorological as well as hydrological water. Shared water, for instance, involves acid rain where one nation emits the pollutants into the atmosphere and another receives the polluted rain.

Flowing water is one of the unique features of this planet, as the clouds and seas so evident in the space photographs reveal. The flow of water is a cultural resource that, however much modified by pipelines and pumps, remains inseparably part of natural meteorological and hydrological systems. But water law can be exercised in politically fragmented jurisdictions, unintelligently related to the hydrology of the landscape. We may buy and sell "water rights," we must also use water in responsible harmony with natural systems. With water, one has to be a resident of Earth, not just a citizen in a city. One turns on the tap to get a glass of water, that is acting locally, and the results depend on the county water board. But one taps into the evolutionary and ecological miracle of water; that is thinking globally. Both levels are required for valuing water appropriately.

From a biospheric perspective, ecological problems typically have little to do with national boundaries, but they cannot be solved without political agreements, and these agreements are difficult to arrange because nations wish to treat as national resources what are also part of the common natural heritage. Resources that are more clearly owned by nations (ores, minerals) are accidentally located. National boundaries were drawn for political reasons, often with minimal attention to natural resources—nearly all drawn before many of the modern essential resources were resources at all: coal, electric power, uranium, copper or iron ore.

Petroleum on Earth is highly concentrated; one-quarter of the world's known reserves are in Saudi Arabia; and more than half in the Middle East. The need for petroleum, however, is dispersed over nations around the globe. People find it difficult nowadays to be either productive or free without it. But the divisions of nation-states, only accidentally related to the location of this most valuable natural resource, only compound the problem.

Many modern nations (England or Japan, for instance) often have economies that require imports of natural resources and exports of manufactured goods. The manufacturing skills are not where the resources lie; the manufacturing requires resources from locations in dozens of nations. Indeed, few, if any, nations are self-sufficient in all of the natural resources that they need or desire, and many are quite deficient. Divisiveness, struggle, even wars can result.

People are fighting for what is of value in nature, but they are also fighting as citizens of nations that have economic policies and political agendas, demanding loyalties in support. Their access to natural resources comes filtered through political units that are not formed, or continued, with these ecologies in mind. They want resources, but the political alignments can often mean suboptimal and unjust solutions to the problems of resource distribution. *Natural* resources have to become *national* resources, and "nationalizing" natural resources can be as much part of the problem as part of the answer, especially when the sovereign independence of nations is asserted without regard for the interdependencies of these nations—both their interdependencies with each other and their interdependencies through the global natural ecosystems. When biological resources are taken to be national possessions in dispute, rather than an Earth commons to be shared, it is difficult to find a fabric in which to share them.

In an Earth ethics that provides for a shared commons, the international fabric will have to be stable and dynamic enough that a nation which is not self-contained can contain itself within the network of international commerce. This involves living in a tension within a community of nations where there is access that redistributes resources across national lines sufficiently for nations to repair their own resource deficiencies in international trade. Unless such commerce can be arranged, the environment will suffer. The rights to a decent environment, to a fair share of the world's resources and goods, will be denied.

If the controlling interest is national sovereignty and welfare alone, we may be prevented from an Earth ethics by the fallacy of misplaced community. This mistakes the nature and character of the communities to which one belongs and gives such disproportionate emphasis to some communities that one becomes blind to others. With the wrong premises about community, the wrong conclusions and inappropriate actions follow. An effort by a developed country (in the so-called North) to aid a developing nation (in the South) is typically interpreted, for example, as "foreign" aid, when such effort could better have been interpreted by the developed country as saving their "home" planet. National sovereignties divide us when we need deeper solutions, respecting the larger communities of life on Earth. On the global scale, none of us are aliens; we are all at home.

"The common heritage of mankind" is the classical category for this global commons. Lately, much that was formerly tacit in this rich natural heritage has become explicit, owing to our new powers for modifying and degrading the biosphere. We are coming to realize that this heritage is, ultimately, the creative, prolific system that we inhabit. Dealing with an acre or two of real estate, perhaps even with hundreds or thousands of acres, we can think that the earth belongs to us, as private property holders. Dealing with a landscape, we can think that the earth belongs to us, as citizens of the country geographically located there.

But on the global scale, Earth is not something we own. Earth does not belong to us; rather we belong to it. We belong on it. The question is not of property, but of community. That is why going from earth to Earth is not a matter of quantitative aggregation of clods of dirt, of real estate instrumental to our preference satisfaction, but of a qualitative change going from the ground under our feet to the ground

---

* Earth is the ground of our being, but this need not preempt the larger religious question whether, ultimately, there is a Ground of Being that transcends the planet.

of our being.* We commit a fallacy of misplaced value to see this common ground as nothing but a national resource.

3. INTERNATIONAL LAW AND ENVIRONMENTAL ETHICS

One may welcome the view of Earth from space, which symbolizes the commonwealth of natural values, but be surprised to find that an account of natural value leads to international law. I myself experienced such surprise. I started out loving mosses, orchids, and butterflies in the wilderness and ended up having to go to a conference in Rio de Janeiro with 4,000 diplomats and 118 heads of state! In conserving natural value one is driven from nature to politics, and, in politics, from local and state to national and international levels. Moving to the international level, one might think that environmental law and policy will increasingly displace ethics and philosophy, but in fact ethical and philosophical value issues become more, not less, important.

Critics say that international law is not really law because it lacks coercive authority. Powerful self-interested states will obey the rules only when it suits them. But that is seeing the glass half empty; from another perspective it is half full. International environmental law will be filled with mixed moral, prudential, political, legal, economic, and ecological arguments, but a vital part of this is the moral force, just because the coercive legal force is reduced. Consider, for instance, the force of moral concern for human rights, even though there is no international government to enforce sanctions against violations. No nation wishes to stand morally condemned by the rest of the world (like South Africa has been with its apartheid). An environmental ethics can persuade, too.

Nine classical principles that have come to undergird the code of international law, and two more recent ones are especially revealing:

1. sovereign equality of states;
2. territorial integrity and political independence of states;
3. equal rights and self-determination of peoples;
4. nonintervention in the internal affairs of states;
5. peaceful settlement of disputes between states;

6. abstention from the threat of the use of force;

7. fulfillment in good faith of international obligations;

8. cooperation with other states; and

9. respect for human rights and fundamental freedoms.

In addition, the two that have emerged since World War II are:

10. an equitable international economic order; and

11. protection of the environment (Jones 1991).

The last has become especially forceful in recent years, culminating in the UNCED Earth Summit. The last two go together, since environmental conservation is coupled with a more equitable sharing of the economic productivity based on natural resources.

These are, so to speak, the eleven commandments of international law. They are universally agreed upon in principle, though often honored in the breach as well as in the observance. People break the ten commandments too, but they nevertheless are an ideal that shapes much behavior. Nations, though they may break these commandments when push comes to shove, nevertheless reluctantly break them, and the ideal is there. They go to considerable efforts to avoid doing so; and other nations, where there are violations, readily condemn and, on occasions, introduce sanctions intended to reform behavior.

The one Earth has no one government, and this seems impossible in the foreseeable future. Since sovereign nations are unwilling to cede any sovereignty to a world government, common issues have to be negotiated in a political system where nations are defending the rights of their citizens, but the fragmented system prevents an integrated, global solution. In pollution cases, for example, the polluted nation, downwind or downstream, does not have any control over the polluter, upwind or upstream, while the polluter does not have any incentive to curb its pollution, since the damages are external to the nation. Cooperative action is difficult where there is little opportunity to regulate and police. The institutions that can take action internationally on global scale environmental problems are weak (Magraw and Nickel 1990; Dryzek and Hunter 1987). That is why moral persuasion becomes more important.

Compare, for instance, the way in which within the continental United States environmental standards can be set on a national basis, enforced, and adjusted to local circumstances as required. Compare also the way in which resources within the United States can be readily redistributed across state lines. The state political lines seldom bear any significant relationship to ecosystem units, and this does create problems even within the continental United States, but at least resources can flow rather freely across those irrelevant lines. The continent can operate, to some degree, as a political and an ecological unit.

Resources flow among the nation-states of Europe, with more difficulty, but increasingly in a common market. They flow with considerably more difficulty still among the nation-states of Africa. We are still looking for an ethic by which the global commons can be fairly shared in ways that make ecological sense. When nation-states are politically operated as if geography and ecology are irrelevant, there will be disaster for both nations and nature. Such nations are essentially misfits on their landscapes.

Keeping each nation oriented to global perspectives by instruments of international law is a major role of the United Nations. Since the United Nations is not a sovereign state, its appeal must be largely persuasive, negotiatory, ethical—based on rights and responsibilities, more than on military force or political power. Laws will be soft laws, but still they will be aspirational and can orient nations. The World Charter for Nature has as a guiding principle that renewable natural resources "shall not be utilized in excess of their natural capacity for regeneration" (UN General Assembly 1982:II.10.d). The United Nations Environment Programme played an important role in negotiations leading to the 1987 Montreal ozone protocol.

The UN International Law Commission has been studying international liability and international watercourses, affecting environmental issues. The Third UN Conference on the Law of the Sea, which produced the United Nations Convention of the Law of the Sea, was significant, even though not enough nations have yet signed for the convention to enter into force. There are over one hundred and fifty international agreements (conventions, treaties, protocols, etc.) registered with the United Nations that deal directly with environmental problems (UNEP 1991). The United Nations facilitated the designation of biosphere reserves.

The United Nations Conference on Environment and Development was convened in Rio de Janeiro in June 1992 in the hopes of launching a number of more environmentally responsible international agreements. Unfortunately, national sovereignties tended to constrain the effectiveness of the conference when it sought to protect the global commons. Nation-states defended the interests of their own citizens, and this cast nation against nation, often the developed nations versus the developing nations. The question of responsibilities to Earth got addressed often rather marginally, if at all. Sometimes the problem was developing countries demanding their rights; more visibly, the United States proved quite unyielding of its national interests and those of its citizens.

Still it was an Earth Summit, and there was much rhetoric and morality play. The Rio Declaration, the was-to-have-been Earth Charter, insisted that humans are at the center of concerns while the secretary-general closed with his insistence that it not enough to love our neighbor; we must also learn to love our world. In, with, and under the rhetoric and aspiration, there will be the ongoing negotiations of international law, facilitated by the Rio conventions, and these do provide increasing opportunities to make an environmental ethics international and binding.

The oceans of the planet illustrate how the one Earth is a biosphere, and also provide an opportunity for realizing this in policy. Almost all the global land area is claimed by one or another of the one hundred and seventy-eight sovereign nations, who also claim territorial waters, but the high seas belong to no nation. Nor do their fauna and flora. It is going to be difficult to reduce the sense of sovereignty on land. But nations do not claim sovereignty over the high seas, any more than they do over the atmosphere, and oceans may be places where we can begin to emphasize how there are natural givens that belong to no one because they belong to us all. A marine ethic could thus be a precursor to a global land ethic. That can extend beyond responsibilities to other persons, to include the marine fauna, flora, and ecosystems, in respect for life on the planet. After all, the oceans cover 70 percent of the Earth's surface and are critical to the planet's health.

A harbinger of how the oceans can unite nations is the surprisingly comprehensive treaty produced by the Third UN Conference on the Law of the Sea. Nations were affected by access to and the health of the seas in so many diverse ways that there was no polarization of sides. There were so many issues so important to so many and they cut so many ways that differently voting blocks could not materialize; everyone had entwined destinies. A concept that dominated the conference is that the oceans are part of the common heritage of humankind. That is a good beginning for a common heritage of land, sea, and air.

Perhaps we are ready now for a UN-initiated Conference on the Law of the Atmosphere. Agreements on global warming could be part of this picture. There is only one atmosphere, and every nation needs this atmosphere; it is needed by wildlife as much as by humans, and kept functional by plants in the carbon dioxide and oxygen cycle. There is no better example of a commons in which we all have entwined destinies.

This sense of ethical responsibility in international law does not always remain only at the prudential, national, or even anthropocentric level. The International Whaling Commission was established in 1946 to benefit an endangered industry, which required the cooperation of the whaling nations. So these nations at first cooperated in their own interests, hoping to share an ongoing resource in which each had a stake. But that commission over the years evolved into a commission with the goal of saving endangered whale species. The emphasis of the commission shifted over the years from commerce that was to the advantage of the mutually consenting nations to conservation and even preservation of the whales, with growing sympathy for the cetaceans themselves (Birnie 1985; Scarff 1977).

The idea of wildlife as both common heritage and good in themselves has produced a number of treaties that involve migratory birds, as well as regulate or prohibit commerce in such goods as ivory, animal skins, and plant products. There cannot be warblers in New England without habitat in Central America; there cannot be elephants in Africa unless importing ivory into the United States is illegal.* One hundred and twelve nations are party to the Convention on International Trade in Endangered Species of Wild Fauna and Flora (CITES). After the Law of the Sea and the Law of the Atmosphere, we could be ready for a Law of World Wildlife. The Convention on Biological Diversity and the Framework Convention on Climate Change contain

---

* Some elephants need to be culled from herds for the good of the herds, and if a way can be found to separate illegal from legal ivory, this policy might change.

open sections that need to be filled out with ongoing negotiations. Reaching international consensus of these kinds is often prudential, but prudence spread out over the larger community, both of humans and of fauna and flora in terrestrial and marine ecosystems, is a step in the direction of an Earth ethics.

4. MOTHER EARTH?

The original meaning of *nature*, "to give birth" (Latin:*(g)nasci, natus)*, is a root in such words as *native, nation, natal, navel*. The root goes back to the Greek word for giving birth, *ginomai*, surviving in such words as *genesis, gene, progeny, pregnant, genius, gentile, generate*. Such origins have given nature a feminine cast, which is not surprising, since females give birth. Generalizing, the whole system is Mother Nature.

Taken to the planetary level, that projection requires some analysis. We are specifying the fertility and creativity, not the gender. We do not really think that ecosystems are feminine, much less that Earth is a feminine planet. Those are category mistakes, rather like thinking of God as being male. The origin of sexuality in evolutionary natural history is a puzzle. Many species propagate by cloning, but this is disadvantageous for most species because it does not permit sufficient interchange of genetic information. Sexuality provides more adept generativity, and that does characterize life on our planet. We may speak of the whole genesis rhetorically or symbolically as feminine, Mother Earth; we also need to translate this into claims that are more philosophically and scientifically exact. We mean that there are generative forces in the Earth natural system that have produced the biota that surrounds us. Nature is the primal fountain of being and value. There is a programmatic tendency to produce such value (see chapter 2, sec. 3).

Consider forests, for instance. The phenomenon of forests is so widespread, persistent, and diverse, appearing almost wherever moisture and climatic conditions permit it, that forests cannot be accidents or anomalies in the Earth processes but rather must be a characteristic expression of the creative process. Likewise with grasslands. Consider species. One does not go from zero to five or ten million species, over several billion years, setbacks notwithstanding, by accident. Consider photoreceptors and eyes, which have evolved independently perhaps forty times (Salvini-Plawen and Mayr 1977). Flight has evolved on several occasions.

Something is at work additionally to species regenerating as they aimlessly track changing environments. The Earth is potential unfolding, and, whatever the accidental elements, the story as a whole is no accident. We need to put an arrow on evolutionary time, and more; we need to put fertility into the system. Speaking of Mother Earth is the rhetorical, popular, classical way of doing this. Further, since nature is not particularly self-explanatory, this has often also been coupled with a Father God, who authorizes and undergirds this earthen creativity. But neither the female nor the male gender is the issue; the issue is parenting, come to focus on Earth, the only place where we know that this birthing has taken place. We need an ethic adequate for this creativity by which more comes out of less.

There is the epic story—eucaryotes, trilobites, dinosaurs, primates, persons—and the drama is enough to justify our conclusions that there is prolific potential in the system. We want a genetic account in the deeper sense, one that tells the full story of the genesis of value. There is a systemic process, profoundly but partially described by evolutionary theory, a historical saga during which spectacular results are achieved. This value, commonly termed "survival value," is better interpreted as valuable information, coded genetically, that is apt for "living on and on" (*sur-vival*), for coping, for life's persisting in the midst of its perpetual perishing. It is this fecundity that was classically termed "Mother Earth," or "Divine Creation." The fact of the matter is literally true, whatever we may think of the mythology used to explain it. Earth is a fertile planet, and in one sense fertility is the deepest value category of all. Dismissing the mythology does not dissolve the valuable facts.

A more recent name for this Earth system is Gaia, and here the need for separating fact and mythology returns. Gaia was an ancient Earth goddess, now reincarnated as the theory that "the entire range of living matter on Earth, from whales to viruses, and from oaks to algae, could be regarded as constituting a single living entity, capable of manipulating the Earth's atmosphere to suit its overall needs and endowed with faculties and powers beyond those of its constitutent parts." "Then we may find ourselves and all other living things to be parts and partners of a vast being who in her entirety has the power to maintain our planet as a fit and comfortable habitat for life" (Lovelock 1979:9,1).

> Gaia is a theory of the atmosphere and surface sediments of the planet Earth taken as a whole. The Gaia hypothesis states that the temperature and composition of the Earth's atmosphere are actively regulated by the sum of life on the planet—the biota. This regulation of the Earth's surface by the biota and for the biota has been in continuous existence since the earliest appearance of widespread life. The assurance of continued global habitability according to the Gaian hypothesis is not a matter merely of chance. The Gaian view of the atmosphere is a radical departure from the former scientific concept that life on Earth is surrounded by and adapts to an essentially static environment. That life interacts with and eventually becomes its own environment; that the atmosphere is an extension of the biosphere in nearly the same sense that the human mind is an extension of DNA; that life interacts with and controls physical attributes of Earth on a global scale—all these things resonate strongly with the ancient magico-religious sentiment that all is one. (Sagan and Margulis 1984:60)

Well, yes and no. Yes, there is a dynamic Earth where the biota is inextricably linked to atmospheric, oceanic, and terrestrial processes. Yes, it is notable how, once the life forces are under way, they remake the environment out of which they first came, molding it further in a prolife direction. Life is not passive before geological and meteorological vicissitudes, but is interactive with these forces. The soil with its humus results from what otherwise would be only mineralogical earth. The atmosphere with its oxygen, carbon dioxide, and ozone shielding layer is a product of plant and animal life. The rivers and springs flow moderated by runoff control due to vegetative cover, plant respiration, and evaporation rates. Life to some extent modifies its climate. There are feedback loops set up between the organic and the nonliving world, and these sometimes become feedforward loops. The phenomenon of organism on the planet does not simply accept a random physical nature, but selects from its possible routes those that are more favorable to life. The physicochemical environment is rebuilt biologically (Kerr 1988).

On the other hand, the hypothesis suggests that Gaia is not Earth, but came into being with and after the origin of life. Gaia is an integrated process, warranting a proper name, that takes over an otherwise rather recalcitrant nature and rebuilds it contrary to its physicochemical, merely geological nature. There is dialectic between Gaia and Earth; the home planet is not very homey until after Gaia has remade it so. What we rather want is an account by which life unfolds from the potential of the geophysics and geochemistry, the destiny of these elements that, though they may seem inert, are, when viewed over evolutionary history, spectacularly fertile.

We already have a name for the place, Earth; and there is no one on Earth who doubts this proper-named place exists. Gaia, by contrast, is, or was, the name of a mythical goddess, and there is really no one on Earth who thinks that the Gaia of Greek mythology exists. Perhaps the ancient mythical proper name will serve with a new meaning, which we can stipulate. Gaia is the systemic Earth, and the new name helps us break away from the old, inert, passive view that earth connotes. If so, well and good. But it is not so easy to convert a mythical goddess into a scientific concept. There will be forever an educational problem, explaining and re-explaining what Gaia means, that she is not who she used to be, but that she, or it, is now a symbol for philosophical ecology at the global level, harmonized with the equilibrating global climatic, meteorological, hydrological, thermodynamic, photosynthetic, metabolic system.

Believing in Gaia is like believing in Mother Nature. We really do not believe there is one more mother over and above all the other mothers. Mother Nature is a symbolic term, like Uncle Sam or Santa Claus, that does stand for something real: the prolific creative system to which we give the more mundane name Earth (like Uncle Sam stands for a real nation, and: "Yes, Virginia, there is a Santa Claus"). They remain mythical terms even while they stand for something real. Meanwhile we do not think that Earth is a mythical term, though it is a symbolic term, because it is a real place. Gaia, a proper name used for a systemic feature of planetary history, will remain arguable. We are perhaps better advised to pack this re-understanding into the undeniably real term, *Earth*.*

---

* This confusion will be compounded by the fact that Gaia was introduced originally as "the Gaia hypothesis"—provisional, tentative, arguable. That is commendable scientifically, where one erects hypotheses and tests them. But it is difficult to convert such a hypothesis into the solid ground of terra firma.

If we want an older word, at once primitive and modern, mythical and real—the "genius" of the system does lie in its fecund creativity. A "genius" is a power that animates—and, if we want to be mythico-religious about it—haunts a place. Late in the drama, that comes to include the human genius, but must the human genius, expressed and flourishing, shut down the biological and geological genius that is its predecessor and support? The questions "What shall I do?" and "What shall I value?" do depend on answers to the question "What is going on?" The *ought* depends on the *is*. The Earth is not some cosmic rockpile, not just the stage on which the human drama is played; Earth is the womb from whence we come and which we really never leave. When we really do understand what is going on, all this storied achievement taking place on our "small pearl in a thick sea of black mystery," an *ought* arises from an *is* that is of *value, valuable,* able to generate momentous value.

5. MANAGING THE PLANET?

It is all very well, in philosophical moments, to muse over Mother Earth; but—comes the protest—in practice, when we really come down to earth, we humans have got to manage the planet, especially from here onward. William C. Clark writes, in a *Scientific American* issue devoted to "Managing Planet Earth," "We have entered an era characterized by syndromes of global change that stem from the interdependence between human development and the environment. As we attempt to move from merely causing these syndromes to managing them consciously, two central questions must be addressed: What kind of planet do we want? What kind of planet can we get?" (1989:47–48). Those questions do not preclude nonanthropocentric answers, but, coupled with the "management" intent, they strongly suggest that humans are being asked what they want out of the planet, and the planetary managers will figure out how to get it for them. That puts humans "at the center of concerns," consciously manipulating the planet's future. The root of *manage* is the Latin "manus," hand. Humans will handle the place. Now this does begin to sound like the end of nature, the replacement of spontaneous nature with a new epoch of deliberate control, humanizing the Earth.

This urge to manage may be coupled with doubts about Mother Nature. Once we had visions of a Mother Nature that was "sensitive, efficient, purposeful, and powerful," but now, thanks to science, we know the cold truth: "Mother Nature cannot keep the environment in tune because she does not exist." So claims Frederick E. Smith, a Harvard professor of ecology. Though this is spaceship Earth, "in the final analysis nothing is guiding the ship" (1970). No wonder, then, that human-introduced changes, when they reach levels of global significance, unsteady the Earthship all the more. The only answer is to take control. *Homo sapiens* is the professional manager of an otherwise drifting, valueless world.

We live in a new age, continues another Harvard professor, Emmanuel G. Mesthene, director of the Program on Technology and Society. Because of our power and our conscious management, "our age is different from all previous ages. We are therefore the first age that can aspire to be free of the tyranny of physical nature that has plagued man since his beginnings." "Nature is coming increasingly under control as a result of restored human confidence and power" (1966:482, 491–492).

While the UNCED Earth Summit was meeting in Rio de Janeiro, 218 scientists, including 27 Nobel laureates, issued an appeal to the 118 heads of state gathered there to "beware of false gods in Rio."

> We want to make our full contribution to the preservation of our common heritage, the Earth. We are however worried, at the dawn of the twenty-first century, at the emergence of an irrational ideology which is opposed to scientific and industrial progress and impedes economic and social development. We contend that a Natural State, sometimes idealized by movements with a tendency to look toward the past, does not exist and has probably never existed since man's first appearance in the biosphere, insofar as humanity has always progressed by increasingly harnessing Nature to its needs and not the reverse. We fully subscribe to the objectives of a scientific ecology for a universe whose resources must be taken stock of, monitored and preserved. But we herewith demand that this stock-taking, monitoring and preservation be founded on . . . Science, Technology and Industry whose instruments, when adequately managed, are indispensable tools of a future shaped by Humanity, by itself and for itself, overcoming major problems like

overpopulation, starvation and worldwide disease. ("Beware of False Gods in Rio," *Wall Street Journal*, June 1, 1991, p. A12)

There is an almost religious fervor here, indicated by the warning against false gods, against irrational romanticism, and by capitalizing Science, Technology and Industry. But the trouble is that we can also idolize the latter too, and humanity by itself and for itself may be only another irrational romanticizing, now of the human place in the world.

Now we have turned almost 180° from the view we had before, even though both views pretend to come out of science. "Managing the planet by and for ourselves" commits the opposite error to "the Gaia hypothesis." The one view is managerial: the earth is inert like the clay on a potter's wheel, worked by the potter's hands. Science is said to teach us that. The other view is mythical: there is something spooky about the planet, best caught by echoes of an ancient goddess, and this can be demythologized and verified by hard atmospheric and biological science. The planetary manager is still a Cartesian at heart, with a dualist worldview: the objective planet out there, matter in motion, contrasted with the self-conscious, human subject, the "I" collected now into a "we" who manage. The image is of a driver in an automobile, of a mind in a body, with humans the minds who manage the otherwise managerless and often recalcitrant world. The Gaia view is of a world that can manage itself, and has done so for several billion years.

Well, all that is philosophically interesting. But let's face the facts. Humans now control 40 percent of the planet's land-based primary net productivity, that is, the basic plant growth that captures the energy on which everything else depends (Vitousek et al. 1986). The whole point of the worry that we have reached "the end of nature" is that humans have affected everything; there is no pristine nature anymore. Those effects are, the would-be managers worry, more often than not detrimental. We intervene ineptly. Robert Goodland, in a study for the Work Bank, found that 35 percent of the Earth's land now has now become degraded (1992). Surely our only option is to intervene more intelligently—to manage the planet.

Now certainly no one wishes to oppose more intelligent intervention, and we have everywhere in our argument advocated culture in harmony with nature, both remaking landscapes and fitting in, relatively, with the natural givens. We want a sustainable society, with its health and integrity, superposed on a natural world, also with its health and integrity. But we are not so sure that managing the recalcitrant planet is the apt paradigm, besides which all the other ideologies are backward romanticisms. Why not, for instance, think of ourselves as authors who are writing the next chapters, or residents who are learning the logic of our home community, or of moral overseers who are trying to optimize both the cultural and the natural values on the planet? Is our only relationship to nature one of engineering it for the better? Perhaps what is as much to be managed is this earth-eating, managerial mentality that has caused the environmental crisis in the first place.

Penultimately, management is a good thing; but, ultimately management is no more appropriate for Earth than for people, because it only sees means not ends. The scientific managers still have the value questions on their hands. On planetary scales, and even on continental and regional scales, it is not so clear that we really do want to manage the environment; rather we want to manage human uses of the environment so that they are congenial to letting the planet go on managing itself. We do say of an Iowa farmer who plows and plants his fields that he is managing his land, but when the sun shines and the rains fall, and the seed grows in the ear, the farmer is fitting his operations in with what is going on over his head and outside his managing hands. We do not just conserve natural value by managing it; we manage ourselves to let natural values continue to flow.

Managers do not really dwell in an environment; they only have resources, something like the way in which bosses, as such, do not have friends, only subordinates. Even the most enlightened exploiters, *qua* exploiters, do not live as persons in a community; they are not citizens of a world, only consumers of materials. They reduce their environment to resource and sink. The environment, of course, must be this much, but it can be much more. But proportionately as the development ethic increases, the environment is reduced to little more than exploited resource.

Let us envision a greatly accelerated management of Earth. Keeping people well fed seems like a good thing, as does the cure of human diseases—but if and only if we can manage ourselves to keep populations within the capacity of their landscapes. We will need to manage our soils, to keep irrigation systems in repair, and so on. But after that, do we want more rain here and less there? More rainforest and less desert? Do we want to modify the climate, and have our weather programmed by the meteorologists? Or by national policy? Would we like to have more summer and less winter, or the other way around? More spring and less fall? Less wind? More clouds? More or fewer islands? Mountains? Plains? Canyons? Volcanoes? We want more lakes, apparently, for we often build them. But do we want more rivers? Do we want different species of fauna and flora, or here more and fewer there? More birds? Fewer snakes? Bugs? We want fewer earthquakes and hurricanes, presumably, but do we want fewer forest fires? Snowstorms? Would we like to have nature less spontaneous and more orderly, or more spontaneous and less orderly? More diverse? Less complex? Should we leave these decisions to the planetary engineers?

We are not so sure; it is already a rather congenial home planet. We cannot take nature ready to hand, but we can remake it for the supporting of agriculture, industry, culture. After that, perhaps, on the larger planetary scales, it is better to build our cultures in intelligent harmony with the way the world is already built, rather than take control and rebuild the planet by ourselves and for ourselves. Donald Ludwig, Ray Hilborn, and Carl Walters say, rather provocatively, "It is more appropriate to think of resources as managing humans than the converse" (1993:17). We worry a little about those who would play God—not that we should not intervene in nature's course for our own good. But there is indeed a danger of false gods, and an overweening trust in "Science, Technology, and Industry" may result in too little trust in "Mother Earth" after all.

If the symbol of "Mother Earth" still seems unscientific, we can use our alternate vocabulary: the aim of the planetary manager is to have human genius manage the system, but there is already a considerable "genius" in the system. Is man the engineer in an unengineered world? The word *engineer* comes from the root *ingenium*, an innate genius, an inventive power, and hence our word *ingenious*, "characterized by original construction." Etymologically again, *nature* and *genius* (and hence *engineer*) come from the same root, *gene (g)nasci, natus*, to give clever birth. In that sense there is ample inventive and engineering power in nature, which has built Earth and several billion species, keeping the whole machinery running, with these species coming and going, for billions of years.

Who built the engineers, with their clever brains and hands, with which they propose now to manage the planet? Isn't building people out of protons a rather ingenious natural achievement? Maybe we should reconsider our models. Nature is not the antithesis of engineering; it is the prototype of ingenuity. Engineers and managers cannot know what they are doing until they know what they are undoing. We ought to spend adequate effort making sure we know what a place is, especially if it is the only home planet, before we decide to remake it into something else. Hands are for managing, but hands are also for holding in loving care.

6. BALANCING GLOBAL NATURAL AND HUMAN CULTURAL VALUES

We began with ten principles to help achieve a balance of culture and nature (see chapter 1, sec. 9); as we close our inquiry, we expand those to ten more.

1. *Conserving natural value is a fundamental principle of international law.* The first ten principles of international law are all humanistic and nationalistic, understandably so, since relating people to people, nation to nation, has been the chief task of ethics. That imperative continues. The eleventh principle is novel because it moves outside the human and national sectors to the natural history that makes human life possible. Before, people and nations hardly had any duties at the global level, because they hardly had any powers to act for worse or better. But now they do; and that is why, during our lifetimes, protecting the natural environment is becoming a new, fundamental principle. Protection of the environment, which is the last, because the most recent, should be the first, because most fundamental international interest. The fate of the Earth is more important than nation, or sovereignty, or rights, or freedom, or democracy, or economics, because it is foundational to them all.

2. *Emphasize global nonrival cultural and environmental values.*

We began with this principle and met it again with ecosystem health (chapter 1, sec. 9; chapter 3, sec. 6). Now we apply it at the planetary level. Viewing Earth from space, there really is no doubt that nature and culture have entwined destinies. There are two truths to be kept in tandem: culture is a radical emergent from spontaneous nature; and culture forever requires the support of spontaneous nature. We cannot be free from our environment, only free within it. The oceans, the ozone layer, the atmosphere, the waters, the continents, shorelines, islands, landscapes, the world heritage of biodiversity, the wildlife, species, germplasm lines, the universal right to an environment with integrity—none of these can, from here onward, be compromised without deep, long-term cultural loss that outweighs any modest, short-term gains. On global scales, no nation, no culture, no people really win when the whole Earth loses. With the goalposts in the right place, no evil comes to those who care for the Earth.

3. *Foreign affairs are domestic affairs in a global Earth ethics.* If the issue is saving the Earth we do not have any foreign policy, because Earth is not a foreign country. If a particular action affects the Amazon, that is Brazilian domestic policy, but it is inseparable from the domestic policies of the other eight nations whose boundaries include the Rivers Amazon. And, since the Amazon drains nearly a quarter of all the freshwater runoff on Earth, and since the photosynthesis in the Amazon is significant on global scales, and since a disproportionate percentage of the Earth's biological richness is at stake there, what happens there is really domestic policy for Earthlings in the United States. Voting as Earthlings is more important than voting as Americans, Brazilians, or Germans.

4. *Common natural resources are more fundamental than national and private resources.* The health and integrity of the global environment are not values that people or nations should let themselves become rivals about because they are not national or private resources. We need to think of these as world resources that belong to us all, even though nations and persons may legitimately control access to propertied natural resources. On global scales, nations are almost as ephemeral as persons. The common natural heritage is only temporarily to be appropriated as national property, under the constraint of its conservation for the good of the whole planet. In a fundamental sense, Earth, and its richness, is something

that belongs to no one because it belongs to us all.

5. Ecological sustainability is more fundamental than economic sustainability. Sometimes it is said that for economists the numerator can be a public or environmental good, but the denominator must be a dollar sign. Perhaps that is true if one is left to business pressures alone; but, when we add policy imperatives, it is truer to say that, while the numerator can be a dollar sign, the denominator must be an ecosystem. We really cannot have a sound economy in a sick environment. We can seem to get by with that sometimes, because a seemingly sound economy in one country may be stealing environmental integrity from another country. One can rape and run, and seem to prosper, until one finds that there is no longer any place to run to.

The limits become evident from the global perspective. There is no place left to run to. We cannot have sound human cultures on a sick Earth. Economists may think that the bottom line must be green—in the greenback sense. Ecologists knows that it has to be green—in the photosynthetic sense.

6. Do not jeopardize global natural values to avoid solving social problems. We applied this principle to biodiversity (chapter 2, sec. 7) ; now we emphasize it for Earth as a whole. Earth does not have any problems, even though life has for billions of years been a struggle for survival. All the problems that Earth now faces are people-created problems. People exploit people. People make more people, too many people. No one thinks that the present human population growth continued without abatement, will be a good thing, or even a possible thing. People escalate their desires; they never learn to say, Enough. People make short-term choices that are irrational in the long term. People judge risks poorly, and so on.

And these people with their problems are regularly tempted to take the easy way out: to conquer more nature, to exploit their holdings more resourcefully. This will be the more tempting because this has, in the past, sometimes been a way out. It is easier (we think) to make more wealth than to redistribute what wealth there already is; the former only requires hard work, the latter requires what the wealthy, and powerful, regard as the sacrifice of what they got (they maintain) through hard work and cleverness. It is impossible (we think) to revise national boundaries. It is counterproductive (we think) to place taxes on domestic and transnational corporate production that reflects the real environmental and social costs of what industry is doing. It is unrealistic, even inhumane to ask people to curb their escalating desires. So we continue business as usual, politics as usual, and destroy the Earth, and ourselves with it. But we cannot solve our problems so long as we fall into the fallacy of mislocating the problem. The problem is not a managerless home planet; the problem is humans who cannot manage themselves.

7. *Avoid global irreversible change.* This was another introductory principle (chapter 1, sec. 9), especially true as we approach the carrying capacity of the commons. Ultimately, that commons lies at the global level. In natural history, of course, all change is irreversible; time never runs backward. Viewing Earth from space, we can see the dynamism soon enough, with the changing cloud cover. But we would watch quite a while to see large-scale system changes. Back on the ground and watching, the natural history on Earth likewise is dynamic: day, night, wet season, dry. But, then again, one watches quite a while to see large-scale pattern changes, climate change, or respeciation.

Nor have we any reason to think that humans want to speed up such global pattern changes or rearrange them. There is no national or business agenda so important as to risk irreversible global change, even if this is an incremental risk. Scientists predict global warming, but are unsure how much. And so? Business as usual until we know how much? No, because if we are wrong we risk so much. The burden of proof does shift to those who want to risk planetary changes. Our capacity to produce changes is an order of magnitude greater than our capacity to reverse them, and several orders of magnitude greater than Earth's spontaneous capacity to reverse our damages.

We can cut down more forest in a day than Earth can grow in five hundred years. We can lose more soil in a year than Earth makes in a millennium, kill more species in a decade than Earth makes in ten thousand years. We can pollute groundwater with radioactive isotopes for almost forever. Given this differential in pace of change, it is both rational and moral to claim, despite our living on a historical Earth, that we want to avoid irreversible planetary change.

8. *Plan for seven generations.* A human lifespan is seven decades, more or less; and seven generations past is almost beyond our scope

of memory. For that one has to go to the library and dig out a history book. Seven generations in the future is beyond our ordinary scope of anticipation. In a world with the pace of change of the twentieth century, we are foolish to predict interest rates or the price of gasoline four centuries from now. But just the planetary view that the twentieth century has given us, just the pace of change that is so accelerating means that it is more, not less urgent, to act now with seven generations in mind, or seventy-seven generations. That is, Earth has been here for generations almost infinite, and we want Earth to remain a home planet for the perennial future. Of course we cannot know specifically what the seventh generation will value in goods and services, but we hardly doubt that they will need air, water, soil, rain, photosynthesis, or enjoy sunsets, mountains, seashores—or birdwatching. There are some perennial givens and needs on Earth, and our recently reached capacities to jeopardize these generate new and increasingly complex responsibilities on the home planet.

9. *Think globally, act locally.* This is a bumper sticker slogan, but philosophically profound. You will perhaps have been uneasy about an Earth ethics; it is at once vaguely reasonably and unreasonably vague. Who can deny an Earth ethics? Who can act on it? An Earth ethics is difficult because there are no clear opponents; no one is against the Earth. On a global scale, there are no immediate effects of our allegedly bad actions. I continue to use fluorocarbon sprays, and nothing happens that I can see. It is hard to organize for worldwide, abstract issues. So much depends on our acting in concert that one person's efforts are washed out. I do not have any options for acting globally; only a handful of people have such power—the heads of state in the G-7 nations, or CEOs in transnational corporations.

But we each do have power to act locally, and it is false to think that acting well beneficially does not accumulate, too. Environmentalism has, often as not, been a grassroots movement before it became a political movement. Alas, the heads of state in G-7 nations and CEOs of transnational corporations have hardly initiated any conservation of natural value at all on global scales; they have largely responded to groundswells of concern mounting up from below. Humans inhabit the Earth, and we are able to think on global scales; we inhabit local environments, and we can and must act there.

10. *Earth is more important than people.* Critics may allege that

this is a misguided, because misanthropic principle. Humans are the glory of Earth, superior (if we must so assert) both in the evolutionary achievements present in their brains and bodies and in the cultural achievements that this natural endowment has made possible. One on one, a person is worth more than a grass plant. People have more intrinsic value. But humans are not more important than grass, ecologically speaking, in the sense that photosynthesis, epitomized in grass and green plants, is what supports everything else. In the systemic patterns, photosynthesis is more important than people.

No persons are so important than they can shut down, even incrementally, the system, when myriads of other persons, with the same inflated self-importance, are doing the same thing. We have little difficulty seeing this Earth-over-people principle if we begin with the claim that conserving the Earth is more important than having *more* people. Almost no one would argue the contrary. But why not then admit that conserving the Earth is more important than the needs, or even the welfare, of *existing* people? If (as seems rather likely) the numbers of people now on Earth threaten, through their otherwise legitimate desires, to degrade the planet (global warming, species extinction, soil degradation), and if we are really committed to optimizing values on Earth, we can only conclude that no people are that important. Thinking globally, human rights are welcome where they are nonrival with the health of the system. But human rights that claim to trump the system are doubtful rights. That kind of arrogance does not win

Someone might protest that this principle confuses the actual loci of value. What we mean is that no people have the right to infringe on the rights of other people, including future generations, as they will do if they degrade Earth's life-support capacity. It is not Earth over people, but people constrained by other people. That is a humanistic way of approaching what we are trying to say, but what we are claiming goes deeper, a naturalistic ethic. Earth is not just important as *our* human home. Earth is important because it can be a *home planet* for all the biota, and that, ultimately, is the most important value of all. In the end, we refuse to put humans at the center of concerns. We cannot even put them on top, unless there is something down under; people have to be grounded in their Earth. The only consolation we offer is that refusing to place humans at the center does not make humans losers; to the contrary, only then can they inherit the Earth.

7. INHERITING THE EARTH

Inherit the Earth! That is really what the preceding maxims are all about. At this scale of vision, if we ask what is principally to be protected, the value of life arising as a creative process on Earth seems a better description than Earth as a human resource, and a more comprehensive category. Humans who see nature only as a resource for their human development are not yet true to their Earth. They do not understand biological conservation in this deep sense. To elevate human intrinsic values is authentic development; but to elevate human values above all else, degrading nature in result, is retrograde. Human "responsibility" on Earth is a better word than human "dominion" over Earth, for it captures what dominion originally meant in the famous Genesis charge to Adam and Eve, or what it ought to mean, a stewardship over something entrusted into one's care, the prolific Earth with it swarms of creatures found to be very good.

Land is not where we *make* a living; it is where we *live*, seen if we enlarge the scope from earth to Earth. Earth is not just where we *make* a living; it *is* where we live. The animal who builds a *polis* still inhabits an *oikos*, a whole world; humans have an ecology. We are natives, naturally born on Earth, before we are nationals, citizens of a political state. The human is first and always an Earthling. Once the mark of an educated person could be summed up as *civitas*, the privileges, rights, responsibilities of citizenship. People ought to be good citizens, productive in their communities, leaders in business, the professions, government, church, education. That was the responsibility that went with your rights.

But the mark of an educated person is today, increasingly, something more. It is not enough to be a good "citizen," it is not enough even to be "international," because neither of those terms have enough "earthiness" in them. "Citizen" is only half the truth; the other half is that we are "residents" dwelling on landscapes. We are natives on Earth. Our responsibility to Earth might be thought the most remote of our responsibilities; it seems so grandiose and vague beside our concrete responsibilities to our children or next door neighbors. But not so: the other way round, it is the most fundamental of our responsibilities. Though foreshadowed in the past by the sense of belonging that many peoples have had on their landscapes, loyalty to the planet is the newest demand in ethics, a new possibility that can also prove the highest level of duty. A century ago, a call for community was typically phrased as the brotherhood of man and the fatherhood of God. Now such a call must be more ecological, less paternalistic, a call for appropriate respect for this home Earth.

The view from space gives us that vision, but we have yet to make it operational. The view from space eliminates boundaries; Earth is a seamless dynamic whole. Two Arab astronauts sensed this: "The first day we all pointed to our countries. The third or fourth day we were pointing to our continents. By the fifth day we were aware of only one Earth." "From space I saw Earth—indescribably beautiful with the scars of national boundaries gone" (Sultan Bin Salman al-Saud and Muhammed Ahmad Faris, quoted in Kelley 1988:82, 76). Our national loyalties and cultural identities can assist in giving us this principled responsibility to the biospheric Earth, but they can just as often get in the way. Our operative values tend to become fragmented, political, economic; the needed values are global, ethical, and ecological. But increasingly from here onward, just this threat to natural systems at the planetary level can produce more global consensus, because now nations have a common interest that is entwined with the integrity of natural systems.

Nature has equipped *Homo sapiens*, the wise species, with a conscience to direct the fearful power of the brain and hand. Only the human species contains moral agents, but perhaps conscience is less wisely used than it ought to be when it exempts the global community of life from consideration, with the resulting paradox that the sole moral species acts only in its collective self-interest toward all the rest. Among the remarkable developments on Earth with which we have to reckon, there is the longstanding ingenuity of the myriads of species that compose natural history; there is the recent, explosive human development; and there ought to be, and is, a developing environmental ethic that optimizes natural values. In this sense, being a naturalist is more important than being an nationalist or even an internationalist.

Feel the ground under your feet, hear the water in the stream, feel the wind in your face and know that land and water and air reach around from your west and come back from the east, circle around from your south over two poles and come back from the north. Feel your biology within and think back across the millennia. Know that you are standing in the midst of planetary circulations that are far more real, far more vital, and almost everlasting compared with the national citizenship that you hold. The geophysical and biological laws, the evolutionary and ecological history, the creativity within the natural system we inherit, and the values they generate, are the ground of your being, and we all owe that Earth system far more than we owe obedience to the civic laws, the national history, or even the heritage of our cultural system.

In that sense, an Earth ethics is not the *reductio ad absurdum* of silly and peripheral concern about chipmunks and daisies, extrapolated to rocks and dirt. To the contrary, it is the elevation to ultimacy of an urgent world vision. Perhaps there is a God above, and this marvelous Earth creation may witness to that God, but meanwhile what cannot be doubted is that on this enthralling Earth we live and move and have our being. On the home planet, we can hardly be responsible to anything more cosmic. If there is any holy ground, this is it.

It was feared by some that the space flights, reaching for the stars, was an act of human arrogance, hubris in extreme, more of the conquest and dominion by *Homo sapiens* that has already ravaged the planet. But people responded unexpectedly. The haughty, the high, and the mighty of spirit failed to materialize with the flight into space. Rather humility—from *humus*, meaning "earthy," also the root of "human"—was the dominant experience. The value and beauty of the home planet, and our destiny in caring for it was the repeated reaction. Perhaps that is a truth in the beatitude: "Blessed are the meek, for they shall inherit the Earth." For earth is indeed a planet with promise, a promised planet, and we humans have both the right to share in and the responsibility to help to keep that promise. This is the biology of ultimate concern.

References

Anderson, Terry L., and Donald R. Leal. 1991. *Free Market Environmentalism*. Boulder, Colo.: Westview Press.

Ayala, Francisco J. 1974. "The Concept of Biological Progress." In Francisco J. Ayala and Theodosius Dobzhansky, eds., *Studies in the Philosophy of Biology*, pp. 339–355. New York: Macmillan.

Bacon, Francis. 1968 [1620]. *Novum Organum* in *Works*. New York: Garrett Press.

Ballentine, R. Kent, and Leonard J. Guarraia, eds. 1977. *The Integrity of Water*. Washington, D.C.: U.S. Government Printing Office.

Bekoff, Marc, and Dale Jamieson. 1991. "Sport Hunting as an Instinct," *Environmental Ethics* 13:375–378.

Birnie, Patricia. 1985. "Role of Developing Countries in Nudging the International Whaling Commission from Regulating Whaling to Encouraging Nonconsumptive Use of Whales." *Ecology Law Quarterly* 12:937–975.

Botkin, Daniel B. 1990. *Discordant Harmonies*. New York: Oxford University Press.

Boutros-Ghalli, Boutros. 1992a. Extracts from closing UNCED statement, in an UNCED summary, *Final Meeting and Round-up of Conference*, p. 1. UN Document ENV/DEV/RIO/29, June 14.

——. 1992b. Text of closing UNCED statements, in *Report of the United Nations Conference on Environment and Development*, vol. IV, pages 66–69. UN Document A/CONF.151.26.

Bunn, Henry T. 1981. "Archaeological Evidence for Meat-Eating by Plio-Pleistocene Hominids from Koobi Fora and Olduvai Gorge." *Nature* 291:574–577.

Cain, Stanley A. 1971 [1944]. *Foundations of Plant Geography*. New York: Hafner.

Callicott, J. Baird. 1980. "Animal Liberation: A Triangular Affair." *Environmental Ethics* 2:311–338.

——. 1984. "Non-Anthropocentric Value Theory and Environmental Ethics." *American Philosophical Quarterly* 21:299–309.

——. 1986. "On the Intrinsic Value of Nonhuman Species." In Bryan G. Norton, ed., *The Preservation of Species*, pp. 138–172. Princeton: Princeton University Press.

——. 1991. "The Wilderness Idea Revisited: The Sustainable Development Alternative." *Environmental Professional* 13:235–247.

—, ed. 1992a. "The Intrinsic Value of Nature." Special Issue of *The Monist* 75(2) (April).

——. 1992b. "La Nature est morte, vive la nature!" *Hastings Center Report* 22(5):16–23.

Campbell, John H. 1983. "Evolving Concepts of Multigene Families." In *Isozymes: Current Topics in Biological and Medical Research*, pp. 401–417. Volume 10. *Genetics and Evolution*. New York: Alan R. Liss.

Causey, Ann S. 1989. "On the Morality of Hunting." *Environmental Ethics* 11:327–343.

Clark, William C. 1989. "Managing Planet Earth." *Scientific American* 261(3):46–54.

Coale, A. J. 1983. "Recent Trends in Fertility in the Less Developed Countries." *Science* 221:828–832.

Colinvaux, Paul A. 1978. *Why Big Fierce Animals Are Rare: An Ecologist's Perspective*. Princeton: Princeton University Press.

Collins, Michael. 1980. "Foreword." In Roy A. Gallant, *Our Universe*. Washington, D.C.: National Geographic Society.

Costanza, Robert, ed. 1991. *Ecological Economics*. New York: Columbia University Press.

Costanza, Robert, Bryan G. Norton, and Benjamin D. Haskell. 1992.

Ecosystem Health: New Goals for Environmental Management. Washington, D.C.: Island Press.

Council on Environmental Quality. 1980. *Global 2000 Report to the President.* Washington, D.C.: U.S. Government Printing Office.

Cowell, C. Mark. 1993. "Ecological Restoration and Environmental Ethics." *Environmental Ethics* 15:19–32.

Craig, Raymond S. 1992. "Land Ethic Canon Proposal: A Report from the Task Force." *Journal of Forestry* 90(8):40–41.

Crick, Francis. 1988. *What Mad Pursuit: A Personal View of Scientific Discovery.* New York: Basic Books.

Darwin, Charles. 1903 [1858]. "Letter to J. D. Hooker," December 30. In *More Letters of Charles Darwin,* edited by Francis Darwin, vol. 1, pp. 114–115. London: John Murray.

———. 1964 [1859]. *On the Origin of Species.* Cambridge, Mass.: Harvard University Press.

———. 1895 [1871]. *The Descent of Man.* New York: D. Appleton.

Dobzhansky, Theodosius. 1974. "Chance and Creativity in Evolution." In Francisco Jose Ayala and Theodosius Dobzhansky, eds., *Studies in the Philosophy of Biology,* pp. 307–337. New York: Macmillan.

Donaldson, Thomas. 1989. *The Ethics of International Business.* New York: Oxford University Press.

Douglas, T. J., and I. A. Schirmer, eds. 1987. *Agricultural Sustainability in a Changing World Order.* Boulder, Colo.: Westview Press.

Dryzek, John, and Susan Hunter. 1987. "Environmental Mediation for International Problems." *International Studies Quarterly* 31:87–102.

Duffy, David Cameron, and Albert J. Meier. 1992. "Do Appalachian Herbaceous Understories Ever Recover from Clearcutting?" *Conservation Biology* 6:196–201.

Durning, Alan B. 1990. *Apartheid's Environmental Toll.* Washington, D.C.: Worldwatch Institute.

Elliot, Robert. 1982. "Faking Nature." *Inquiry* 25:81–93.

Elton, Charles S. 1958. *The Ecology of Invasions by Animals and Plants.* New York: Wiley.

Engel, J. Ronald. 1990. "Introduction: The Ethics of Sustainable Development." In J. Ronald Engel and Joan Gibb Engel, eds., *Ethics of Environment and Development,* pp. 1–23. London: Belhaven Press.

Garvin, Lucius. 1953. *A Modern Introduction to Ethics.* Cambridge, Mass.: Houghton Mifflin.

Gómez-Pompa, Arturo, and Andrea Kaus. 1992. "Taming the Wilderness Myth." *BioScience* 42:271–279.

Goodland, Robert. 1992. "The Case That the World Has Reached Limits." In Robert Goodland, Herman E. Daly, and Salah El Serafy, eds., *Population, Technology, and Lifestyle*, pp. 3–22. Washington, D.C.: Island Press.

Goodman, D. 1975. "The Theory of Diversity-Stability Relationships in Ecology." *Quarterly Review of Biology* 50:237–266.

Gould, Stephen Jay. 1980a. "Chance Riches." *Natural History* 89(11):36–44.

——. 1980b. *The Panda's Thumb*. New York: W. W. Norton.

——. 1989. *Wonderful Life: The Burgess Shale and the Nature of History*. New York: W. W. Norton.

Goulet, Denis. 1990. "Development Ethics and Ecological Wisdom." In J. Ronald Engel and Joan Gibb Engel, eds., *Ethics of Environment and Development*, pp. 36–62. London: Belhaven Press.

Griffin, Donald R. 1981. *The Question of Animal Awareness*. Rev. ed. Los Altos, Calif.: William Kaufman.

——. 1984. *Animal Thinking*. Cambridge, Mass.: Harvard University Press.

Gunn, Alastair S. 1991. "The Restoration of Species and Natural Environments." *Environmental Ethics* 13:291–310.

Halliday, Tim. 1978. *Vanishing Birds*. New York: Holt, Rinehart and Winston.

Hendee, John C., George H. Stankey, and Robert C. Lucas. 1990. *Wilderness Management*. 2d ed. Fort Collins, Colo.: International Wilderness Leadership Foundation.

Huntley, Brian, Roy Siegfried, and Clem Sunter. 1989. *South African Environments into the 21st Century*. Cape Town: Human and Rousseau, Ltd. and Tafelberg Publishers Ltd.

James, William. 1925. *Varieties of Religious Experience*. New York: Longmans, Green.

John Paul II. 1989. "Peace with All Creation." *Origins:* CNS Documentary Service 19 (no. 28, December 14):465–468.

Jones, Dorothy V. 1991. *Code of Peace: Ethics and Security in the World of Warlord States*. Chicago: University of Chicago Press.

Jordan, William R., III. 1991. "Ecological Restoration and the Reintegration of Ecological Systems." In D. J. Roy, B. E. Wynne, and R. W. Old, eds., *Bioscience—Society*, pp. 151–162. San Francisco: John Wiley and Sons.

Jordan, William R., III, Michael E. Gilpin, and John D. Aber, eds. 1987. *Restoration Ecology: A Synthetic Approach to Ecological Research*. New York: Cambridge University Press.

Karr, James R., and D. R. Dudley. 1981. "Ecological Perspective on Water Quality Goals." *Environmental Management* 5:55–68.

Katz, Eric. 1992. "The Big Lie: Human Restoration of Nature." *Research in Philosophy and Technology* 12:231–241.

Kelley, Kevin W., ed. 1988. *The Home Planet*. Reading, Mass.: Addison-Wesley.

Kerr, Richard A. 1988. "No Longer Willful, Gaia Becomes Respectable." *Science* 240:393–395.

King, Roger J. H. 1991. "Environmental Ethics and the Case for Hunting." *Environmental Ethics* 13:59–85.

Knickerbocker, Brad. 1991. "Biodiversity: Top Concern in Saving Species." *Christian Science Monitor* (December 23):8.

Krider, E. Philip. 1986. "Lightning Damage and Lightning Protection." In Robert H. Maybury, ed., *Violent Forces of Nature*, pp. 205–229. Mt. Airy, Md.: Lomond Publications (in cooperation with UNESCO).

Krukeberg, Arthur R., and Deborah Rabinowitz. 1985. "Biological Aspects of Endemism in Higher Plants." *Annual Review of Ecology and Systematics* 16:447–479.

Leopold, Aldo. 1968 [1949]. *A Sand County Almanac*. New York: Oxford University Press.

——. 1966. "The Round River." In *A Sand County Almanac*. Enlarged ed. New York: Oxford University Press.

Leopold, A. S., S. A. Cain, C. M. Cottam, I. N. Gabrielson, and T. L. Kimball. 1963. *Wildlife Management in the National Parks*. Report of the Advisory Board on Wildlife Management, March 4. Washington, D.C.: U.S. Government Printing Office.

Loftin, Robert W. 1984. "The Morality of Hunting." *Environmental Ethics* 6:241–250

Lotan, James E., Bruce M. Kilgore, William C. Fischer, and Robert W. Mutch, eds. 1985. *Proceedings-Symposium and Workshop on Wilderness Fire*. Missoula, Mont., November 15–18, 1983. Ogden, Utah: USDA Forest Service, Intermountain Forest and Range Experiment Station, General Technical Report INT-182.

Lovelock, James. 1979. *Gaia: A New Look at Life on Earth*. New York: Oxford University Press.

Ludwig, Donald, Ray Hilborn, and Carl Walters. 1993. "Uncertainty, Resource Exploitation, and Conservation: Lessons from History." *Science* 260:17–18.

MacArthur, Robert. 1955. "Fluctuations of Animal Populations and a Measure of Community Stability." *Ecology* 36:533–536.

McKibben, Bill. 1989. *The End of Nature*. New York: Random House.

Magraw, Daniel Barstow, and James W. Nickel. 1990. "Can Today's International System Handle Transboundary Environmental Problems?" In Donald Scherer, ed., *Upstream/Downstream: Issues in Environmental Ethics*, pp. 121–157. Philadelphia: Temple University Press.

Magurran, Anne E. 1988. *Ecological Diversity and Its Measurement*. Princeton, N.J.: Princeton University Press.

Mares, Michael A. 1988. "Conservation in South America: Problems, Consequences and Solutions." *Science* 223:734–739.

Maslow, Abraham. 1968. *Toward a Psychology of Being*. 2d ed. Princeton, N.J.: Van Nostrand.

May, Robert M. 1973. *Stability and Complexity in Model Ecosystems*. Princeton, N.J.: Princeton University Press.

——. 1988. "How Many Species Are There on Earth?" *Science* 241:1441–1449.

Maynard Smith, John. 1972. *On Evolution*. Edinburgh: Edinburgh University Press.

Mayr, Ernst. 1988. *Toward a New Philosophy of Biology*. Cambridge, Mass.: Harvard University Press.

Meine, Curt. 1988. *Aldo Leopold: His Life and Work*. Madison: University of Wisconsin Press.

Mesthene, Emmanuel G. 1966. "Technology and Religion." *Theology Today* 23:481–495.

Miller, Peter. 1982. "Value as Richness: Toward a Value Theory for an Expanded Naturalism in Environmental Ethics." *Environmental Ethics* 4:101–114.

Muir, John. 1916. *A Thousand-Mile Walk to the Gulf*. Boston: Houghton Mifflin.

Murie, Martin. 1972. "Evaluations of Natural Environments." In W. A. Thomas, ed., *Indicators of Environmental Quality*, pp. 43–53. New York: Plenum Press.

Myers, Norman. 1979. *The Sinking Ark*. New York: Pergamon Press.

Naess, Arne. 1984. "A Defense of the Deep Ecology Movement." *Environmental Ethics* 6:265–270.

Norton, Bryan G. 1984. "Environmental Ethics and Weak Anthropocentrism." *Environmental Ethics* 6:131–148.

——. 1987. *Why Preserve Natural Variety?* Princeton, N.J.: Princeton University Press.

Orians, Gordon H. 1975. "Diversity, Stability and Maturity in Natural Ecosystems." In W. H. van Dobben and R. H. Lowe-MConnell, eds.,

Unifying Concepts in Ecology, pp. 139–150. The Hague: Dr. W. Junk B. V. Publishers.

——. 1980. "Habitat Selection: General Theory and Applications to Human Behavior." In Joan S. Lockard, ed., *The Evolution of Human Social Behavior*, pp. 46–66. New York: Elsevier North Holland.

Ortega y Gasset, José. 1972. *Meditations on Hunting*. New York: Scribners.

Packard, Steve. 1990. "No End to Nature." *Restoration and Management Notes* 8(2) (Winter):72.

Passmore, John. 1974. *Man's Responsibility for Nature*. New York: Scribners.

Perry, Ralph Barton. 1954 [1926]. *General Theory of Value*. Cambridge, Mass.: Harvard University Press.

Pielou, E. C. 1975. *Ecological Diversity*. New York: John Wiley.

Power, Jonathan. 1992. "Despite Its Gifts, Brazil Is a Basket Case." *Miami Herald* (June 22):10A.

Prall, David W. 1921. *A Study in the Theory of Value*. University of California Publications in Philosophy, vol. 3, no. 2. Berkeley: University of California Press.

Preston-Whyte, Rob, and Graham House, eds. 1990. *Rotating the Cube: Environmental Strategies for the 1990s*. Durban: Department of Geographical and Environmental Sciences and Indicator Project South Africa, University of Natal.

Rapport, David J. 1989. "What Constitutes Ecosystem Health?" *Perspectives in Biology and Medicine* 33:120–132.

Raup, David M. 1991. *Extinction: Bad Genes or Bad Luck?* New York. W. W. Norton.

Raup, David M., and J. J. Sepkoski, Jr. 1982. "Mass Extinctions in the Marine Fossil Record." *Science* 215:1501–1503.

Redclift, M. 1987. *Sustainable Development: Exploring the Contradictions*. London: Methuen.

Regan, Tom. 1983. *The Case for Animal Rights*. Berkeley: University of California Press.

Reganold, J. P., R. I. Papendick, and J. F. Parr. 1990. "Sustainable Agriculture." *Scientific American* 262(6):112–120.

Reilly, William K. 1990. "A Strategy to Save the Great Water Bodies." *EPA Journal* 16(6) (November/December):2–4.

Rescher, Nicholas. 1974. "The Environmental Crisis and the Quality of Life." In William T. Blackstone, ed., *Philosophy and Environmental Crisis*, pp. 90–104. Athens: University of Georgia Press.

Roberts, Leslie. 1993. "Wetlands Trading is a Loser's Game, Say Ecologists." *Science* 260:1890–1892.

Rolston, Holmes, III. 1988. *Environmental Ethics*. Philadelphia: Temple University Press.

——. 1991. "The Wilderness Idea Reaffirmed." *The Environmental Professional* 13:370–377.

——. 1993. "Rights and Responsibilities on the Home Planet." *Yale Journal of International Law* 18:251–279.

Roman Catholic Bishops. 1991. "Renewing the Earth: An Invitation to Reflection and Action on the Environment in the Light of Catholic Social Teaching." *Origins: CNS Documentary Service* 21 (no. 27, December 12):425–432.

Rothenberg, David. 1992. "The Greenhouse from Down Deep: What Can Philosophy Do for Ecology?" *Pan Ecology* 7(2) (Spring):1–3.

Sagan, Dorion, and Lynn Margulis. 1984. "Gaia and Philosophy." In Leroy S. Rouner, ed., *On Nature*, pp. 60–73. Notre Dame, Ind.: University of Notre Dame Press.

Salvini-Plawen, L. v., and Ernst Mayr. 1977. "On the Evolution of Photoreceptors and Eyes." In Max K. Hecht, William C. Steere, and Bruce Wallace, eds., *Evolutionary Biology*, vol. 10, pp. 207–263. New York: Plenum Press.

Scarff, James E. 1977. "International Management of Whales, Dolphins, and Porpoises: An Interdisciplinary Assessment." *Ecology Law Quarterly* 6:323–427, 571–638.

Shiva, Vandana. 1991. *The Violence of the Green Revolution*. London: Zed Books.

Smith, Frederick E. 1970. "Scientific Problems and Progress in Solving the Environmental Crisis." *Denver Post* (February 20):8A.

Stebbins, G. Ledyard. 1980. "Rarity of Plant Species: A Synthetic Viewpoint." *Rhodora* 80:77–85.

Stone, Charles P. 1985. "Alien Animals in Hawai'i's Native Ecosystems." In Charles P. Stone and J. Michael Scott, eds., *Hawai'i's Terrestrial Ecosystems: Preservation and Management*, pp. 251–297. Honolulu: Cooperative National Park Resources Studies Unit, University of Hawaii.

Stone, Christopher D. 1987. *Earth and Other Ethics*. New York: Harper and Row.

Sylvan, Richard. 1994. "Mucking with Nature." In Sylvan, *Against the Main Stream*. Discussion Papers in Environmental Philosophy, no.21. Canberra: Research School of Social Sciences, Australian National University.

Terborgh, John. 1988. "The Big Things that Run the World." *Conservation Biology* 2:402–403.

Thompson, Daniel Q., and Ralph H. Smith. 1971. "The Forest Primeval in the Northeast—A Great Myth?" In *Tall Timbers Fire Ecology Conference, Annual Proceedings*, no. 10. Tallahassee, Fla.: Tall Timbers Research Station.

United Nations. 1990. *List of National Parks and Protected Areas*. New York: United Nations.

United Nations Conference on Environment and Development. 1992a. *Convention on Biological Diversity*. New York: UNCED Document no. DPI/1307.

——. 1992b. *Principles on General Rights and Obligations*. New York: UNCED Document A/CONF.151/PC/WG.III/L.33. March 31.

——. 1992c. *The Rio Declaration*. New York: UNCED Document A/CONF.151/5/Rev. 1, June 13.

United Nations Environment Programme. 1991. *Register of International Treaties and Other Agreements in the Field of the Environment*. Nairobi: Document No. UNEP/GC.16/Inf.4, May.

United Nations General Assembly. 1948. *Universal Declaration on Human Rights*. In UN General Assembly, Third Session, First Part, *Official Records*, "Resolutions," pp. 71–77.

——. 1982. *World Charter for Nature*. UN General Assembly Resolution no. 37/7 of October 28. New York: United Nations.

United Nations World Commission on Environment and Development. 1987a. *Environmental Protection and Sustainable Development: Legal Principles and Recommendations*. London/Dordrecht, Netherlands: Graham and Trotman/Martinus Nijhoff.

——. 1987b. *Our Common Future*. New York: Oxford University Press.

U.S. Congress. 1964. *Wilderness Act of 1964*. Public Law 88–577. 78 Stat. 891.

——. 1969. *National Environmental Policy Act of 1969*. Public Law 91–190. 83 Stat. 852.

——. 1971. *Wild Free-Roaming Horses and Burros Act of 1971*. Public Law 92–195. 85 Stat. 649.

——. 1972a. *Federal Water Pollution Control Act Amendments of 1972*. Public Law 92–500. 86 U. S. Stat. 816.

——. 1972b. *Marine Protection, Research, and Sanctuaries Act of 1972*. Public Law 92–532. 86 U.S. Stat. 1052.

——. 1973. *Endangered Species Act of 1973*. Public Law 93–205. 87 U.

S. Stat. 884. Codified with amendments in U.S.C., 1988 ed., vol. 6, title 16, chapter 35.

——. 1976a. *Federal Land Policy and Management Act of 1976*. Public Law 94–579. 90 Stat. 2743.

——. 1976b. *National Forest Management Act of 1976*. Public Law 94–588. 90 Stat. 2949.

——. 1990. *Eighth Report to Congress on the Administration of the Wild Free-Roaming Horse and Burro Act*. Washington, D.C.: U.S. Government Printing Office.

Valentine, James W. 1969. "Patterns of Taxonomic and Ecological Structure of the Shelf Benthos During Phanerozoic Time." *Paleontology* 12:684–709.

——. 1973. *Evolutionary Paleoecology of the Marine Biosphere*. Englewood Cliffs, N.J.: Prentice-Hall.

Van Voris, Peter, Robert V. O'Neill, William R. Emanuel, and H. H. Shugart, Jr. 1980. "Functional Complexity and Ecosystem Stability." *Ecology* 61:1352–1360.

Varley, John, and Schullery, Paul. 1983. *Freshwater Wilderness: Yellowstone Fishes and their World*. Yellowstone National Park, Wy.: Yellowstone Library and Museum Association.

Vitali, Theodore R. 1990. "Sport Hunting: Moral or Immoral?" *Environmental Ethics* 12:69–82.

Vitousek, Peter M., Paul R. Ehrlich, Anne H. Ehrlich, and Pamela A. Matson. 1986. "Human Appropriation of the Products of Biosynthesis." *BioScience* 36:368–373.

Walker, Brian. 1989. "Diversity and Stability in Ecosystem Conservation." In David Western and Mary Pearl, eds., *Conservation for the Twenty-First Century*, pp. 121–130. New York: Oxford University Press.

Weir, Jack. 1992. "The Sweetwater Rattlesnake Round-Up: A Case Study in Environmental Ethics." *Conservation Biology* 6:116–127.

Wells, Martin J. 1978. *Octopus*. London: Chapman and Hall.

Wenz, Peter. 1989. "Democracy and Environmental Change." In Niger Dower, ed., *Ethics and Environmental Responsibility*, pp. 91–109. Aldershot, U.K.: Gower.

Westman, Walter E. 1991. "Ecological Restoration Projects: Measuring Their Performance." *Environmental Professional* 13:207–215.

Westra, Laura. 1994. *An Environmental Proposal for Ethics: The Principle of Integrity*. Lanham, Md.: Rowman and Littlefield.

Whitman, Walt. [1860] 1961. *Leaves of Grass*. Ithaca: Cornell University Press.

Wildlife Society. 1988. *Conservation Policies of the Wildlife Society*. Bethesda, Md.: Wildlife Society.

Wilson, Edward O. 1983. "Introduction." "What's a Species Worth?" Special issue of *Nature Conservancy News* 33(6) (November–December):4.

——. 1984. *Biophilia*. Cambridge, Mass.: Harvard University Press.

——. 1992. *The Diversity of Life*. Cambridge, Mass.: Harvard University Press.

Wordsworth, William. 1798. "Lines Composed a Few Miles above Tintern Abbey."

World Conservation Union (IUCN). 1990. *Caring for the World: A Strategy for Sustainability*. Gland, Switzerland: World Conservation Union.

Index

Aber, John D., 88, 240
Adaptation, 44–45, 71, 92, 174
Adenosine triphosphate (ATP), 94
Adirondack mountains, 31, 200
Aesthetics, aesthetic value, 136; of wildlife, 118–22
Affirmative action, 30
Africa, 76, 152; and elephants, 127; South Africa, 148–49, 185, 186, 214
Agenda 21, see United Nations
Agriculture, 8, 25, 54, 72, 77, 85–86, 95, 100, 133–44, 149, 199, 227
Allied Chemical Company, 31
Alligators, 127, 130–31
al-Saud, Sultan Bin Salman, 235
Amazon, 54–55, 96

America, 9, 229; as geographical and economic unit, 215; nature sacrificed to build, 144–45; primitive America, 75*n*, 86
Anderson, Terry L., 155, 237
Angel hair, in Mammoth Cave, 182
Animals, 79, 83, 101–32, 144, 172; animal rights 106–14; animal welfare, 108, 110–14; charismatic megafauna, 63, 103, 116, 118–19; as conservation systems, 168–71; lower and higher, 102–6, 165; virtues, 105; *see also* Values, wildlife; Wildlife
Antarctica, 31, 72, 181–82

Anthropocentrism, 133–66, 233;
    see also Values, anthropocen-
    tric
Aristotle, 12, 121, 169
Arizona, 189
Ash Meadows, Nevada, 51, 53
Audubon Society, 15
Australia, 185
Ayala, Francisco, 47, 237

Bacon, Francis, 4, 237
Ballentine, R. Kent, 69, 237
Bananas, 57
Bats, 2, 60, 104
Bears, 80, 110, 111, 112, 113,
    131, 132
Beetles, 37, 39
Bekoff, Marc, 122, 237
Biodiversity, 17, 34–67, 73, 84,
    136, 137; and the commons,
    54–58, 210–14; diversity
    indices, 35–40; extent of,
    35–40; at threat, 36–37
Biology, see Science
Birds, 117, 120, 130, 131, 135,
    141, 227
Birnie, Patricia, 218, 237
Bison, 86, 121, 124, 132; attempt-
    ed rescue in Yellowstone Park,
    110
Bixby State Park, Iowa, 51
Bobcats, 120
Botkin, Daniel B., 74, 237
Boutros-Ghali, Boutros, 203, 217,
    237–38
Bracken Cave, Texas, 104
Brain, mind, 194, 227; complexity
    of human, 41–42, 102–3,
    138–39, 232
Brazil, 95–96, 148, 229
Bristlecone pine, 51
Bunn, Henry T., 123, 238

Burden of proof, 31, 93, 153,
    231
Bureau of Land Management,
    115
Burros, feral, 114–15
Butterflies, 50, 103

Cain, Stanley A., 50, 238
California, 83
Callicott, J. Baird, 4–5, 159–60,
    171, 187n, 238
Campbell, John H., 47–48, 238
Capitalism, see Economics; Mar-
    kets
Cardinals, 10
Cattle, on public lands, 115n; and
    wolves, 132
Causey, Ann, 122, 238
Caves, 183–84
Chance, see Contingency
Chaos, chaos theory, 75, 138–39
Chesapeake Bay, 8, 31–32
Chicago, 5
Chimpanzees, 37, 103
Cities, 12, 15
Citizens, 30, 210–13, 234; and
    consumers, 30; and residents,
    10–12, 234
Clark, William C., 223, 238
Clean Water Act, 5, 88
Clearcuts, 90
Climate change, 31, 73, 149, 218,
    231
Clinch River, 102
Coale, A. J., 151, 238
Coffee, 57
Colinvaux, Paul A., 50, 238
Collins, Michael, 203, 238
Colorado, 183
Colorado River, 9
Columbia (nation), 151
Columbia River, 118

Commodities, 14–15; and communities, 9

Commons: biodiversity and, 54–58; common heritage of mankind, 213, 217; environment as, 26, 31

Communities, 11, 26, 59, 85, 143; biotic, 77–82, 173–74, 176, 189; and commodities, 9; Earth as community of life, 203–10

Compassion, for animals, 112–13

Complexity, 34–67, 227; kinds of, 40–44; evolution of, 44–50, 102–3

Compromise, 26–27

Conscience, 3, 186

Consciousness, in animals, 59–60, 107, 179

Conservation, 75; and life, 168–71; and restoration, 93

Consumption, 97, 143, 145–50, 226, 230

Contingency: and lack of animals in Hawaii, 117–18; in natural history, 40, 45, 59, 75, 79, 139, 180, 219–20

Convention on Biodiversity, see United Nations

Convention on International Trade in Endangered Species (CITES), 35, 218

Costanza, Robert, 69, 71, 155, 238–39

Costa Rica, 58, 60

Council on Environmental Quality, 37, 239

Cowell, C. Mark, 88, 239

Coyotes, 2, 7, 11, 110, 111, 139, 172

Craig, Raymond, S., 168, 239

Cranes, sandhill, 88; whooping, 50

Creativity, 183, 195, 219–23, 236; see also Values, systemic

Crick, Francis, 42, 239

Crustaceans, 45, 60

Crystals, 182

Culture: and nature, 1–6, 82, 106, 202, 204–5, 226; nature sacrificed for, 143–44; supported by nature, 6–9, 228; nature as symbols, 137; and rights, 18; transmissible culture, 2, 19, 20; wildlife in culture, 130–32, 137

Cybernetics, see Information

Cytochrome c molecules, 94

Darwin, Charles, 20, 102, 139, 239

Deer, 88, 111, 112, 114, 116, 132; albino, 52

De Maria, Walter, 183

Democracy, 228; and environment, 154–58

Development, 12, 15–16, 22, 54–58, 89, 234; and human rights, 150–54; see also Sustainable development

Dialectical value, 139

Dignity, human, 164; see also Excellences, human; Virtues, human

Dirt, 11, 206, 208–9, 236, earth and Earth, 206–7

Diversity, 34–67, 138, 227; evolution of, 44–50; and pluralism, 40, 43, 78; and stability, 74, 139; see also biodiversity

Dobzhansky, Theodosius, 47, 239

Dolphins, 63

Donaldson, Thomas, 210n, 239

Douglas, T. J., 83, 239

Drift, in evolution, 45, 47

Dryzek, John, 215, 231

Dudley, D. R., 69, 70, 241
Duffy, David Cameron, 90, 239
Durning, Alan B., 148*n*, 239

Eagles, 88, 102, 103, 119, 121, 130, 132, 137
Earth, 77, 100; as home planet, 11, 175, 191, 203–36; inheriting, 233–36
Earth Charter, *see* Rio Declaration
Earthlings, 11, 41, 234
Ecology, 40–41, 113, 140
Economics, 13–14, 19, 28, 35, 65–66, 134, 154–58, 210*n*, 215, 228, 229–30
Ecosystems, 7, 13, 18, 52, 60, 62, 139–40, 170, 196; as biotic communities, 77–82, 196; constant, 74; cyclic stability, 75; Earth, with ecosystems, 203, 209, 219; elastic, 75; diversity and complexity in, 34–67, 227; feral animals in, 114–15; generating value, 175–76; inertia, 74; integrity and health in, 19, 68–100, 229; like markets, 155–56; organisms integrated into, 173–74; persistent, 74; succession, 92, 188; trajectory stability, 75; trophic pyramids, 42–43, 175
Ecuador, 57, 151
Egoism, ethical, 21
Elegance, lack of in biology, 42, 43
Elephants, 76, 127, 218
Elk, 113, 120, 121, 122
Elliot, Robert, 90, 239
Elton, Charles S., 106, 239
Endangered Species, 19, 64, 136; *see also* Biodiversity
Endangered Species Act, 35, 88, 156, 168

Endemism, 37–38, 51
Engel, J. Ronald, 85, 239
Engineers, 227–28; *see also* Management
Entropy, 169
Entwined destinies, 6–9, 22, 140, 228
Environmental Impact Statement, 28
Environmental Protection Agency, 7, 168
Emergence, 4–5, 180–81, 194
Ethiopia, 57
Eucaryotes, 43
Evolution, 72, 76, 103, 176, 207–8, 227; and contingency, 42, 139; of diversity and complexity, 44–49, 102, 207–8, 219–23; and drift, 45; Earth in a post-evolutionary phase, 8, 87, 145; humans evolving out of nature, 4–5; reset by catastrophic extinctions, 48–49; resuming after restoration, 92; of values, 181
Excellences, Human, 162–66; *see also* Virtues
Exotics, plants and animals, 39
Experience, centers of, 105, 161–62, 181, 192–97
Extinction, 19, 36, 51; catastrophic, 48–49; anthropogenic (artificial), 49

Faris, Muhammed Ahmad, 235
Finger Lakes, 8
Florida, 75n
Florida Department of Natural Resources, 75n
Forest fires, 50, 76, 99, 188–89, 227
Forests, 16, 55, 64, 76, 89–90, 99, 143, 151, 181, 219, 231; old

growth, 27, 62, 69, 89–90, 143; tropical, 151
Foxes, 120–21, 131
Framework Convention on Climate Change, *see* United Nations
Freedom, 3, 139, 228–29
Fund for Animals, 64–65
Future generations, 10–11, 19–22, 83–84, 86, 231–32

Gaia, Gaia hypothesis, 220–23, 225
Garvin, Lucius, 4, 239
Genes, 2, 20, 47, 80–81, 105, 113–14, 138; as a cognitive system, 47–48, 168–71, 172–73, 194; and history, 179
Genetic fallacy, 4, 44
Genetic resources, 54–58
Genius, on Earth, 222–23, 227
Geography, 178–79, 210
Geology, geomorphology, 179, 221–22
Geysers, 183
Gila Wilderness, New Mexico, 185
Gilpin, Michael E., 88, 240
Glacier National Park, 111
Goats, feral, 64–65, 116
Goodland, Robert, 225, 240
Goodman, D., 74, 240
Goods, *see* Values
Gómez-Pompa, Arturo, 188, 239
Gorillas, 63, 128
Gould, Stephen Jay, 38–39, 42, 240
Goulet, Denis, 7, 240
Grand Canyon National Park, 182
Grand Caverns, Virginia, 183
Grandfather Mountain, North Carolina, 183

Grasses, 45, 91, 106, 175, 232; and fire, 190; grasslands, 85–86, 143, 181, 219; *see also* Prairies
Great Barrier Reef, 5
Great Smoky Mountains, 75
Griffin, Donald R., 103, 240
Grouse, 119, 132
Growth, 83–88, 145–50; *see also* Sustainable development
Guarraia, Leonard J., 69, 237
Gunn, Alastair, S., 91, 240

Halliday, Tim, 117, 240
Harvey, Paul, 111
Haskell, Benjamin D., 69, 71, 238–39
Hawaii, 37, 38; lack of animals on, 116–17
Hawks, 92, 119
Health, ecosystem, 68–100, 229
Heizer, Michael, 183
Hendee, John C., 185, 240
Hilborn, Ray, 227, 241
History, 30–31, 44, 92, 93, 97–98, 121, 136, 137, 178–80, 207–10; historical genesis, 72, 92; organisms as historical systems, 173; and stability, 74–77, 139
Holism, 175, 210
Horses, feral, 114–15
House, Graham, 148*n*, 243
Hoyle, Fred, 204
Humility, 236
Hunter, Susan, 215, 239
Hunting, 114, 122–26
Huntley, Brian, 148*n*, 149, 240

Identity, personal, 19–21, 137–38
Illinois, 201
Indians, Native Americans, *see* Indigenous peoples

Indigenous peoples, 86, 150–54; and development, 191; effects on wilderness, 187–91

Industry, and environment, 25, 26–33, 62, 83, 96, 224, 232; and control of nature, 224, 227; and relocation of labor, 153

Information, 41, 47, 75, 78, 155; genetic contrasted with cultural, 2–3; organisms as cybernetic systems, 168–72, 207–10, 220

Instincts, 105

Instrumental values, see Values, instrumental

Integrity, 205, 225; in ecosystems, 68–100, 229; site (place) integrity, 174, 181–84; in wilderness, 184

Interests, 210; in animals, 108; self-interest, 156

International Law, 214–18, principles of 214–15, 228

International Whaling Commission, 218

Intrinsic values, see Values, intrinsic

Invertebrates, 63, 102, 103, 210

Iowa, 51, 85–86, 226

Irreversible change, 30, 231

Jaguars, 63

Jähn, Sigmund, 100

James, William, 192, 240

James River, 31–32

Jamieson, Dale, 122, 237

Jesus, 20

John Paul II, Pope, 17

Jones, Dorothy, 215, 240

Jordan, William R. III, 88, 240

Judaism, 9

Jupiter, 34

Justice, 65, 70, 84, 87, 141–42, 147–50, 230

Kariba Dam, Africa, 152

Karr, James R., 69, 70, 241

Katz, Eric, 90, 241

Kaus, Andrea, 188, 239

Kelley, Kevin W., 100, 204, 235, 241

Kepone, 31–32

Kerr, Richard A., 221, 241

Keystone species, 62–63

King, Roger J. H., 122, 241

Knickerbocker, Brad, 7, 241

Krider, E. Philip, 189, 241

Krukeberg, Arthur, R., 50, 241

Labor, 13–14, 56–57, 70, 134–35, 140

Land ethic, 69, 106, 143, 168–69, 204–10

Leal, Donald R., 155, 237

Lemurs, 158, 160, 161, 165

Leopold, Aldo, 31, 69, 71, 74, 76, 105–6, 131–32, 185, 186, 191–92, 205, 241

Leopold, A. Starker, 75n, 189n

Life, value of, 140–41, 172–73

Lightning, 92, 99; and forest fires, 188–91

Lions, 103, 107, 120, 130

Loftin, Robert W., 122, 241

Lotan, James E., 188n, 189n, 241

Lovelock, James, 220–21, 241

Lucas, Robert C., 185, 240

Ludwig, Donald, 227, 241

MacArthur, Robert, 74, 241

Macgraw, Daniel Barstow, 214, 242

McKibben, Bill, 197, 241–41

Madagascar, 160

Magurran, Anne E., 37, 40, 242

Malaysia, 57

Mammoth Cave National Park, 182

Management, 73, 77, 230; of
    Earth, 8–9, 223–28; of nature,
    201, 224; of wilderness, 187; of
    wildlife, 113–14
Mares, Michael A., 151, 242
Margulis, Lynn, 221, 244
Markets, 13–14, 54–58, 155; *see
    also* Economics
Maslow, Abraham, 166, 242
May, Robert M., 36, 74, 242
Maynard Smith, John, 45–46,
    242
Mayr, Ernst, 43, 102, 219, 242,
    244
Maximizing, and optimizing, 28
Meier, Albert J., 90, 239
Meine, Curt, 192, 242
Merck Pharmaceuticals, 58, 60
Mercy killing, 111
Mesthene, Emmanuel G., 224,
    242
Michigan, Lake, 5
Miller, Peter, 59*n*, 242
Mind, human, *see* Brain, human
Minerals, 182
Minnesota, 132
Mississippi River, 137
Mitchell, Edgar, 204
Mongoose, 116
Monkeys, 5, 41, 82, 103; rhesus
    macaques, 116
Monocultures, 72
Montreal ozone protocol, 216
Mosses, 90
Mountains, 10, 34, 106, 119, 141,
    181, 183, 227, 232
Muir, John, 106, 185, 242
Murie, Martin, 200, 242
Muskrats, 92
Mussels, 102, 103, 132
Myers, Norman, 36, 242

Naess, Arne, 106, 242

Narrative, and natural history, 22,
    43, 137
National Environmental Policy
    Act, 23–24, 156
National Forest Management Act,
    35, 69
National Wildlife Federation, 16
Nations, 9, 24–25, 68, 77, 168,
    210, 214, 216–17, 229; domes-
    tic and foreign affairs, 229;
    invisible from space, 235; and
    natural resources, 54–58,
    210–13, 229; and the oceans,
    217
Natural Bridge, Virginia, 183
Nature: ; control of, 224; and cul-
    ture, 1–6, 70, 78, 106, 201–2,
    204–5, 226; degrees of natural-
    ness, 72–73, 91; differing sens-
    es of, 4–5, 88–89; end of
    nature, 197–202, 224–25;
    faked nature, 89–90; laws of
    nature, 4, 14, 74, 139, 179–80;
    meaning of, 179, 219; "Mother
    Earth," 219–23, 227; "Mother
    Nature," 87, 209, 223–24;
    plural natures, 1–2, 78, 138,
    178, 210; pristine, 73, 98,
    188–91, 225; sacrificed for cul-
    ture, 143; supporting culture,
    6–9, 228; the unnatural, 4, 14,
    49, 72, 197–98; unity in, 78,
    138; *see also* wilderness
Nature Conservancy, The, 21
Nevada, 115
Newton, Isaac, 20
New Mexico, 189
New Zealand, 185
Nickel, James W., 215, 242
North Carolina, 183
Norton, Bryan G., 69, 71, 163,
    238–39
Nova Scotia, 137

Oceans, 205, 207, 217, 229
Octopus, 104–5
Oklahoma, 10
Ontario, 137
Optimizing, and maximizing, 28
Organisms, 168–71
Orians, Gordon, 11, 242–43
Ortega y Gasset, José, 125, 243
Otters, 92
Ozone layer, 31
Owls, 27, 62, 92, 121

Packard, Steve, 201, 243
Pain, in animal suffering, 112–13
Palestine, 9
Panthers, 103, 107, 120
Pappendick, R. I., 83, 243
Parr, J. F., 83, 243
Passmore, John, 81–82, 243
Perry, Ralph Barton, 192, 243
Peru, 54, 57, 151
Petroleum, 212
Pielou, E. C., 37, 46, 243
Philosophy, 3, 23, 46, 59, 140–41,
   158, 180, 185, 198, 214
Photosynthesis, 72, 103, 161, 193,
   232
Place, sense of, 181–84
Platte River, South, 87–88
Plato, 101n
Pogonia, Whorled, 64
Policy, environmental, 3, 8,
   23–26, 26–33, 83, 156–57,
   210–13
Population growth, policy, 84,
   145–50, 233
Potatoes, 57
Poverty, 84, 145–50, 230
Power, Jonathan, 148, 243
Prairie dogs, 129
Prairies, 86–87, 89; restoration of,
   88, 201
Prall, David W., 193, 243

Preston-White, Rob, 148n, 243
Prince Edward Island, 8
Procaryotes, 43
Progress, 47, 102; see also Com-
   plexity, evolution of
Protagoras, 101
Protected Areas, 68
Pumas, 63
Pupfish, Devil's Hole, 51, 53, 63

Rabbits, 7, 10, 120, 130, 132,
   139
Rabinowitz, Deborah, 50, 241
Rapport, David J., 72, 243
Rarity, 50–54, 64, 90
Raup, David M., 48–49, 243
Recreation, 15, 35, 59, 135, 185;
   and hunting 122–26
Redclift, M., 83, 243
Regan, Tom, 107, 243
Reganold, J. P., 83, 243
Reilly, William K., 167, 243
Religion, 3, 9, 15, 58, 59, 126,
   140–41, 154, 158, 164, 185,
   213, 221, 224, 236
Rescher, Nicholas, 98, 243
Residence, on landscapes, 9–12,
   25, 213, 225–26, 234
Resources, 9–12, 28, 58, 84, 119,
   134, 141, 150–54, 155, 181,
   216; Earth as resource, 204;
   natural and national, 54–58,
   210–13, 229
Restoration, 73, 88–93, 114; and
   end of nature, 201; and replicas, 90; and restitution, 93
Rhinoceroses, 128
Richness, 35, 58–61, 67, 162–63
Rights, human, 70, 87, 97, 106,
   145–50, 150–54, 210, 214,
   229; animal, 106–10; and environmental values, 16–19,
   210–14, 233

Rio Declaration, *see* United Nations

Risk, 96

Rivers, 10, 12, 34, 92, 102, 106, 118, 119, 137, 181, 182; multinational, 211, 227

Roberts, Leslie, 90, 244

Rocky Mountain National Park, 106

Roman Catholic Bishops, 164

Roosevelt, Theodore, 168, 182

Rothenberg, David, 198, 200, 244

Royal Gorge, Colorado, 183

Rural environments, 13–14, 162–63, 188

Rushmore, Mount, National Park, 183

Sagan, Dorion, 221, 244

Salamanders, 118

Salvini-Plawen, L. v., 219, 244

San Clemente Island, 64, 116

Satisfaction, 87

Saudi Arabia, 57, 210

Scarff, James E., 218–44

Schirmer, I. A., 83, 239

Schullery, Paul, 118, 246

Science, 35, 59, 134, 135–36, 158, 194; biology, 171, 178; and control of nature, 224; physical sciences contrasted with biological sciences, 2, 71, 138–39, 168–71; pure and applied, 179; in wilderness, 185

Self, 20, 103, 137–38; and excellence, 162–66; self-actualizing, 166; self-identity in organisms, 170; self-interest, 156, 225; *see also* Identity, personal

Self-organizing systems, 73, 168–71, 180–81, 207–10, 219–23

Sentience, 107; and value, 159–60; *see also* Consciousness

Sepkoski, J. J., 48, 243

Shiva, Vandana, 55–56, 244

Sheep, bighorn, 106, 108, 121, 132, 137; and pinkeye in Yellowstone Park, 112–13

Shenandoah Valley, 8

Siegfried, Roy, 148*n*, 149, 240

Sierra Club, 15, 185

Simplicity, and complexity, 42–43

Smith, Frederick E., 223–24, 244

Smith, Ralph H., 188, 244–45

Snail, Iowa Pleistocene, 51

Snakes, 119, 227; Sweetwater Rattlesnake Roundup, 129

Society of American Foresters, 167–68

Socrates, 20, 141–42, 163

South Dakota, 137, 183

Speciation, 63, 97, 176, 219; *see also* Complexity; Diversity; Evolution

Species, 5, 35, 71, 73, 92, 110, 176, 209, 219; charismatic, 63; duties to, 113; keystone, 62–63, 98; ownership of, 54–58; *see also* endangered species

Spillover, 29

Stability, 205; and historical change, 74–77, 139, 179

Stakeholders, 29

Stankey, George H., 185, 240

Stebbins, G. Ledyard, 50, 244

Stone, Charles P., 117, 244

Stone, Christopher D., 182, 244

Stone Mountain, Georgia, 184

Storied achievement, 174, 178–81, 207–8, 219–20, 227–28

Subjects, subjectivity, 105, 176; objective and subjective, 192–97; and value, 158–62, 176

Sunter, Clem, 148*n*, 149, 240
Sustainable development, sustainability, 7, 12, 22, 24, 30, 83–88, 225, 229
Sylvan, Richard, 91, 244
Systemic value, *see* Values, systemic

Technology, 30–32, 54–58, 67, 224, 227
Telos, in organisms, 169–70
Tennessee River, 102
Terborgh, John, 63, 244
Teton Wilderness, 99
Thompson, Daniel Q., 188, 244–45
Tigers, 62, 125, 174–75; Siberian, 113
Tomato; *Lycopersicon chmielewskii*, 54–56
Triage, 66–67
Tsunamis, 71

United Nations, 16, 216; *Agenda 21*, 24, 65; Commission on Human Rights, 17*n*; Conference on Environment and Development (UNCED), 24, 65, 68, 81, 203, 214, 215, 216–17, 224; Convention of the Law of the Sea, 216, 218; Convention on Biodiversity, 24, 35, 55, 57, 65, 136, 218; Framework Convention on Climate Change, 24, 218; International Law Commission, 216; Rio Declaration, 24–25, 133, 167, 217; World Charter for Nature, 167, 168, 216; World Commission on Environment and Development, 17, 83, 84, 86, 210; United Nations Environment Programme (UNEP), 216

Universal Declaration on Human Rights, 16–17
Urban environments, 12, 162, 188; *see also* Cities
U.S. Congress, 9, 16, 23–24, 28, 62, 69, 114–15, 168, 185
U.S. Constitution, 16
U.S. Fish and Wildlife Service, 64, 88
U.S. Forest Service, 35, 90, 185
Utah, 115

Valentine, J. W., 47, 246
Value and values, 21, 22; anthropocentric, 3, 133–66, 210, 233; anthropogenic, 3, 158–62, 186; dialectical, 139–40; disvalues, 39, 42, 50, 74; diversity and complexity, 34–67; of Earth, 223; ecosystem integrity and health, 68–100; extrinsic, 192–93; fallacy of misplaced values, 177, 213; instrumental, 71, 79, 140, 171–77, 206–7, 232; intrinsic natural, 3, 71, 103, 131, 136, 140, 159–60, 162–202, 206–7, 232; latent value judgments, 32–33; minority, 28; multiple uses, 26, 33; multiple values, 26, 155; natural and cultural, 1–33; ownership, 160–61; projected onto nature, 159–60; and objectivity and subjectivity, 158–62, 192–97; survival, 108, 220; systemic, 71, 81, 98, 171–77, 180–81, 219–23; transformative, 163; types of natural value, 134–41; "urban values," 15; wildlife, 101–32
Van Voris, Peter, 74, 246
Varley, John, 118, 246

Virtues; animal, 105; human
   excellences, 162–66
Viruses, 50, 220
Vitali, Theodore R., 122, 246
Vitousek, Peter M., 225, 246
Volcanoes, 71, 169, 182, 227

Walters, Carl, 227, 241
Walker, Brian, 76, 246
Warblers, 11, 120, 122, 132, 172,
   175, 177, 195, 218
Warming, global, see Climate
   change
Wastes, toxic, 5, 16, 88, 96,
   148–49, 215, 231
Water, role of on Earth, 205, 207,
   211
Water Quality Act, 88
Wells, Martin J., 105, 245–46
Weir, Jack, 129, 246
Wenz, Peter, 157, 246
Westman, Walter E., 90, 246
Westra, Laura, 69, 246
Whales, 3, 63, 164–65, 218, 221;
   rescued in Alaska, 110
Wheat, 57
Whitman, Walt, 162, 163, 246
Wild, meanings of, 102
Wild and Free Roaming Horses
   and Burros Act, 114
Wilderness, wild environments,
   10, 14–16, 27, 73, 77, 99,
   109–10, 137–38, 141, 158–59,
   160, 184–92; and end of nature
   197–98

Wilderness Act, 69, 184–85
Wilderness Society, The, 15
Wildlife, 59, 101–32, 148, 229;
   aesthetic appreciation of,
   118–22; feral and exotic,
   114–18; commercial value,
   126–30; as common heritage,
   218, 229; as hunters 125; sym-
   bols in culture, 130–32
Wildlife Society, The, 131, 246
Wilson, Edward O., 5, 35, 36,
   151, 209, 246–47
Winning and losing, 6, 26,
   141–45, 162–66
Wisconsin, 205
Wolverines, 111, 113
Wolves, 6, 105, 130, 132, 142
Wonderland, nature as, 184, 208
Woodcock, 131–32
Wordsworth, William, 141, 247
World Bank, 225
World Charter for Nature, see
   United Nations
World Conservation Union
   (IUCN), 7, 34, 247

Xerces Society, 103

Yellowstone National Park, 76,
   99, 110, 113, 183, 199; and
   barren waters, 118
Yosemite National Park, 183, 184